Also by Dave Bidini

On a Cold Road (1998)

Tropic of Hockey (2001)

Baseballissimo (2004)

For Those About to Rock (2004)

The Best Game You Can Name (2005)

The Five Hole Stories (2006)

For Those About to Write (2007)

Around the World in 57½ Gigs (2007)

Home and Away (2010)

Writing Gordon Lightfoot (2011)

A Wild Stab for It (2012)

Keon and Me (2013)

MIDNIGHT LIGHT

A PERSONAL JOURNEY TO THE NORTH

DAVE BIDINI

McCLELLAND & STEWART

First edition published 2018

McClelland & Stewart and colophon are registered trademarks of
Penguin Random House Canada.

Library and Archives Canada Cataloguing in Publication

Bidini, Dave, author
Midnight light: a personal journey to the north / Dave Bidini.

Issued in print and electronic formats.
ISBN 978-0-7710-1775-9 (paperback).—ISBN 978-0-7710-1779-7 (EPUB)

1. Bidini, Dave—Travel—Northwest Territories.
2. Journalists—Travel—Northwest Territories. 3. Yellowknife
(N.W.T.)—Description and travel. 4. Northwest Territories—
Description and travel. I. Title.

FC4167.4.B53 2018   917.19'3044   C2018-900565-3
                                                C2018-900566-1

Photographs are courtesy of the author.

Typeset in Perpetua by M&S, Toronto
Printed and bound in Canada

McClelland & Stewart,
a division of Penguin Random House Canada Limited,
a Penguin Random House Company
www.penguinrandomhouse.ca
1 2 3 4 5   22 21 20 19 18

To journalists everywhere.

And to Dene Nation.

"To write is, in some metaphoric sense, to go North.
To go North is, in some sense, to write."

Robert Kroetsch, *A Likely Story*

"It's a shame to leave this masterpiece
With its gallery gods and its garbage-bag trees"

The Tragically Hip,

"Looking for a Place to Happen"

CONTENTS

≡

1

WE'LL MAKE IT, I SWEAR

Among the capital cities of Canada, Yellowknife is easily the least celebrated. No one has ever written a popular poem or song about the place. No one can pronounce, nor remember, the name of the region's emblematic flower—this is, literally, true, since it's the *Dryas octopetala*, although its floral grouping, the *subshrub*, is almost too fun to say—and no famous hockey or baseball or soccer player has come from here, even though many players were born in smaller places. No one ever started a bar fight because the Ingraham Trail or Somba K'e Park or the old KFC across from the Independent grocery store—all local signposts—were insulted. No one has ever defamed incumbent mayor Mark Heyck—who, when asked on national television one New Year's Eve if he had a message for Canadians, shouted, "People live here!"—and no eco-terrorist has ever scribbled down the name of the town's main intersection—50th and 50th—as a place to stage an attack in an effort to draw attention to man's abuse of the natural world, a crusading principle that wouldn't make sense in Yellowknife seeing as many of the city's wooden homes—brick being too expensive to import—fit into great unyielding shards of steep, 2.7-billion-year-old Canadian Shield granite like arrows of cardboard into a bookcase's shelving (Yellowknifers also live in long, narrow trailers—a.k.a. modular or manufactured homes—plunked on undiggable permafrost while a whole shoreline section, called The Woodyard, consists, more or less, of shacks). No matter where you stand, your feet are sloped at an angle, the product of dinosaur-hump-like terrain that rolls into two pronounced bodies of water—Back Bay and Yellowknife Bay, and its attendant wine-gum-coloured houseboats—on the northern arm of Great Slave Lake. To echo a Cape Breton drywaller who swayed next to me at a urinal one night at the Black Knight, a British identikit down-town pub: "Nothing in this town is fookin' level," as good a slogan as any for the largest settlement close to the Arctic Circle—437 kilometres south, to be exact—and the people who live in it.

I first came to Yellowknife in 2014, twenty-five years after setting out as an itinerant musician in the 1980s. Those early, epiphanous journeys yielded a parcel of albums and a handful of books, after which I strutted about the land declaring myself an authority on this type of travel, carving tracks through endless prairie towns too small for a single horse and ocean hamlets smashed flat one season only to rise the next. I felt like I'd been everywhere, man, but I hadn't; not really. While I'd visited Iqaluit and Dawson City and Whitehorse, I'd never been *up there,* which is how people in the Territories describe the white ribbon across the top of North American maps, found beneath a paper crease still crisp at the fold.

I told myself that ignoring Canada's neglected northern middle was probably a matter of logistics, but getting to Yellowknife and the Northwest Territories isn't especially challenging. A plane will take you there and you can drive, too, provided you're willing to shuttle eighteen hours north from Edmonton through Hay River. After arriving at the airport's bag-gage carousel for the first time—I'd been invited to read at the city's NorthWords literary festival—I stood atop an enormous coloured floor-tile map of the Territories' vast region—as big as Alberta and Saskatchewan combined, or twelve Belgiums, if that's your preferred metric—and wondered if I knew anything at all. What if the Northwest Territories was everything Canada wasn't? What if people spat out maple syrup, hated hockey, and considered Mr. Dressup a fraud? Perhaps my entire sense of Canada would go to hell, and maybe that's why I'd never gone there. I wondered who the real fraud was.

NorthWords ended up being one of the strangest—and thus, best— literary festivals I'd ever attended. Save for a handful of writers from elsewhere, it eschewed the temptation of imported authors in favour of local scribblers, many of whom had never been published. This was partly because organizers couldn't afford to fly guests so far north and partly because very few publishers lobbied for their writers to read in a tiny market with zero influence on the tastemakers of Canada. In this and many other ways, the location and conditions of Yellowknife—north of 60 and minus 45 down 50th Avenue in the wintertime—acted as a kind of filtering agent. Those who visited traversed great distances through multiple airports for as much as it cost to get to Tunisia, and those who stayed did so because the North doesn't ask questions of its visitors (the average stay for newcomers is five years, which is to say, five winters). In this sense, the Northwest Territories is a microcosm within a microcosm. If Canada is a country of vast spaces pinned with the occasional city, the Northwest Territories had but one major centre whose population had dwindled in the twenty-first century, owing to the declining mining industry. It's a small busy place within an enormously empty place, so whenever anyone arrives, they're noticed. They're talked about in the supermarkets and Elks Club, and within five minutes, everyone knows their name, where they're from, and why they're in Yellowknife (also, whether they're single. They are usually single). In the early days of the town, the local paper published a "Who's Leaving? Who's Arriving?" section. Getting to know people was the least of anyone's problems.

Before coming to town, I asked a friend who'd spent some time there what he thought of the city. He shrugged and told me, "I dunno; it's kind of goat." "Kind of goat" may or may not have been an expression used by contemporary youths (my friend is forty-three), but it's what a lot of people thought about Yellowknife. At first glance, I saw how they might have arrived at this conclusion. During the festival, I stayed at a hotel overlooking a stand of small jack pines and spruce—at the 62nd parallel, Yellowknife is where Canada's receding floral hairline begins—but after heading out for a closer look, I noticed the ground strewn with garbage: smoke packs and beer cans and a few crumpled condoms. Beside the hotel, a crane gouged the foundation of what I discovered would be another hotel, its jaws chewing into the surrounding rock and working to destroy what I thought, at first, was the only truly grand and beautiful thing about Yellowknife: Precambrian skulls of rock rearing up at you whenever you turned a corner. There were times around the city when I found myself fanning my hands against the rock's lichen-plastered stone and feeling closer to an eternity of time than anywhere else I'd been, although this sensation was somewhat conflicted by the city's social decay: vampires in torn parkas lurking in store doorways; stoned Inuvialuit giants asleep in the mouth of a parking garage; and hives of truant kids pooling weed money or, worse, looking for whatever harder stuff was being supplied to them by the 856 boys, a B.C. drug gang that sold to easy and isolated marks up north. Because of them—and because of other things, too—tourists hadn't flooded the city even though it was, perhaps, the last unself-conscious social hub in Canada, built in a thundering and mystical natural setting, no less.

In 2014, Yellowknife boasted—perhaps "boasted" is the wrong word here—the country's highest rate of violent crime per capita. Things were bad enough that "suicide-by-cop" was a known term, one invented, according to some locals, by RCMP brass trying to justify their occasionally questionable tactics. The city also had a homeless population magnetized around its dive-bar row; the sun holidayed elsewhere for more than half the year; the city's modern downtown sections were mostly grey with mining company offices and government buildings; the Internet sucked; there were more overweight chronic smokers in the Northwest Territories than anywhere in Canada (you could look it up); and the RCMP operated with zero oversight, lacking a police services board and no local force, filling the jails with Indigenous men and women scarred after centuries of residential school abuse and geno-cide. Yellowknife didn't even have 911. One woman, Audrey Henderson, a nurse at Stanton Territorial Hospital, printed sets of vehicle magnets to remind people of the appropriate emergency numbers: 1111 for police; 2222 for ambulance and fire; and, naturally, 4111 for the hospital. Even though 911 didn't exist—Bell charged residents for the phantom service—people kept calling it, and those who didn't simply drove to the fire department to tell them that their business was ablaze, which is what happened during an incident at a local carpet store.

My first reading at NorthWords took place at an old-age home (okay, "seniors facility") alongside a large moustached man in his fifties wearing grey sweatpants who told a story about what it felt like to kiss a woman who'd just eaten a hunk of walrus meat. He was followed by a teenager in a Metallica shirt and Coke-bottle glasses who read an angry, spittled poem about how his dad abandoned the family when he was young. The next reader talked about pooping on the tundra while on a two-day snowmobile journey. The Edinburgh Festival of Authors, it was not. It was better.

For certain events, NorthWords employed a young woman to sit on stage in front of her electronic keyboard and play awful Richard Clayderman–style piano musings whenever the reader went past the five-minute limit: death by minor fifths padded with painted fingernails. Veterans of the literary racket were able to navigate through the Middle-of-the-Road assault, but new readers grew unsettled at the sound of the first B diminished chord. Their voices tightened. Their words became rushed and papers fell out of their hands. It was awful. Finally, a brutal woman in a glittering blue dress with a Phyllis Diller voice walked from behind a screen like a demented matron and waved for them to get off. It was humiliating and terrible and the crowd laughed their asses off.

For my last night in the city, I went with two of the other visiting writers—Edmonton's Todd Babiak and Vancouver's Billeh Nickerson—to what is, possibly, the most famous place in Yellowknife: the Gold Range tavern. Built in 1958 by the early business pioneer Jacob Glick above his root cellar, and, in the beginning, the only place in town where you could place a long-distance phone call, the Range—a beer hall lit by neon BUD signs washed over aging wood-panelled walls with rows of tables running to a small stage—possessed a whole other level of goat-ishness. Inside the bar, a sallow light suggested the middle of January around 11 p.m. on a Tuesday, even in the warmth of the two-month summer. Sitting below a rooming house with forty apartments, the Range was like an old, smoking lady—menthol darts—who swore a lot and never took off her parka holed at the elbow with grease stains along the fringe. Still, once you started talking to her, you were drawn into the complicated and tragic wealth of her story. This was also a little what Yellowknife was like. It concealed very little about itself. For better or worse, it rarely pretended to be something it was not.

The Range smelled, on first rush of stale air, like an old stained carpet (that it sold more beer than any other tavern in Canada in the entirety of the 1980s probably had something to do with it, and so did its notorious "two and a juice," a combination drink that married two glasses of draft beer with a tomato juice mixer). Having toured rooms like this for the early parts of my musical life—and some of the later parts, too—my reaction wasn't so much regret as nostalgia. Among the taxidermied pike and the twirling ceiling fans—there was no AC at the Gold Range—we found a cover band playing: Colt 45 from Kelowna, British Columbia. The band had a barrel-chested, goateed, and razor-skulled singer-drummer with a headset mic, somebody's uncle on bass, and a guitar player with a withered picking hand shaped like a claw who played the bejesus out of his instrument. They were ungainly misfits in the same way that a lot of the people in the bar were—in the same way that we, as Canadian writers, were, I thought—although, like many of the patrons, the band was at home playing whatever they wanted without the airy demands of an airy crowd. The people in the bar appeared grateful for the noise. At one point, a willowy dude from N'dilo—a nearby Dene community—(pronounced "DeeLo") sat on a barrel near the stage and barked something at the guitar player. The guitar player gave him the thumbs-up with his good hand and went over and talked to the drummer. The drummer nodded—dwarfed by cymbals from behind the kit, he looked like an enormous goateed egg— and said into the microphone, winking at the crowd, "It's time to play Ray's favourite song." Ray clapped with such enthusiasm that he fell off the barrel. The drummer clacked his sticks to start what I assumed would be something by Toby Keith or Skynyrd, but, instead, the band laid into an unlikely song by INXS, the Australian pop ensemble. Ray climbed to his feet and waved his hands over his head. I hadn't heard the song before, but Babiak had, which he thought made him look cool, but did not.

A few people joined Ray on the dance floor, if only to try to coax him off it. He waved them away. They turned and made "Oh that Ray!" gestures with their palms turned skyward, and the band played on. I left my table for a moment and went to the bar at the back of the club: only bottles, only cash. I looked to my right and to my left. I looked over to the washrooms and to the archway leading to a few pool tables around the corner. I looked at the bar staff—gregarious, pony-tailed, Dene—slinging drinks across the counter. I looked at a group of people in fancy dress—a wedding party—seated at tables with dozens of empty bottles surrounding flowery centrepieces. I looked to the stage and at the band, who'd begun a thirty-two-minute Creedence Clearwater Revival medley. I looked at Ray, who'd fallen to the dance floor and was wriggling about on his knees, his pants pulled down to his bum. I looked at the writers.

Everyone was smiling.

It got better. The medley concluded with Bon Jovi's "Living on a Prayer"—not, actually, a CCR song—and the dance floor filled. It was in the Gold Range that I stood witness to a scene that, I believe, only could have happened in this tavern in this city: dancing elders in moccasins and braids; a tuxedoed groom and a gowned bride; three enormous bearded Inuvialuit men from the high Western Arctic wearing denim jackets with eagles stitched across the back; an ancient swaying woman with three teeth, leaning on a cane and closing her eyes in rapture; two young white guys in suits (government types, I assumed); a surreal First Nations' stagette in which the guests—young Dene women in their twenties—wore mini-skirts and fifties greaser jackets with "Pink Ladies" written in "Laverne and Shirley" script on the back; a sexy N'dilo woman in a black dress, her bosom spilling out of her top; a crew of men in workboots clacking Budweisers; and a bouncer with an unlit smoke hanging from his mouth who reached in to find Ray, hiked him up by his collar, and pitched him out the door of the club (he would later return for the band's encore), all in one steady motion.

My friend Loren McGinnis, the relocated CBC broadcaster who'd moved home after years working abroad, appeared in the joyful middle of this northern hurricane. I hadn't seen Loren in a while so we exchanged hugs in the fray. While the band kept playing—"Take my hand/We'll make it, I swear"—he turned to me and said in my ear, "Don't stare, but look behind you." I did, and found three young women—their faces lit by the neon glow of the room—with ancestral tattoos—half-moons, scythes, small indigo blots and tiny arrows—inked across their cheekbones. "Kids are starting to do it," said Loren. "Embracing things that are fading." The bearded egg sang, "We're halfway they-yair!!" and Loren's words echoed in my thoughts: *Embracing things that are fading.* What I'd seen in Yellowknife was beyond any Canada I'd known, where time, scale, and distance were their own concepts. I left town the next morning, but my flight was a series of considerations about what I could possibly do to get back.

2

A THOUSAND SHINING EYES

With the exception of the Dene—whose families have been in the region for ten-thousand-plus years—Yellowknife's social milieu was largely about people trying to begin again after a complicated life down south (in many ways, Yellowknife is Canada's last resort, although there's nothing resort about it). Returning to Toronto, I hadn't planned on being similarly challenged or set adrift, but after continuing a job I'd held for years—Saturday columnist for one of Canada's national newspapers—I found my work clawed away, the victim of prevailing changes in an industry I'd known my entire life. The appeal of being elsewhere felt more profound than ever.

I've always loved newspapers: the smell of the ink and the rough of the newsprint weighted in my hands, their broadsheets flapping like Viking sails. When I was a kid, our family read them all—the *Globe and Mail*, the *Toronto Star*, the *Sun*, and before that the *Telegram*—at the kitchen table with each person drawing out whatever they needed: Comics, Sports, Business, Entertainment (and yet never "Wheels," the *Star*'s automotive supplement). Dark three-inch headlines told the world's story in a shriek of splashed ink, creating a singular deep impression that carried through the day. To some, this might sound like a memory from the 1800s—it's been a long time since people cared about newspapers beyond the metrics of their demise—but it was the 70s and 80s. These days, I still descend bleary-eyed down the staircase to read two papers. People ask me how or why I became a writer and this is what I tell them: every day, I started with a story.

I used to write fake columns about fake things—PYTHON FOUND ON MARBLEHEAD ROAD!—on my father's old iron typewriter in the basement, hammering away with elbows hiked and shoulders hunched, rattling the house in a clanging symphony of pounding metal bars and cricket-leg type rods inking sheafs of literary nonsense. I started writing way before I ever picked up a guitar. Prose came to me more easily, and it didn't require bleeding fingertips or difficult notation or lessons in a music shop hotbox trying to learn impossible solos played by British dudes with rattlesnake hair. Writing meant I could pour my imagination onto the page without wrestling a guitar neck or leaving the nest to make art. I could be at home and do what I loved to do. It probably wasn't until I wanted or needed to be away that rock and roll became desirable—fighting through sore fingertips, callouses toughened me for the road ahead—although the typewriter was never far from reach. I hauled around a portable Underwood on Canadian tours—grey with black trim housed in a tortoise-shell suitcase—tapping and chiming while the country rolled past on the other side of the window.

The year I turned eleven, I submitted a poem about a hockey player— at my mother's insistence—to the *Toronto Sun*'s "Young Sun" section, a folio that appeared every Sunday. The poem was accepted, and I won a T-shirt, which seemed like the greatest thing ever. Later, I contributed to high school newspapers; sent unsolicited, and abjectly terrible, writing to the few rock magazines I found at our local suburban plaza; and scribbled for Toronto fanzines that were mimeographed and stapled together at copy shops across the city. I wrote for *Nerve*, a music monthly hacked into shape across paste-up boards in the basement of Ryerson Polytechnical, and stumbled into some legitimate work for the *Village Voice*, whose sports editor kindly published whatever small posts I sent him, typewritten at my parents' kitchen table, then enveloped and stamped to his office in New York City.

The first time I was published in one of the papers of my youth was in the summer of 1991. I was asked to write a regular column in the *Toronto Star*. The idea was born out of some work I'd done for a *Star* satellite weekly called *Metropolis*, whose editors suggested to the parent company that they give me a shot. The morning of my first story, I drove to the *Star* building—a grey colossus at the bottom of the city standing like a pointer finger refuting the lake—expecting to find my way to the printing press, where I might watch the moment produced in real time. Unable to find it—and too out of my depth to look any harder—I waited near dawn behind a parade of idling taxis, determined to be at the column's birth as it sucked its first breath from the world. I imagined the printing press shuddering somewhere in the basement of the building: a subterranean floor whirring with machines where sluiceways shat bundles into loading bays, the papers falling into the hands of crust-faced Popeyes who slugged them onto skids sagging with each stack. Later, these fat, roped squares were stuffed into tin houses poled to sidewalks and delivered to a bleary mass unleafing them over bed covers, breakfast nooks, diner counters, and arena benches. This day, they'd find something new in there. Me. My writing. In the *Toronto Star*.

I sat in the car and waited as the day announced itself: a flan of sunshine layered across the horizon and over the orange glow of the lake. Five a.m. became 6 a.m. as a truck coughing black tailpipe smoke rumbled and bounced around a corner. A man swung from the vehicle's running board: Tarzan in utility greys. He jumped to the ground and cranked open the face of a windowbox in front of the *Star* building and stuffed it with newsprint. I climbed out of my car and moved across the street jangling my coins through the slot to release the glass facing. I walked back, holding the paper in my arms as if I were an altar boy carrying a priest's vestments. In the car, I pulled out every other section, throwing them on the passenger side. I found the Arts, and there it was on the first page: my column. My heart beat like a malleted kettle drum. I read the story once, twice, a third time, closed the paper, opened it, read it again, touched it, smelled it, read it some more, put it down, picked it up, then put it down again.

I looked up.

The sun had climbed above the lake, brightening the *Star* building with a thousand shining eyes. Across the street, a tall figure with tangled hair and a tired face walked out of the revolving front doors wearing a belted trench coat. She lit a smoke, looked at the sky, then flicked away the smoke. She clacked down the steps into a taxi, slid across the back seat, and leaned against the window. When I think of her now, and how it felt to hold the newspaper in my hands, I return to what is probably the single most seductive moment of my life. The woman looked back at the building. The driver pushed down the meter flag and pulled from the curb.

He took the writer away.

I wrote for the *Star* for two years, if at a distance. Because freelance writers weren't given desks at the paper—they still aren't—I needed permission from my editor to walk the floor. I came in on slow days to write, or pretend to write, at a borrowed desk. I found myself surrounded by journalists sitting at their terminals pecking out prose under a low ceiling, green letters blinking over black screens. Bodies moved about, page mock-ups were shuffled from one station to another, and loose-tied editors walked the cubicles waving pages in one hand and smoking with the other before bending at a desk to discuss this or that detail with a writer whose bitten lip and savaged nails told him that she was hard pressed to make her deadline and could we settle this quickly? Whenever news broke, journalists stood over their partitions like kids at a fence, trying to find out what had happened: a plane, Chilean, downed, hundreds feared dead; a minister caught in a scandal; a gun death in the north corridor of the city. I tapped my keyboard with a make-believe furor, pretending to do something more substantial than writing a column about sports and rock and roll.

I was the section's second hire after the legendary Pierre Berton. I took our pairing as a challenge—in my mind, I pitied the veteran author as a fusty old-guard writer whom I was required to knock off his perch—but, in the end, my column was cursed, having to appear opposite the great columnist of fifty years. While the quality of my work swung wildly—trying to hit targets I invented week to week—the master created with strength and poise and a word store stocked after a lifetime working at the craft. My default was always to punk the column—inciteful writing for the sake of inciting—and I learned the hard way that no matter how strong the note, you need more than one, especially when writing often. I had no stamina and only a few ideas. Whenever anyone told me that they read my column—and whenever a pause came where their effusive praise was supposed to be—I assumed they hated it. I worked self-consciously, which is the artist's death knell. I was overcome with such anxiety as a writer that, despite the triumph of those first moments, I was poisoned, knowing that I was learning my craft in full view of the public, friends, and family. The columns got worse and the section folded. I couldn't shake those rookie blues.

It was after my demise at the *Star* that I started writing books. The record shows that I sold a few, sold many, didn't sell any at all (you know how it goes). It wasn't until Michael Jackson died that I started writing again for newspapers, beginning my life at the *National Post* on the evening of June 24, 2009. After the news broke, I received a phone call in the early evening from the paper's arts editor, who asked if I'd write an obituary for the King of Pop, and could he have it within the hour? I thought it was a stretch, but as I sat at my computer, eight hundred words found me. I called the editor and told him that I had something, and when I walked to the store the next day to buy the paper, the story was on the front page, my byline centred over a radiant photograph of the late musician. The editor asked if I wanted to contribute a regular column to the newspaper, and I said okay. He promised to let me do whatever I wanted.

I loved writing for the paper. The editor kept his word, facilitating a wild and free creative arrangement. After a few years of columnizing—and writing other things as well: a Record of the Month Club feature, the occasional film review, and sports dispatches from Stockholm, Russia, and elsewhere—I met the paper's editor-in-chief for coffee and asked if I could write even more, feeling like journalism was what I was supposed to be doing. *A career. A focus for what I needed to say.* Maybe I could sit at my own desk, spend some time in a lively newsroom chewing on a cigar, a bottle and glass rolling around in a metal drawer that I'd lean over to open.

While I pledged my devotion and argued for more work, I got the sense that the boss had no idea what my column was about. The occasion was fretful and alarming. Leaving the café, I wondered if they'd confused me with someone else. I told myself that, being the new head of a national newspaper—the paper was also transitioning, having just acquired a larger media chain, and some writers had left for the competition—they were probably too busy with other things to know every writer working there. I decided we were both confused and waited to hear what happened next.

Time passed—a lot of time—and then, finally, I pressed them for word on my future. I was sent an email in which the editor-in-chief said that I'd be appearing in the paper less, not more. I was flummoxed. My arts editor was moved upstairs, and his replacement told me that he didn't particularly like my work ("Too poetic," he told me, bluntly). Emails arguing my defence lapsed for weeks and were never returned. I was slowly, inexorably gouged from the paper. I wondered if I'd ever called anyone a terrible name or made fun of their children. To this day, I still don't know what happened.

I wouldn't have been the first writer to suffer through these vagaries, not in modern times, anyway. Soon after I was downsized, the paper—its majority stake having been sold to a U.S. hedge fund company that traded in debt—laid off hundreds of staff, and then, a year later, hundreds more, amalgamating newsrooms across the country. Although there may have been an existential or philosophical shift away from my style at the paper—to be fair, the section also thinned from twenty-five to eighteen to twelve pages—writers losing work was, and is, the result of more base and controlling editorial decisions, falling ad revenue, cheaper online alternatives, media mergers that compromise jobs, winnowing print sizes, everybody rushing to digital, and, I think, less value for the depth of writing in a world of finger taps and tongue-wagging emojis (in the last days of my column, emphasis was put on trailing the heat of the popular story as opposed to good writing, whatever it happened to be about). After I groused about my disappearing presence in the paper's pages, someone said, "Maybe they just don't want to—or can't afford to—pay you?" I ignored the point, but they were partly right. Whatever the case, my life in journalism was fading like a palm smudge.

I slunk about the Earth wondering what in the frig I was going to do next. I could have poured myself deeper into the rock and roll game, although after thirty years, I wasn't sure how much deeper I could go. I'd already proven myself, I thought, as a musician with fourteen albums and so many shows under my belt that, on a recent trip to Buffalo, New York, I sat in a bar called Nietzsche's where, after several hours hanging with friends and admiring the intimacy of the room, I realized I'd played there back in the early 1990s. Rock and roll was glorious Providence. But I wasn't sure how much more I had to learn.

By contrast, newspaper writing was something I was digging into as a daily act—new art, new possibilities—but because the state of journalism was so precarious, and because I'd been punted from my regular column, I wondered whether all I'd done had been nothing more than a prelude to failure. Had being published as an eleven-year-old in the "Young Sun" meant nothing? Had being harassed at home a few years later by Styx fans angry at my giving a negative review to their Grand Illusion show at the Gardens ("Styx's Cheap Illusion") while writing as a teenager for the *Sunshine News* in the 70s hardened me for a life *out of* print? Had stories about Manon Rhéaume, the first female hockey player to sign an NHL contract, in the *Village Voice* and an op-ed about the NHL lockout for the *New York Times* ("NHL Goes for a Skate") and two years of writing opposite Pierre Berton guided me into a post-journalism vacuum crafting ad copy and sponsored content? Had I been left behind, like so many others, by the newspaper industry's desire for "conversations on social media" and "digital harmonizing" and "vlogs" and "paywalls," abandoning the idea of wild writing flung on doorsteps about the life of a place and its people and who'd died and where were Saturday's garage sales and would it rain or snow tomorrow? Was my tenure in papers some kind of cheap illusion? Would Styx get the last laugh?

And then I remembered.

Hey.

Yellowknife had a newspaper.

3

SHARPER THAN MOST GRAVEL

Yellowknife's longstanding twice-weekly independent newspaper—the *Yellowknifer*—didn't look like much. It was a maquillaged *Penny Saver*—half as wide as the *Star* and barely as thick as a single section—and you could get it everywhere, including most downtown street corners, where newsgirls and newsboys hawked it out of shoulder bags in whatever kind of weather consumed them. Other than a small-run francophone folio called *L'Aquilon*, the *Yellowknifer* was still the town's only printed broadsheet newspaper—a new online organ and magazine, *Edge YK*, had recently appeared to challenge it, while two very good papers, the *Northern Journal* and the *Native Press*, had both folded—and its writing lived in the deep veins of the city. Its founders' edict established that it would never use wire copy and that, unless news came from within the city, international stories—no matter how huge—were forbidden. This devout localism gave the paper its identity, making it a true micro-press in all that that term implied (and, indeed, before it was invented), requiring it to meet the needs of the community whenever possible, transforming into a commemorative yearbook in spring (photos of high school graduates commanded a two-page folio every June); a city entertainment provider in the summer (the front page BUZZ department as well as longer features like "FORMER CROONER PENS MURDER-MYSTERY"); a sports round-up; an op-ed stompbox with a rotating set of contributors; and, at its best, a probing investigative journal that held the government, RCMP, and the mining industry—the city's three main employers—accountable. This is to say nothing of Saturday's coloured garage sale map; the Whatsit? graphic riddle ("There was no winner for the June 3rd Whatsit"); Tundra comics; Sutherland Drugs "Capsule Comments"; the Top 5 Videoland DVD rental list; Frame Lake clean-up drives; a summer beach safety manual; and one of the *Yellowknifer*'s most popular, and curious, columns, "Tales from the Dump" by artist and writer Walt Humphries (Yellowknivers called the dump their "YKea"). There were also headlines like GIANT TROUT HOOKED INYK BAY, identifying the newspaper as coming from nowhere else.

One of the remarkable things about the *Yellowknifer*'s operation—two floors in an old automobile dealership showroom and garage in the fraught heart of the city—was that the paper had grown while the greater newspaper industry collapsed around it. After calling Loren to explore the possibilities of going there to work—and to write about working there—he suggested that I contact the *Yellowknifer*'s managing editor, Bruce Valpy, and suggest embedding at the paper. Our arrangement took a shockingly, and suspiciously, short amount of time to compose after a handful of emails and one phone conversation in which I explained my curiosity about the North and the fact that I'd been pushed from the pages of my former employer. Bruce cleared his throat and said, "Sure, okay, come," and that was that. I ran the idea past my wife and kids. We pressed some numbers and figured out what could get us through the summer with the help of a grant or two, and my kids shrugged, secretly delighted that there'd be only one adult left to tell them to clean their room.

Bruce Valpy's approach to an outsider sitting along press row reflected the prevailing attitude of both the paper and the city it covered. A curious man with a cool hand and a watchmaker's barometer who was thin, fifty-something, and greying at the temples, his approach was "If you want to commit to coming and dedicating your writing to Yellowknife, it proves that you want to be here. That's good enough for me." His attitude was likely tied to the fact that the place possessed a carousel citizenry ("How I ended up in Yellowknife . . ." was something you heard a lot in town), reflected when a minor hockey coach was asked how to best define the city during a recent *Hockey Day in Canada* broadcast, finding the word "transient," a term better used to describe a vagrant or serial killer than a town where people stayed forever.

I set out making arrangements to stay the summer. While some people might hike their eyebrows over my decision to come here during the fairer season, I was loath to—and, let's face it, incapable of—writing a typical northern book, the kind born after travelling into inhospitable parts of the country while suffering through hellacious winter. These books are the domain of healthy men in beards with a "zest for the outdoors," and even though I wasn't not healthy, I, like many men and women my age, swore when approaching broken escalators or discovering that the washroom was on the third floor. I didn't paddle and I didn't hike and I considered the term "natural splendour" doublespeak for "place where no one lives." Besides, I wanted to learn less about the wild and more about people being together in a small city, one that I hoped to know—at least partly, and through a refracted literary view—during my time *up here*.

I searched for accommodations beyond the downtown core, partly so I wouldn't spend every night at the Gold Range, and partly because I wanted to be as close as possible to the majesty of Great Slave Lake. Yellowknife is divided into four hunks: the city proper, New Town—suburbs that stretch out to the airport and beyond—Old Town and N'dilo, connected via the Latham Island bridge to the Yellowknife limits (another community, Dettah, is a greater distance away). Old Town was the city's original 1930s settlement, a hardscrabble former mining camp tight to the shoreline. Prospectors gathered there after gold was discovered and, over the years, the enclave had become a riot of shacks, country cottages, and bizarre Bauhaus apartment constructs. It was as if someone had cupped the whole of cottage country in their hands, then blindly scattered it like board-game pieces over mounds of rock. The few strange and incongruous modern buildings in Old Town included a round, steely grey condo dwelling that looked like a Russian submarine and, behind it, a glassy vertical home stuck like gum to the Shield's rock face as if it had been picked up by a tornado and spun out of a trendy Manhattan enclave before landing in the North. But these dwellings were anomalous. Old Town was mostly preserved to its roughened core, although not finely preserved in the way Old Montreal was, and certainly not like Whitehorse, with its trees ringed with frilly garters. According to author and photographer—and unofficial city biographer—Fran Hurcomb, it was only recently that cab drivers had stopped driving around Yellowknife with "handmade maps of Old Town clipped to their visors . . . the houses known either by those who lived in them or next door to them, or in many cases, by colourful nicknames like Slant 6, Moulin Rouge, Johnny's Highrise, and the House of Horrors," an old rooming house run by the miner Alphonse "Frenchie" Cyr, which got its name after a partygoer drowned while reaching into a flooded basement for a can of beer.

Most of the homes in Old Town and Peace River Flats had thorny yards and bent porches, where an old coot might sit in the shadows with a shotgun across his lap. You couldn't walk twenty feet without coming across a motor vehicle or fishing boat swallowed in weeds, and every property seemed to have a shed that looked as if a hacking cough might send it collapsing to the ground. Yet the closer I studied them, the more I discovered the occasional artisanal touch: woodcuts screwed to the faces of homes; little hand-painted gnomes, one of whom wore a Quebec Nordiques sweater; and, in some instances, small greenhouses with plants in bloom. For all of the sloping ruggedness of the land and the perpetual shade cast by the rising chunks of Shield, it seemed as if the coots were going soft in their dotage.

Old Town had but a single long-term option for visitors: a plywood-walled cabin in Peace River Flats, a small neighbourhood named after a group of Albertans who once floated down a barge—the *Beulah 1*—from the Peace and Slave rivers to the Northwest Territories. I was brought to the cabin on a bright cool spring day by a Somalian cab driver named Assan, whose radio played a local CBC news report about a mammoth skeleton being reassembled in N'dilo. I counted the number of times in my life—the number would be zero, it turned out—that I'd heard a paleographic artist describe the spinal details of an extinct beast while I was sitting alongside an immigrant from Mogadishu driving beside ancestral Dene shorelines. Even better was what happened when Assan took a call from a friend during our ride: the woodpecking timbre of his voice chattering against the baritone of the paleo-artist while a flurry of gulls cried over Yellowknife Bay, the waters shining green-blue as we rumbled down the Franklin Avenue hill into Old Town.

It was during Assan's phone call that I realized we were lost—my cabin had no actual address, its location described, generally, as being behind the Narwal B&B owned by Cathy Allooloo—but it was okay with me. If other occasions might have seen me grow frustrated with not having arrived at our destination, I was lost in the bliss of being in a new place, all the while wondering why the rest of Canada had never heard of Old Town, although it's not as if it went out of its way to tell anybody, left on its own to be, well, old. There were only a few plaques—including one at Pilot's Monument, which sat atop the largest hill in the centre of the village and commemorated the opening of the North by float planes— and locals occasionally pointed tourists to the area's first dry goods store (a small green mollusk of a building called Weaver and Devore, still thrumming with business), the North's finest fish restaurant (Bullocks), and Canada's oldest café, the Wildcat, built by Willie Wylie and Shorty Stout and recently appropriated by local government, who'd turned it into more of a museumed keepsake than a lively heart of the neighbourhood. In distant times, locals were married there by a priest who also doubled as the town magician, and funerals were facilitated by a perpetually tippled man named "Burial" Smith, who drove around Yellowknife in a van operating as both a taxi and a hearse, with a sign on the dashboard that read:

$15 LYING DOWN
$2.50 STANDING UP

Eventually, we stopped the cab on one of the dirt roads honey-combing through Old Town so that Assan could chirp at his dispatcher. He rubbed his face, apologizing profusely for being lost (he'd only been in town a few months). Finally, after a series of tight turns along loop-ing roads, we travelled down a shaded cul-de-sac toward a hunk of rock that loomed in the distance like a Sinbad giant rising from the earth. Had we been travelling at wild speeds, our lives would have ended like crash test dummies in a slow-motion instructional, but instead the car grumbled to a lazy halt in the shadow of the rock, rest-ing at the Narwal porch.

Because the Narwal website yielded little information—or any photos—of the cabin, I wasn't entirely sure what kind of accommoda-tion was being offered, and Cathy's grounds did little to illuminate. The property possessed all the requisite expectations of a place on the shores of Great Slave Lake: axes, two of them, driven into a tree stump; a hammered-together table with muskrat pelts spread across it; a chainsaw propped against the side of the cabin; a few mangled bicycles lying one over the other; Ski-Doos hooded against a fence at the back of the property; two long nylon-sheltered rectangular tents housing more axes, chainsaws, and Ski-Doos, as well as a huddle of life preserv-ers and bouquets of paddles; and, slanted on a mound of granite rock in the shade of the skull, a dozen kayaks and canoes. After climbing the porch and ringing the doorbell, then knocking on the door, then trying to open the door, I did what any traveller would have done, stepping back and calling out "Helloooooo?" There was no answer, but some-thing better happened: I heard my voice echo around the edge of the bay, which, I discovered, lay between a stand of tall weeds along a scrub path on the other side of the road.

After a while, a truck roared outside, tapping its horn. A blond-haired woman called to me from the passenger side: Cathy Allooloo. Cathy was the implacable, short-statured, and pony-tailed fifty-something proprietor of the Narwal and my summer cabin landlord. Traces of winters past were dug into her expressions as if by the steady hand of an artist working to reflect a rough sense of beauty born after a time in the North. Having passed through her adolescence in suburban Mississauga, Ontario, Cathy had spent most of her life in Pond Inlet, Nunavut before coming to the Narwal with her two kids—Devon and Tiffany (Ayalik), both young adults—and operating an adventure tourism outfit whose scale of experience included challenging week-long canoe trips as well as short paddles where guests were treated to elk stew, bannock, and maple butter on the rocks and bits of northern dinner-theatre starring young actors who recreated famous local scenes in which, inevitably, a bush pilot met his fate despite rallying to save the passengers. Most times I saw her, Cathy was either sandalled and in camping shorts, standing atop a large van roping two or three kayaks to the roof; picking up a canoe from the ground's stone embankment, then putting it on her head and guiding it to a truck's flatbed; or unflinchingly descending into the frigid waters of the bay to pull out whatever had fallen overboard during a trip: a theatre prop, a passenger's paddle, a bag of cutlery. Cathy was incapable of doing less than seventeen things at once, including making arrangements for visiting Europeans; organizing fiddlers for an overnight ceilidh on nearby Jolliffe Island; taking care of her three huskies whom she kennelled on a landing next to my cabin; or tending to the clueless writer from Toronto, who, every now and then, arrived home tippled and keyless—living in a place with the most bars per capita in Canada, it was impossible not to run into a pint of ale, and someone to drink it with, on the way home—asking his pyjamaed landlord to please let him in.

Cathy found me a set of keys, and I made my way through a green wire gate beside the B&B—the angled granite of Old Town made sure that nothing was fookin level here, either—and went to the cabin at the back of the grounds, dragging my suitcase behind me. For some, the idea of a place on a remote shoreline may conjure dreams of Muskoka chairs and a perfect wooden dock toothpicked with Bose speakers playing The Tragically Hip's "Bobcaygeon," but my summer abode presented its set of challenges. I'd also chosen the cabin over a city apartment as a sop to friends and advisers who suggested I try a modicum of "roughing it," and, even though it wasn't exactly the equal of explorer Samuel Hearne, who ate his sealskin jacket for nourishment after his food stores were raided, there was no running water or proper kitchen in the cabin, and you had to stork in the middle of the room to get the Internet. Holes gouged in the wall revealed tangles of unfinished electrical wiring; a pipeless sink caught dishwater poured from a bucket before expressing it on my feet; and there were curtainless windows, light fixtures that didn't work, and, hardship of hardships, a coffee maker that turned on, lit up, then sat there as if it were a commuter slumbering on a transit bench. Previously, the cabin had been used as a meeting space and bunkie for workers passing through Yellowknife, and I thought I could sniff a wet wool odour and traces of burly-assed men flung across two pleather couches and a small bedroom at the back. My first instinct was to draw my little transistor radio from my suitcase and click it on. I put the radio on top of an old wall heater and listened to an announcer read the news in French about a fishing boat that had gone missing on the Sylvia Grinnell River in Iqaluit. The transistor brightened the room as if I'd just hung a Chagall canvas. I sat on a couch and mulled over the pleather. Outside, an army of dark bugs flung themselves at the window.

During my first evening in the cabin—the day before I started at the paper—I shouted up from the bottom of the Narwal landing, wondering whether I might have some sort of cooking device (a toaster oven and microwave were on the way), and what I was supposed to do about a bathroom and shower (I could use the guest toilet in the B&B). Cathy asked if I wanted to come up to her loft for a visit, and I said I did. There, my landlord and Tiffany were sitting on a couch in a room on the second floor with a window overlooking the lake, the sun bobbing in the sky as it would for most of the daylight-only heart of the summer, which recalled one of the great Northwest Territories saws: how, in the 1970s, the Canadian government congratulated itself for sending forty thousand dollars' worth of July 1 fireworks to a place where there was almost zero darkness for the three-month summertime.

Tiffany was a master paddler who did tours for the Narwal, but she was also a musician—throat-singing and otherwise—whose face was like the moon at dusk, her eyes constellations of light. We were joined in the loft by a fellow in his work clothes named Bob Draxel (not his real name), which made me wonder why, in every situation set in the Canadian North, there was always a guy sitting around in his work clothes named Bob, and they were almost always saying things like "You see that gravel out there? That isn't normal gravel. That gravel is different, different than what you people are used to."

Bob continued, pointing through the window: "Now this is sharper than most gravel. It's got quite an edge on it!" (Bob really liked gravel.) He told me this, I think, as a warning, but also as a point of boastful pride, and before I could rally to defend the honour of Ontario gravel, I let it go. "You watch these roads," said Bob, before adding, "I mean: be careful or they'll get ya." I had no choice but to tell him, point blank, that since we had hundreds of thousands more people and towns in Ontario, it only stood to reason that we probably had sharper gravel, at which point he fell silent and starting humming a melody that suggested he was dreaming of this impossibly sharp gravel, which made me kind of like Bob, even though he'd said the thing about the roads.

There was an elevated bunk in the corner, and above that, an enormous five-foot polar bear pelt stretched out on the wall. It's perhaps an obvious statement that it wasn't every day that I found myself socializing in front of a polar bear pelt, but, as we've seen with Bob's deadly gravel, there was always a sense of adventure, or misadventure, at hand. The surrounding region's names suggested as much: Vampire's Peak, Broken Skull River, Bear Rock sinkhole, Scimitar Canyon, the Rapids of the Drowned, the Lake That Fell off a Cliff, Hell Roaring Creek, and so on. One Old Town resident, the filmmaker, social advocate, and addiction counsellor Emily Lawson, told me that a person I would like to have met was the late ninety-seven-year-old elder Mike ("Grandpa") Krutko, who, after downing planes in the 40s and 50s outside Fort McPherson, walked through the marauding winter into the nearest town—"nearest" being at least a hundred kilometres away—found a machine part, walked back, repaired his plane, and flew home; routine activity in a place informed by the perils of the land. Grandpa Krutko was heroic in many ways, not the least of which was, after turning ninety-five and publishing the story of his life—*Mike Krutko's Amazing Adventures*—he told a friend, "I'm thinking of driving down the road and maybe selling some books." Now that takes guts.

I asked Cathy about the origins of the pelt. She told me that her son, Devon, had shot it when he was eleven years old, his first kill on the land. She called Devon in from another room, and after telling him how impressed I was, the brawny nineteen-year-old shrugged the way any teenager might have were they singled out by a doting parent. He waited until I'd finishing speaking before announcing that he was "goin' to shoot muskrat," appearing moments later on the road walking to the dock with his shotgun.

Cathy told me that Devon had shot the bear "right between the lungs." Rather than question her about the hows and whys of the kill, I obsessed on the word "bear," asking the group, "Are there bears around here?" Bob stopped humming and laughed a nervous laugh, which made me wish we were talking about gravel again. Cathy put it this way: "It's the North. There are animals everywhere. There was a bear here last summer."

Although I tried to treat the news of a bear being "here" as if she'd said that, occasionally, Bonhomme liked to drop by and leave six packs of Brador on people's doorsteps, I visibly tightened. Cathy said, "Don't worry. It came in, then went right back out again. But this is the Northwest Territories. We have to live with the animals and be among them, always have."

I imagined the headlines back home:

SHARP GRAVEL NOT ENOUGH TO KEEP BEAR FROM EATING WRITER

Tiffany was preparing to take a handful of women on a six-day canoe trip. When I asked her about the details of the adventure, she vented about what the excursion looked like now compared to what it would have looked like twenty years ago. "It's costing $750 in food," she said, exaggerating the number before settling into a parody of one of the paddlers and their macrobiotic needs. Tiffany rolled her eyes and waved her hands, but her outrage became even more animated once I introduced a subject I should have known not to introduce: Whitehorse vs. Yellowknife. As soon as I finished saying the name of Yellowknife's estranged northern cousin, Tiffany leaned over and pretended to spit on the floor.

"People think they're the same place because both cities have colours and a noun in their name," she said, disgusted. "Tourists call us thinking they're calling the Yukon. They want to come to the gold rush town, they say. The rest of Canada can't tell the difference, like we're all one big thing mashed together. But there's only five thousand people in the whole of the Yukon who live outside of you-know-where," she told me. "Here, we're half in the city, half in the Territories. The communities are strong," she said, making a fist.

A few days later, I told Loren McGinnis what Tiffany had said, and he agreed, speaking about the Yukon as if he were chewing on bits of sour rind. "Yellowknife may be hard to define," he said, "but it sure as hell isn't Whitehorse, with its candy corn and manicured boardwalks and can-can shows. The Yukon is Northern Lite. It's a tourist's version of what the North is about. In recent TV ads, there wasn't a single Aboriginal person in them. People spoke out, but the tourism people said that it was part of a planned roll-out, which, of course, it wasn't. The way they want to present themselves is: COME TO THE YUKON. THERE ARE WHITE PEOPLE HERE. But in Yellowknife, people speak South and North Slavey, Tlicho, Dogrib, Gwich'in," he said, listing an excellent set of words I'd never heard before, but which I later learned were all groups of Indigenous peoples of that land. Loren's opinions were supported by a writer named Tim Querengesser, who lived in Yellowknife and whose views were that "in Whitehorse, everyone is trying to live out the gold rush over and over again, but it's so old and tired. The people who got screwed over the hardest there were Aboriginal and they're not celebrating. The Northwest Territories doesn't have a founding mythology, but that's why it's vibrant. Everyone's trying to create an identity rather than rely on one."

In some cases, you couldn't blame people for their confusion about the North. Many southern Canadians still consider it an amorphous and homogenous region. This was confirmed by a local woman who told me that, as a kid in the 70s, she'd watch CBC national weather forecasts and "they wouldn't even mention what was happening in the N.W.T." Even the name "Northwest Territories" told people where it was rather than what it was and if "Saskatchewan" or "Nunavut" were words that jumped on the tongue like a peppery mint, "Northwest Territories" sounded as if it were written on a government-issued manila envelope, which, in fact, it was: created by a group of bureaucrats in Ottawa as a placeholder name for traders and mining companies.

Years ago, the N.W.T.'s former premier, Stephen Kakfwi, whose courageous writings have documented a residential school life where he was raped and abused by his headmaster, started an initiative to rename the Territory "Denendeh," after the Dene, who make up 50 per cent of the Territories' forty thousand citizens. Men and women were canvassed and asked to vote on a new name, but "Denendeh" finished third. Most people voted to keep the existing name, but the second most popular choice was "Bob," which is both funny and not at the same time. Kakfwi took his cause to the federal government, but got no further traction. "Basically, the government said yes to Nunavut and no to Stephen Kakfwi," said Querengesser. "They told us to go fuck ourselves." In writer Shane Koyczan's opinion, it was worse than that, "like a terrible joke," he said. "They looked at Nunavut and said, 'Yeah, we'll take that.' The rest of it: 'Nah, we're good.'"

I asked Cathy, Bob, and Tiffany if anyone ever used the name "Denendeh," and Cathy said, "Some do, but not many. Some Dene do, I guess. But these are small problems," she told me. "There are other things to worry about. Bigger things, I think." I wanted to ask her about these other things, but Tiffany got up from the couch and excused herself, begging off to bed in advance of the cruel early morning departure. She told me that she hoped our conversation was helpful, but that there was still lots to learn. I told her that's why I'd come north: to experience a place I knew almost nothing about.

"Although at least I know the difference between Yellowknife and W . . ." I said, stopping myself in time.

Tiffany leaned over, just in case.

4

FUCK ELSEWHERE

Yellowknife took its time before it ever became a city. It wasn't until 1961 that a road was built connecting Hay River to Yellowknife from the south—goods and supplies were brought in by barge and Cat train before that—and, in 1967, Ottawa finally got around to establishing a capital here the way your aunt gets around to finishing that magazine she's kept beneath the coffee table and has been meaning to read for years (the government of the Northwest Territories was based in Ottawa until moving up north in Canada's Centennial year, bringing eighty-one government employees to town to help orchestrate a council).

If the mid-1940s had seen the rest of Canada surging into modern post-war times, the Hudson's Bay Company was still a controlling presence here, sounding a call for gold diggers almost fifty years after the first chaotic rush to the Klondike (the route to Dawson City came through the area, but few stopped to test the ground for minerals, instead hurrying on to the Yukon). Prospectors filled Old Town and, in 1945, thirty thousand mining licences were issued, with Giant Mine joining Con Mine, the latter originally staked by an itinerant prospector named Murdoch Mosher, who sold his interests early and missed out on millions earned from his discovery (Mosher was among a group of early Yellowknife prospectors that included the city's first female resident, Vicky Lepine, who arrived in 1937 on a motor-powered scow and created a scandal after marrying the RCMP's

Casey McKale, who flouted force standards by marrying early in his career). If the mines created Yellowknife's first workforce—while also creating hazardous levels of arsenic in the air and water due to toxins expelled in the smelting process, an issue that the current government hoped to mitigate by freezing 237,000 tons of the poison underground for the near future—they also established a demand for something that the region never had before: a substantial local press.

Yellowknife's first newspaper was the mimeographed *Prospector*, whose typeface was set by candlelight in a tent on the slope of Pilot's Monument, and after that came the *Yellowknife Blade*, published by a married couple named Jock and Mildred McMeekan (Jock was a notorious former *Prospector* columnist). In its infancy, the *Blade* was stapled together on legal-sized paper with handwritten headlines and ads and a hand-drawn masthead. McMeekan sold copies on the steps of the local coffee shop, and scuttlebutt had him ferrying the money from his pockets to the bar across the street, where he shuttered the parlour at the end of every night.

The *Blade* never evolved into a legitimate press, so the responsibility fell to an RCAF veteran named Duke DeCoursey, the next in a long line of newspaper men with great and ridiculous names. Along with his wife, Maude, they published the erratically produced *News of the North*, a folio assembled in a small, eight-by-ten frame tent where they took turns writing, editing, and cutting ads. They also lived in the tent, so any cooking had to be done with the other person either sitting outside or lying prone on the bed. In his memoir, *The Yellowknife Years*, DeCoursey wrote of "the ecstasy that is the formation of a newspaper from dream to reality," an idea that mirrored the ethereal growth of the city itself, rising out of the earth as if overnight. Initially, the paper was printed in Stony Plain, Alberta, and flown on CP Air to the North, but after a time, DeCoursey purchased a linotype—and other printing apparati—shipping it by train to Yellowknife. The paper appeared in fits and starts, but it lasted until its absorption and sale in 1979, at which point *News of the North* (*NOTN*) became *News/North*, a Territory-wide newspaper.

In 1972, two men—J.W. "Sig" Sigvaldason and Jack Adderley—started a paper to rival *NOTN*. They called it the *Yellowknifer*. Because Sig—an Icelandic Winnipegger—and Jack had both been hired and fired by *News of the North*, the *Yellowknifer*'s inception was a vengeful birth. Because the idea of a newspaper was considered a dubious investment by small business loan groups—even as late as 1972 at the height of North American print culture—it forced Adderley and Sigvaldason to turn to a man named Johnny Rocher (pronounced "Rocker," and considered one of the eccentric longstanding guardians of The Woodyard) for collateral in order to get a proper bank loan. They received three thousand dollars in start-up funding and, on March 22, 1972, the two men produced their first weekly edition of the *Yellowknifer*. Early issues had a column by a writer known simply as The Oldtimer with a cartoon drawing that looked like it had been made on the back of a tavern coaster. One early page-three story was titled "Are the Men of Today Wearing Their Hair Too Long?" (another asked: "What Penalty Should Be Imposed upon Drivers Who Splash Pedestrians?") while, deeper into the issue, a piece called "Stretcher Patient Disappears" recounted how Sgt. Ed Cook and Sgt. Claude Belanger climbed on a B737 aircraft to assist a convalescing man from Edmonton, only to find him gone. "At last report, the whereabouts of the patient was unknown," it said. "He was never seen again."

Early *Yellowknifers* ran notices such as "I, Doris Strade, Hereby State That I Am No Longer Responsible for My Husband's Debts" and "Marital Aids, 1 $ Refundable with First Order." In Mordecai Richler's essay about the city, "North of Sixty," he quoted a *Yellowknifer* want ad in which a lawn mower was being sold: "Reason for selling. No grass. Or would consider purchasing lawn."

The conditions in which the paper was assembled weren't much better than the *NOTN*'s early days. It was cut and pasted over Sigvaldason's kitchen table at his home until they moved into a small building—a skid shack given to them by Rocher—without any running water, and where a single extension cord provided power from a building two blocks away.

According to a commemorative *Yellowknifer* issue published years later, "The nine staff shared a central honey bucket [a toilet pot] and an airtight heater which often exploded, covering finished pages in a layer of soot." Sigvaldason added: "Between the two of us, we had one typewriter, a camera, and one thousand dollars." A former Great Slave MLA, the late Bill Braden, remembered that, as a printer and a photographer, "I did all of the darkroom work in the tiny, cold porch of my parents' house. For the typesetting, there were three or four ladies in town who were very proficient typists. Adderley would scrawl something out, and then we'd bring it around town to these three or four women. The rush was to get the first edition out by Caribou Carnival [the city's wintertime festival]. That was the launch and we did it."

The paper was assembled at the Yellowknife Legion, and its publishing schedule often depended on the availability of supplies in the North. A few years later, the *Yellowknifer* moved into a space bequeathed by Rocher: a 714-square-foot refrigeration shack filled with, according to Adderley, "lots of junk and cast-iron fittings." Still, it gave the paper its footing before eventually moving downtown and passing through a series of editors, although Sigvaldason continued to own the paper in absentia, having moved south to Ottawa in his twilight years.

It was Sigvaldason's idea that the *Yellowknifer* limit itself to local and regional news, resisting the temptation of world events and dogmatically refusing to run wire copy. In 2015, it was hard to argue against that which the *News/North* franchise had become, owning papers across the Northwest Territories and Nunavut—twenty-eight thousand printed weekly from Iqaluit to Inuvik to Fort Simpson—and possessing a thriving news monopoly at the top of Canada (which was a little like being the world's richest pauper, but still). Because the *Globe and Mail* and the *National Post* had stopped delivering to the North, and because the Internet was wonky in large patches of the territory, people still turned to print to find out what was happening. The *Yellowknifer* was an out-of-time media provider in an out-of-time place, protected from whatever modern transgressions had compromised papers in the rest of Canada. If newsrooms across the country were gutting their workforce because of declining revenue amid the panic to become digitally relevant, the *Yellowknifer* maintained a vitality of purpose by simply being itself.

The necessity for original copy meant more opportunity—if more work—for the paper's writers. The staff was chained to a demanding and focused schedule: two or three stories a day—researching, interviewing, writing, then rewriting—for two editions a week plus a weekly *News/North* aggregate of content from the outlying papers as well as some new material. These pressures created a newsroom atmosphere of chattering phone calls and journalists hustling the floor, working the angles of a piece, but the demands also wrenched energy from the writing corps and burned people out (transplanted reporters were allowed to write off two trips home a year, giving staffers a break from the northern grind). The *Yellowknifer* had heavy turnover and, according to one former writer, "you never got too used to working with anyone because, in some cases, they were here one day and gone the next." In one instance, a journalist came from Montreal, was assigned a single story, spent the day writing and filing the story, and left the next day.

The paper's plethora of young writers probably resulted in more learn-on-the-job-utility-prose, but it also helped develop serious and unflinching working writers: people like Jennifer Pritchett of the *Saint John Telegraph-Journal* and the *Globe and Mail*'s Nathan Vander Klippe, both of whom had come through the newsroom. The main requirement seemed to be that you not suck and that you tolerate the paper's peculiarities. The *Yellowknifer*'s entertainment writer, a twenty-something woman named Dana, was interviewed as a general reporter, turned down, and then, a few days later, hired in haste to cover music, dance, theatre, and visual art. Once a writer stepped off the plane, their foot was in the door. How you fucked it up—or didn't fuck it up—was your own business.

More than a few staffers were hired on the phone. Cody Punter, for instance, was offered his job after a chance encounter in a bar. I'd met

Cody on the dance floor of the Range during my initial visit to Yellowknife. He was a bright kid who looked like he was born riding a skateboard and moved about as if he were always two cups of coffee ahead of everyone else. We'd had a conversation in which, between the second and third "movements" of the Creedence medley—although to call them "movements" is to elevate them a little too high—I found out that we'd grown up in the same part of Etobicoke and that he was, for a time, represented by the same literary agent (Cody was a fledgling novelist and photo-journalist).

"A few years ago, I flew here to visit my dad, who works as a crown prosecutor for a Nunavut firm based out of Yellowknife," he told me. "I was one of those people who got off the plane and wondered where the mountains were, thinking I was in Whitehorse instead of Yellowknife. On my first night, my dad took me out to the Black Knight. An inebriated woman came up to the table and introduced herself. After chatting for a while, I told her that I did some writing, and she suggested I work for the local newspaper. I laughed at first, but she was serious. The next day I sent off my resumé—it didn't have any formal journalism experience and no J school—and a cover letter, thinking nothing of it. The next thing I knew, the paper's senior editor, Mike Bryant, sent me out on a trial assignment where I was asked to write a story about whether or not the city should plough a trail on Frame Lake down to the ice or just pack down the snow. It was minus 30 degrees C and I didn't know what I was doing. I got the interviews, took some photos, and filed my copy by 5 p.m. The work was atrocious but they rewrote the whole thing and used it in the newspaper.

"I went in to meet with Mike. He reviewed my stuff and offered me a week-long trial. At the end of the week, I was back in the office. Mike asked: 'Do you want to write for a newspaper?' I said that I'd never written for one before. He cut me off and said something along the lines of 'I didn't ask about your experience. I asked if you wanted to work for a newspaper.' I told him that I did. And that's how I got hired."

The Yellowknifer building was a squat construct in a rough part of down-town, announcing itself from the street on a yellow ribbon sign sitting atop a blue corrugated roof across from the rugged Northern Lites motel, which former writer Jorge Barrera once framed as "the Gaza Strip, where winos gather drinking Hermits and solvents." A few weeks before I arrived, a vainglorious drug dealer had opened fire on his rivals, proving that one way of getting your name in the newspaper is to try and shoot someone within a half block of fourteen editors and journalists.

There was a small gravel parking lot in front of the *Yellowknifer* and a glass door leading to an ante room—the Northern News Service's de facto office—where I sat waiting to be buzzed into the newsroom proper. A huge whiteboard loomed in front of me with little cut-outs of the writers' faces beside their in/out schedule and, above that, a high-definition screen that should have been tuned to the CBC News Network or CNN or BNN, but, instead, showed what looked like a Beckett film: an empty parking lot with a few bikes locked to a rack and a plastic bag tumbling end-over-end through the image. A red-haired woman named Holly, who worked the desk in the ante room, passed a fob to me across the counter. I pressed the small flat square against the electronic grille beside the newsroom door and it bleeped, opening with a *ka-chunk*. I walked into the *Yellowknifer*.

I'd like to report that when I crossed the threshold, the paper's writers and editors stopped mid-keyboard tap to freeze at the sight of my figure— the distinguished fake journalist filling the door frame while delightful fanfare peppered the air—before hurrying to jeuje my writer's station and offer me a disposable cup filled with gin and grapefruit juice. Instead, everybody kept working. Finally, Mike Bryant, the paper's senior editor, turned from his desk in the middle of the room—he was positioned this way, I would learn, to more easily converse with, and occasionally hector, the greatest number of writers at a single time—and said, "So you must be Dave."

"I must be," I said, waiting to see if my insouciance would turn any heads (it would not). Mike came over—thick brush of dark hair over friendly, if discerning, eyes and a rugby back's build—and shook my hand before walking me to my place in the newsroom. Mike had lived in Yellowknife for much of his adult life, moving in 1996 to The Woodyard in Old Town, although he'd spent time in Winnipeg before that. He remembered chopping wood at minus 40 to heat the shack after coming home from the bar, and using honey buckets in the absence of running water. He'd suffered through the tough winters and played in a band, Small Town Rhino, fermenting his reputation as a rough-souled musician who lived along the edges of life. When Gord Downie was in Yellowknife with the Country of Miracles to play the Folk on the Rocks music festival, he asked Mike to help cast the video for "Vancouver Divorce," which the musician shot in town using a sixteen-year-old *Yellowknifer* employee— one of the truck drivers—as its lead. Mike also campaigned for election to city council, posting signs around town that said KEEP YELLOWKNIFE WEIRD (he lost). Whenever the editor's name came up in conversation, people widened their eyes while discussing his days as a wild frontman, a hard piece to fit with how he seemed now: professional, domestic, devoted to his job and young family. I remember coming home after my first day and scanning Facebook for photos, arriving at pictures—none of them posted by Mike—of a bushy-haired, sleeveless hulk sweating and grabbing at the fretboard of his bass like a man trying to strangle a snake.

The *Yellowknifer* newsroom looked as if a paper bomb had been detonated; scribbled-over pages and photocopies and bits of newsprint flowed across every desk corner and around computer terminals. Each station was mummered with coloured Post-it notes, stacks of old *Yellowknifers*, markered folios from long-dead stories, old assignment schedules, and phone numbers scratched on bits of paper that fanned across the flat of the desks. I was encouraged to see that my station was as unkempt and messy as the others, partly because it showed that management didn't view me as someone too precious to mind the disaster (again, no jeujing) and partly because, as an itinerant writer living in a cabin without running water, I wouldn't have to worry about showing up for work spritzed and perfect. I felt even more welcome after deciding that the writer I'd displaced had kept things messy so that I'd feel less self-conscious about worrying the order of his station, even though he'd probably left it this way because he hoped to one day see it again, having been farmed out to Fort Simpson, seven hours southwest of Yellowknife, to work for an NNSL (Northern News Services Ltd.) satellite paper. This was a process through which every young reporter was required to pass: doing time in the communities before returning to their chair at the *Yellowknifer*. Most writers complained about having to do it, but Mike, and Bruce Valpy, believed that it made them better journalists. This was also part of the *Yellowknifer's* ideology: to serve communities around the Northwest Territories with the semblance of a working press.

Along the top of the newsroom walls were small plaques and citations tilted after years of feather-dusting: Atco Gas Photographic Award; Better Newspapers Competition Certificate of Excellence (Mike Bryant, 2nd place); CNA Award Best Technical Photo (3rd place); Air Cadet League of Canada Citation; Certificate of Gratitude from St. Patrick's High School and several Alberta Weekly Newspaper Association awards, even though Yellowknife wasn't in Alberta. In one corner of the room stood a shelving unit with nothing but old papers piled on it, and in another was Valpy's glass-windowed office. He was seen or heard only when a serious issue was at hand: a problem with a writer out of town; a complaint registered by this or that government office; an insubordination by a staffer; or the large water cooler being removed from the office, an issue that seemed to cheese reporters off more than having to pack up and head to Rankin Inlet. Valpy moved quietly and smoothly as if he were drifting across the plane of the world, and because of his slow, easy way and the fact that his authority was parcelled in small measures, his commands were affecting and formidable (whenever Bruce opened his office door and asked a writer to come in, you knew that something was up; I imagined less trumpeting fanfare; more long carving cello strokes). Phones cricketed, printers rumbled, and an army of keyboards were struck like popping popcorn, yet Valpy went about his work in the dim light of his office. If you didn't know him better, you would have thought he was hiding.

As well as managing the paper, Valpy was a writer himself: a playwright who'd staged a show about the life of John Hornby, the early, unhinged Barren Lands explorer who lived to an advanced age despite subjecting himself, and his companions, to starvation in the wild. Valpy had lived by himself for six months in the Far North as a way of understanding the place—and the reality of life in the greater Northwest Territories—after moving from Fredericton, New Brunswick. He possessed an intimate sense of the city. If the metric for people living in Yellowknife was five years, Valpy set a new bar at twenty-six, which he held like a baton above his head. He was resolute in his commitment to the place while also stubborn and unyielding about what the *Yellowknifer* was and how it should serve the city, guarding the ideology set forth by its original editors. If the paper was fatter and more colourful with longer stories than it had been during its monochromatic inception (colour ink was introduced as recently as 2014) it possessed the same cemented notion of who they were writing for and why, ignoring trending stories—the kind that had grown in importance for other city presses—and leaving international events to the rest, no matter how seismic. Valpy told historian Meagan Leonard that stories of people coming and going in town were the stories that still moved papers from the newsstands, "getting cut out and put on the fridge before they go yellow and fall," he said. In this sense, the template of the *Yellowknifer* then and now was strikingly the same. If you still wanted to find out why the cops were on the block a few days ago or where that dark smoke two streets over was coming from or what was going on with Decheco King—a notorious and inveterate criminal who had allegedly slain a man with an ornamental sword before escaping from prison

after bounding over a fence using the top of a barbecue as his vault—
you turned to the city newspaper to find out.

The *Yellowknifer* was a true paper in that it refused to acknowledge
an ethereal media. It had zero digital presence short of a sticky, paywalled
home page. This prevented writers from tweeting links to their work—
occasionally, they photo-capped pages and posted them on Facebook—
and gave the *Yellowknifer* no presence in twenty-first-century media (few
of my friends in the southern media had heard of the publication). Neither
Bruce nor Mike seemed to care. That the paper's stubbornness occurred
at a time when most North American papers were funnelling massive
dollars into building tablet versions of their print editions was astonish-
ingly brazen. If you wanted to read the *Yellowknifer*, you had to buy the
Yellowknifer. You had to walk, drive, cycle, or snowmobile to a newsstand,
or find one of the kids selling papers out of large cloth bags (the paper
became a twice-weekly concern in 1989). The kids made a quarter for each
paper sold and went table to table around bars and restaurants, a gesture
that reminded one how near to the past so much of Yellowknife remained.
I heard a young newspaper seller ask a patron "Hey, mister, do you wanna
buy a newspaper?"—as if he were in a scene from *Bugsy Malone*. "We get
strong kids; strapping kids. Only the best," said NNS publisher Mike Scott,
who I thought was overselling the point a little, but still.

I asked Bruce about being a print-only operation in a time of digital
frenzy (even the paper's computers were old clunky Dells that sometimes
worked and sometimes did not) and the fact that the *Yellowknifer* still
refused to publish any news from elsewhere. He looked at me through
round glasses, tipped his chin forward, tented his fingers and, with the
mellow of his voice couching the violence of his words, meted out a three-
beat phrase:

"Well. Fuck. Elsewhere."

I thought there could be worse phrases or slogans for Yellowknife—
it was at least more effective, I thought, than NWT Tourism's "Gateway
to the North," which implied that Yellowknife was a place that you left

to go somewhere else—and, in this sense, there was no better symbol for the attitude of the city than its paper. There was also the booze and drugs and dysfunction and the time that one *Yellowknifer* writer took ecstasy and passed out by the side of the road near the airport in his underwear and didn't speak for a week. But not to get ahead of ourselves.

5

PHAROAHS OF THE PRESS

The work stations at the *Yellowknifer* were arranged in two rows—writers at the front along the street wall, editors behind them—with a set of desks at the back and along the sides of the room for the photo editor—a taciturn but generous British Columbian named Walter Strong—as well as the sports, entertainment, and business writers. Among the writers, the paper was divided into two camps: either young enough to have been only a year or two removed from J school or veteran hard cases who'd circled back to the small press after years working down south. Mike sat me between two young journalists: Ewan, a late twenties reporter born in Burlington, Ontario, whose dad had been a career reporter in Toronto, and Shawn, an even younger Maritime writer. The two were not alone in their youth. There were a half-dozen other staffers in their twenties who worked at the paper, partly because they worked for cheap and partly because it was hard to get seasoned reporters to uproot their careers for a life in the North. Ewan graduated from Humber College and had worked at a ninety-page paper in Niagara, which he wrote almost entirely himself, while Shawn's last job was in his hometown of Essex, New Brunswick, which came with its own set of complications, having to occasionally report on noted local figures in compromising situations. The *Yellowknifer* provided an elevated experience in that there was a big-city verisimilitude about the news they were required to cover: violent crime, three strata of active government, and an interesting cultural life stewing Indigenous and non-Indigenous citizens. One of Mike Bryant's jobs was to make sure journalists stayed committed to the tenacity and devotion required to write about these areas, even though, a lot of the time, the in-between stories were inevitably about a charity bake-off at the Prince of Wales Northern Heritage Centre or the annual over-fifty N.W.T. tennis championships. This forced the editor to stick pins in their cushions every now and then, but he defended his method by telling me, "When a young writer comes out of the *Yellowknifer*, we like to think they can move on and work anywhere without issue. I know I'm hard. But if I'm not, shit gets out of control. You can't let it become Club Med. You can't let it slide. If you do, it becomes about a loss of discipline and before you know it the same mistakes are being repeated over and over. I mean, Jesus: spell the person's name right. Spell the company's name right. Stuff like that drives me crazy. You can't allow them to get away with things." This was, perhaps, easier for editors to achieve at the *Yellowknifer* than other papers because a lot of writers— especially the younger ones—were low on confidence and self-esteem. They were entering a world and an occupation in which they weren't certain they'd succeed or, in some cases, continue beyond next week.

Whenever a writer was called out by Mike—often in full view of the newsroom—you could tell what they were thinking: "If he's so smart, why the fuck is he working here?" An ex-*Yellowknifer* writer who requested anonymity said, "Mike Bryant always struck me as a guy who took himself too seriously. I was only in Yellowknife for a couple months, but my strongest recollections involve him huffing over to my desk to give me an assignment. Twice he threw year-old press releases at me before giving me a detailed explanation of the story." When I passed this quote by Mike, he immediately guessed who'd delivered it. "That guy was a pussy," he said, expectorating his words. "He couldn't hack it in the North. He couldn't handle Yellowknife. I'm glad he's gone."

Other than their prose style, Ewan and Shawn were complete opposites. Ewan was tall and lanky and wore skinny jeans with a toque plugged over his dark straight hair. He was laconic to the point that his energy was forever idling, and the only time I saw him excited was after he received from his mother a care package that contained more sets of skinny jeans. He was a champion sloucher, sitting impressively low in his chair and staring fitfully at the screen as if looking at questions on a Grade 10 math exam. His casual nature was such that he is remembered in the courts for once wearing pyjama bottoms to cover a trial. Despite the fact that he seemed born from a Richard Linklater film, there was a brightness of thought in his ideas and the modicum of a big dream that, one day, he might work for an English-language paper in Tokyo. If Ewan gave the impression that it mattered less to him that the *Yellowknifer* was merely a parking spot for his career, he also refused to let the rugged work schedule, the demanding editors, the occasionally sophomoric assignments, and the hack work—weather report, horoscope—bother him. Even though I sometimes felt required to pelt him with eraser bits to measure his consciousness, he was never not writing. He filed, and filed well, although there were some issues, including quoting people off the record, something he insisted was never the case.

Shawn was quiet, too, but his muted presence was less slacker and more Presbyterian Maritime: a shy ginger kid, who, as a novice reporter in a lively newsroom, tried not to draw attention to himself. Even though he was a millennial, Shawn had an older way about him. He dressed with a sense of formality—neatly groomed in a button-down window-pane shirt—and possessed a certain fastidiousness about how he went about his business, which, as a quasi-political reporter—Shawn covered the Legislative Assembly—demanded careful order and quality. He spoke more than Ewan, but only at a single volume—around 1 on your Marshall cabinet—and my tinnitus—around 10 on the Marshall cabinet—often forced me to lean in to hear his rejoinders. On the telephone, he was gentle-voiced and polite when dealing with his subjects, although this often pedalled him toward journalistic dead ends, resulting in deep sighs of frustration, the only time I ever saw him especially bothered, or,

I suppose, excited. At home, Shawn kept a police scanner (his own), which he left on while he slept in case news broke in the middle of the night, something that would happen a few times over the summer. During my first week at the paper, he wrote nine pieces and contributed to a photo essay in the paper's centrefold. He said yes to everything, even when it sapped his energy. He had a hill to climb on his way to becoming a great reporter, but if being a decent person and someone with reverence for the craft counted for anything, he was probably on his way, although like everyone else at the *Yellowknifer*, how he would get there was a more interesting question.

There was an unoccupied desk to Shawn's right that was messier than everyone else's: strewn with potato chip bags, Subway sandwich wrappers, bitten take-out cups with dried pools of coffee at the bottom, a soup bowl with cracker crumbs, old bent pens, an uneven stack of ringed notebooks, a packet of bowed business cards elasticked and shoved under a computer terminal, a framed Crime Stoppers certificate, and an open phonebook splayed face down. I asked whose desk it was, and a few of the writers looked at each other without saying anything. Finally, Karen K. Ho, a gifted writer from Toronto who covered business for the paper, turned in her chair and said, "That's where John sits." And then everyone went quiet again.

Although Karen was at least twenty years younger than me, we had something in common: we'd both been squeezed out at the same national newspaper. She was unsentimental and measured when it came to how she viewed her work both here and down south, which isn't to suggest a lack of enthusiasm. She'd moved forward in her writing life the way a paper airplane moves through the air—dipping and darting, if occasion-ally falling to the carpet—and, more than anyone else, she was wired to social media, recognizing who was trolling whom and what flashpoints had appeared in the Canadian media. If the ideology of the *Yellowknifer* reflected a time past, Karen had a modern view of how journalism worked: tracking hits and retweets, and finding out what kind of stories were land-ing and where.

"The *Yellowknifer* was the only place in Canada that hired me to write full-time about what I like to write about," she said, justifying her decision to have travelled so far from her home. She was committed to putting in her hours as a full-time reporter, understanding that it was this kind of work ethic that got one noticed at bigger papers. She also chased freelance work and longer-term projects and created opportunities for herself (a lot of *Yellowknifer* writers did freelance work under pseudonyms to supplement their incomes). Despite these ambitions, she wasn't beyond embracing the charms of being in a small place. "People in this town know who I am," she told me, smiling a quicksilver smile, "and that's new for me. In Toronto, I was never recognized for being a writer, but here it happens a lot. I've written things where the next day everyone talks about it. In Toronto, that's much harder to do because there are so many other voices. It's good for one's confidence, knowing you're being read." While confidence is a struggle for anyone who creates for a living, Karen seemed capable of holding self-doubt at bay (at least publicly), especially with the challenges of living in a remote place. "In the beginning, weeks would pass when people here would go out for drinks and I'd just hide in my room. The thing they don't tell you in J school—right after they tell you that you have to live and work in a small town to start your career—is how hard it is. You're not only far away from everybody and the only place you've known for a long time, but very few people look out for you. If you're used to chicken soup from your mum, there's no way you can get your cultural equivalent. I poured a lot of energy into working on a large freelance piece and had lots of anxiety about the story. Mike told me, 'If you blow your deadlines because of freelance work, it's not going to be good.'" As it stood, Karen's large freelance piece—a parallel narrative about growing up in an Asian family with demanding expectations, and a woman she'd known since high school who'd hired hit men to kill her parents—was on track to be published in the summer by *Toronto Life*, a magazine with eleven times the circulation of the *Yellowknifer*. As it turned out, no amount of poise or steadiness could prepare her for the global response to the story.

Mike and Bruce brought me into a small meeting room at the back of the office and discussed what I'd write for the paper, and how much I'd get paid: a hundred dollars a column, fifty dollars a photograph. "Just so you know," said Bruce, fanning his hands across the table, "I'd have you writing two stories a day if you weren't Dave Bidini," which made me wish I weren't Dave Bidini.

"Well, I'm not precious," I said. "You can work me. Feel free to treat me like everybody here."

"We write to a basic level," he said, trying to let me off the hook. "Besides, writing one column and doing some other things, you'll be plenty busy, I think."

I decided to trust him, grateful that I wouldn't have to go through the neurosis of having to pitch stories or worry about whether my work would live or die week to week. Bruce tented his fingers and said, "We'll call it 'Bidini on the Town,' or something like that," and I nodded, hiding my thoughts that, while it wasn't the best name ever for a column, at least it wasn't the worst. Bruce suggested that I start work on an introductory column to announce my presence in the paper—it seemed like a good idea—and when I got up to return to my station, a great roaring sound found me from the back of the room. Bruce noticed my alarm and said, gesturing with his thumb, "The printing press. Over there." I asked if I could take a look and he pointed me down a small hallway behind the newsroom and a Bunn coffee station with a teetering cone of polystyrene cups. As I followed a perfume of grease and ink, the roaring got louder and then, suddenly, it stopped: *shuuuunk.* I peered around the corner of the hallway behind a thicket of newsprint rolls tipped on their ends.

The printing press was crammed into the whole of the building's rear space, formerly the mechanic's shop at the back of the car dealership. The press was enormous and royal blue—its upper reaches nearly clawed the ceiling—and comprised three towers articulated with jutting sharp angles like a set of robots with their elbows askance. Purchased in 1975 from a paper plant in Mexico, it was part Jetsons invention, part Giger exhibit, its spools of ink drooling colours on the pages that had been threaded through, the current edition suspended in mid-print. The greasy behemoth—brooding when quiet, yet shakingly alive whenever it was powered on—was patrolled by a grey-overalled crew who moved like Pharaoh custodians, examining its contours for signs of weakness. After the press started again—engaged by the thumbing of a great red button at a console in the middle of the room—the workers peered at the newsprint moving into the mouth of the machine, checking for tugs and hitches that might corrupt the paper's flatness as it was fed on an automated track suspended by wires between the towers like dark spider webbing. The papers moved fast, as if they were on some kind of industrial amusement ride—it was here that the process was at its most cinematic—flying copy from on high before being assembled somewhere in the machine's cavity and then burped out on the floor, where a quick-armed, baseball-capped young man picked up the stacks from a tray at mid-waist and bundled them together, sorting them on skids and hauling them out to idling trucks.

After the paper was spat out of the press, a small, overalled man named Jewala opened one of the pages flat on a metal stand-up desk, then leaned in, his face a few inches from the type, studying the work through a magnifying glass. We often think of newspapers as inherently disposable, yet here they were being laboured over with a diamond cutter's focus, the pages hung and clipped across a large easel after being corrected and approved.

After finding me among the stack of newsprint rolls—I'm about as covert as Inspector Clouseau, it turns out—Jewala called me over. He showed me a series of small perforations along the sides of the pages, something he called the "register" which, he explained, had to be punched the right way for the paper to line up and fit together. There were other signs that the paper was, or wasn't, right: the precisely ragged edge of the pages; a set of coloured dots that lay at the bottom of the page, fully bled; and the centrefold at the heart of the paper. If Jewala and his charges—mostly from Cape Breton or Newfoundland, it turned out—didn't catch the imperfections, the edition was compromised; improper alignment cost the company hours of work and wasted newsprint. Electrical outages were also never far away in a city where the winter was a constant challenge, and where soaked power supplies due to freezing temperatures tested the patience of everyone (the cold was so all-consuming that the Dene measure life in winters passed, rather than years. If they want to know your age, they ask: *"Ne hrie tan-nite?"* or "Your winters, how many?").

After examining a set of pages, Jewala told me: "I am making art, you could say. It's something new every day. New words, new pictures. New problems," he said, sighing with a small laugh at the end. I'd worked in factories before, but there was something poetic about seeing men walking around the floor reading newspapers, an offence that, in my teenage days working in a shoe factory in Etobicoke—a job my father secured for me and a place employees called "The Hellhole"—would have been gunpowder for the Philistines. There was also a certain romance about the clarity of creation that passed from writer's terminal to editorial desk to layout station to printing press, all under one roof. No matter how hot or immediate or vital the manifestation of digital news, here a machine roared, a shaking Goliath grinding out the words and pictures of a city press, with a crossword in the back.

Behind the machine was a red metal door, and it was through this door that the workers as well as *Yellowknifer* staff went to smoke, which everyone in the North seemed to do. Through the door frame, the sun snaked into the dim back end of the building and so I followed it outside, where I found a man with a grey goatee and shorts pacing around arguing into his phone while hacking on a dart.

"Well, no, no, no, that's not what I'm saying. No, no, okay, just listen to me for a second, if I can be so bold," he said, laughing nervously and drawing on his smoke.

"No, no, *right. Right.* That's my point," he said, pacing more quickly. "I'm giving you the opportunity here because I feel I owe you that opportunity."

The person saw me and did a double-take, holding up a finger.

"Listen, can I call you right back? Yeah, yeah. Okay, yeah."

John McFadden shoved his phone in his pocket.

"I didn't believe them, but it's true," he said, cracking a smile.

"What's true?"

"It's you."

"Huh?"

"It's you. It's Dave Bidini in Yellowknife," he said.

"Yeah, I guess it is."

John's phone rang again.

"Oh for fuck's sake," he said.

"Yeah, yeah, okay. Lissen, next Thursday I'll have the money."

"That was my weed dealer," he said, lighting another smoke. "But maybe you didn't need to know that."

6

AKAITCHO AND THE WOLF

Yellowknife is home to Dene Nation. The word "Dene" can be halved to find its meaning: "De" being "flow," and "Ne" being "Mother Earth." The Dene origin story centres on two medicine men—Yamoria and Yamagh—who may or may not have been the same person (the myth varies and includes both names). Yamoria and Yamagh were discovered in the bush at the base of a felled tree by a young girl, who brought them home to her parents. As they grew up, the world was revealed to be dominated by warring people, and so the two children worked to end this, Yamoria travelling by spirit flight to the Mackenzie Valley, Yamagh to the mountains. They encouraged elders to lead their communities and stressed that people communicate through words, rather than force. They did this, partly, with mind control, making them both mystical and a little Vulcan, and partly by creating an edict under which they felt the Dene should live. The rules of this edict included "Love each other as much as possible" and "Don't harm anyone with your voice or action" and "Don't make fun of each other, especially in the matter of sex." Yamoria and Yamagh were benevolent figures, and whenever they were challenged by people wielding corrupt medicine power, they clapped their hands and the men expired, avoiding bloodshed or gunfire.

The city proper was named after the Yellowknives—*T'atsaot'ine* in Dene, or "Copper Indians" to others—whose name was anglicized by European explorers like Samuel Hearne—the *kwet'i* or *mola*—drawn to the bright copper used in tools and weapons. The Yellowknives were the descendants of the Athabaskans, the largest Indigenous linguistic group in North America, stretching from the Canadian north to the American south. (The Dene and the Dine—the Navajo—share nearly the same language, leading to the suggestion of a great migration over untold stretches of land at an early point in North American history, while remaining the continent's most compelling linguistic puzzle. In fact, there are prophecies as far south as Guatemala that suggest a return to the ancestral North as a way of making whole the Indigenous people of Latin America.) Through the naked history of Old Town and N'dilo, it wasn't hard to imagine what might have happened had the forebears of the Yellowknivers—the Northern Plano Paleo Indians, who lived eight thousand years ago—thought, "Ah, screw it, let's just leave and not be cold for once, okay?" Instead, the Yellowknives sustained life through long winters and set the foundation for all that came after, including the creation of a communtiy whose white settlers were thought to be very ill because of their skin tone—resembling "meat which had been sodden in water til all the blood was extracted," according to something Scottish explorer Alexander Mackenzie had heard—and who nearly destroyed the first inhabitants.

The Yellowknives of the late 1700s and early 1800s were led by a revered Copper Indian chief named Akaitcho, or *Ekeicho*, both of which translated into "Bigfoot," owing to the fact that he could range over long distances in the snow ("like a wolf with big paws," wrote biographer Ken McGoogan). If Akaitcho—or Bigfoot—wasn't a poetic enough handle, his two brothers were called Humpy and White Capot, and together they were recruited to join the Franklin Expedition on an early search for the Northwest Passage (two other Indigenous men, The Hook and Long Legs, led smaller parties). As described in Peter Steele's book about George Back, the English naval officer and naturalist who survived Franklin's journey, the first encounter between the Brits and the Yellowknives was almost comical, with Franklin and his group dressed in fully medalled uniforms sitting inside a tent beneath a silk Union Jack awaiting the arrival of the Dene chief. According to Steele, Akaitcho "entered the fort wearing a white cloak covered with a blanket," and, after shrugging at the pageantry, "he sat down ponderously, smoked a peace pipe, drank some spirits with his companions, and . . . told Franklin that it was too late in the year to go much further, but that he would escort them some distance north to 'a land where animals abounded.' " Franklin balked at Akaitcho's suggestion, insisting that his orders had come from "the greatest chief in the world [the King], who was sovereign of all the trading companies in the country" (whether he did this as if he were a John Cleese creation pompously clacking his heels together and raising a finger is undocumented). There was more shrugging from the Yellowknife chief, who instructed one of his charges to draw a map in charcoal on the floor. In the end, the Dene were asked to help with a myriad of duties while moving down the Coppermine River to the Arctic Ocean and back again (the Coppermine Expedition of 1819–1822), hunting and guiding as well as ensuring food stores for Franklin's return in exchange for an absolution of debt between the 'Knives and the North West Company plus a cache of cloth, ammunition, tobacco, and other items. These stores of food would prove important with starvation and hardship striking the Franklin group relentlessly.

Stories abound concerning the mortal darkness and terrible desperation by which Franklin and his men negotiated every step. On a cold fall day in 1821 en route to Fort Enterprise, for instance, one of Franklin's guides, an Iroquois voyageur named Michel Terohaute, hatcheted off what he claimed was the frozen offal of a wolf eviscerated by caribou, but which other travellers—including two of Franklin's lieutenants, Dr. Richardson and Robert Hood—believed was the head of a previously frozen member of their group. They ate it anyway since cannibalism was required to survive, although nine men still perished on the trip. In Rudy Wiebe's elegiac *Playing Dead*, he writes that "five Englishmen . . . survived [the journey]. It cannot be because they were physically stronger . . . [rather] they survive because a) they leave behind their dying . . . b) they eat human flesh . . . and c) they kill the strongest man in the party because they are afraid he will kill and probably eat them." Wiebe talks about how two Inuit hunters were found guilty of killing a pair of rifle-wielding priests, while Dr. Richardson (Franklin's medic) was later accused of a murder but never charged. Over time, if Franklin and his men have been romanticized, it's a distinction that is rarely afforded the Indigenous denizens of the North, who, if it wasn't for their art of survival, would have never facilitated the European explorers' navigation through the greater country.

Opinion is divided when it comes to an impression of Akaitcho, and his relationship with Franklin. There's a conflict, and probably bias, of opinion about whether Akaitcho fulfilled his agreement with the explorer, owing to the paucity of supplies left for him on his return journey. Some suggest that Akaitcho warned Franklin that the idea of leaving stores of food along the way was not a fail-safe (there is also a school of thought that believes that Akaitcho was almost certain Franklin would not return alive, telling a confidante after the party's departure that "he has not the least hopes of seeing one person return"). Others have suggested that he neglected to restock depots at Fort Enterprise and other places because he assumed that Franklin would die on his journey. But on their return home, Akaitcho lost three of his own hunters through the ice and was unable to procure lasting ammunition needed to kill game, severely weakening the band's efforts to help the explorers with food.

One afternoon in Old Town, I met a fellow named Travis Mercredi, a Métis electronic musician who grew up in Fort Smith, a small community eight hours south of Yellowknife. Travis helped me understand Akaitcho's legacy, but I also learned a lot about growing up in the Northwest Territories. I asked Travis how a kid from the communities had become a gearhead in a place where, only a few decades ago, people had voted against allowing television into their region.

"We're way geekier and nerdier in the communities than we're given credit for," he told me, proudly. "The first wave of tech was huge for us because it gave us access, and since the place is remote and there isn't much to do, we got *way* into computers. We also geeked-out to music, too, stuff like 'Wish You Were Here,' by Pink Floyd. Whenever we had socials and dances at the Grand Rapids hall—a.k.a. 'Moccasin Square Gardens'— the whole crowd shouted when the band hit the chorus: 'So, so you think you can tell / Heaven from hell.'" I conveyed Travis's story to Richard Van Camp, the Fort Smith novelist, who confirmed the community's love of rock and roll. "For my friends, it was 'Eye of the Tiger,'" he said. "That song would come on and we would all go crazy." Dëneze (pronounced "Den-A-Zay") Nakehk'o, a broadcaster, MLA candidate, and activist from Fort Simpson who wore a dark blue Seattle Seahawks cap and beatnik's Van Dyke, told me that the song for him was Neil Young's "Rockin' in the Free World." "It was our grad song. It's what everyone in the class walked in to."

I asked Travis about the conflicting impressions of Akaitcho and the Franklin legacy, and he told me that, after Franklin's near-starvation at Fort Enterprise, Akaitcho immediately charged into action, amassing a team of hunters carrying hunks of already scarce meat to head out and rescue the explorer and his crew (among the men were the Dene hunters Boudelkell, Crooked Foot, and a person known simply as The Rat). They walked fifty-five miles in two and a half days, cutting across the deadly winter to reach the site where, after witnessing the deplorable condition of the men, the Yellowknives burst into tears while parcelling out food and blankets and starting fires to warm the stranded Englishmen (a second rescue party followed a few days later). "They could not believe the state they were in," said Travis, "and it broke their hearts that people were suffering on Dene land" (Franklin has admitted that Akaitcho showed him the "utmost tenderness" and cooked for them with his own hands, "an office he never performs for himself").

"History will record what it wants to record," said Travis, acknowledging that, in some instances, the Yellowknives have been painted as

almost begrudgingly heading out to save the men. "But if I know anything," he continued, "it's that the Dene are the kind of people that will
help you. They're more interested in getting along than making anyone
suffer, no matter what's been done to them or their culture. Besides, no
matter what the motivation, Akaitcho rescued them. He could have
easily—*easily*—let them die or gone out there and massacred them. But
did he? No. Honestly, you wonder how the history of Aboriginal people
in Canada would have played out had Franklin perished on the land or
been killed. You wonder what would have followed, and whether whatever
happened to Aboriginal people of the North—Aboriginal people everywhere in Canada—would have happened at all. Akaitcho helping Franklin
is a turning point in our history. The rest of Canada needs to hear more
stories like that. True stories."

Was Akaitcho a good or bad dude? Chances are he was somewhere
in between. After learning, in the end, that Franklin was unable to com-
pensate him for his heroics, the Dene chief said, plainly: "The world goes
badly." He said that they should try to settle things in the autumn and
added, daring a wink: "[This will be] the first time that the white people
have been indebted to the Copper Indians."

My first Sunday in Yellowknife ended up being two days in one: the Summer
Solstice and Aboriginal Day. The Northwest Territories is the only jurisdiction in Canada where Aboriginal Day is a statutory holiday. For the city, it
was a chance to twin these celebrations, making the visitor—the visitor
being me—experience the festivities in one fell swoop. They took place at
Somba K'e Park on Frame Lake ("Somba K'e" meaning in Dene "place of
money," which is what they called Yellowknife on its inception). I liked it
there, but couldn't help note the irony of a manicured green space created
in a part of the world where the teeming wild was everywhere. Still, it was
nicely kept with a bike path tight to the shore and in the shadow of the

Prince of Wales Heritage Centre. Aboriginal Day celebrations included a traditional fish fry, feeding of the fire, a cameo by NHL veteran Jordin Tootoo, and performances on a flat asphalt stage under a low white tent by the Scottish Métis dancers of the North Slave. The moccasinned troupe were dressed in red-and-white embroidered cowboy vests and skirts, each with sashaying fringe. During their performance—another hybrid moment where Highland dancers kicked to barnyard Manitoba fiddle music played by Métis with electric guitars—the patriarch of the host family announced the dancers—a parade of sons, daughters, cousins, and sisters—by their scholastic achievements, telling the crowd, "Robert is entering his second year of community college in Lethbridge!" and "Brent wants to study to be an actor. Do you think he's handsome enough?" and "Susan just got back from helping her cousin get settled in Pond Inlet and is going to Toronto for nursing college in the fall!" The dancers' accomplishments were important, especially in light of the North's limited education opportunities, the legacy of residential schools, and the Métis' historical lack of First Nations status, which was finally granted in 2016 ("The government has always been afraid of us!" shouted the patriarch between songs, half-joking, half-not). The crowd applauded the dancers' achievements, and while it might take seven generations to reverse what Indigenous communities have had to suffer through since existing with the non-Indigenous world, a bunch of white folks cheering a kid who was trying to be a nurse wasn't the worst thing that could have happened at this tundra Opry, which concluded with a performance by the casually attired Dene drummers—bluejeaned and baseball capped—striking caribou drums while singing melodies older than any I will hear in my lifetime.

After the show, I was introduced to Snookie Catholique—Bruce Valpy's ex-partner—the CBC broadcaster and former N.W.T. language commissioner. A discussion of her full name—one of the great names, I told her, honestly—led us down a rabbit hole of conversation about the origins of other colourful Dene handles—Chocolate, Football, Six

Pack—and how many of them were applied during colonial posts by lazy trading agents. According to the brilliant writer and historian, and Oblate priest, Bern Will Brown, one fellow in particular, Charles Gaudet, who managed a trading post at Fort Good Hope, almost single-handedly wreaked havoc on Indigenous names, establishing longstanding family patronymics after the nature of goods purchased at the post: Tobac ("tobacco"), San-Couteau ("no knife"), and Kochon ("pig"). Another person named Abe Okpik—more sensitive than Gaudet—is also responsible for the integrity of the Territories' family names, having been entrusted in 1969 by former Territorial Commissioner Stuart Hodgson (whom Inuit called "Oomemak," i.e., "muskox") to correct the scourge by which Inuit and Inuvialuit families had been issued numbers by the Canadian government rather than unwieldy—to white officials, at least—given names. When Okpik asked them to choose surnames, many reached for the handful of English words they knew, which is how we ended up with men and women named after traded dry goods and words like "Norwegian" and "Greenland."

As outdoor civic festivals go, the Aboriginal Day event was fun, but I returned to Peace River Flats, where I borrowed a bike from the Allooloos and took off. It was just after 8 p.m., but it might as well have been early morning. One of the things uppermost in my mind before coming to Yellowknife was how, beyond the obvious readings and local resources, I might learn about, and make contact with, the Dene community. On my ride, one swooping Old Town road led to another which led to another. And then I was in N'dilo.

Novelist Elizabeth Hay tells us that, before the bridge, N'dilo was accessed by a row boat paddled by a woman named Bertha, who charged travellers one nickel per ride to get to the other side. N'dilo had street signs written in Weledeh (a Dene dialect) and wood cuts in the shape and colour of the city's name (in the 1800s, the Slaves massacred the Yellowknives, their old aggressors, forcing them to resettle in another part of the lake). The neighbourhood had a little bit of everything: mansions with backyards leading down to the water, falling-down shacks, and bungalows tucked one against the other. There were porches and satellite dishes and SUVs and curtained windows and garden ornaments and kids' tricycles tipped over on manicured front lawns. There were magazines and flyers left on doorsteps and, in one case, a Habs flag flying over a garage, which meant that the Dene had to put up with jerks who like the Montreal Canadiens, too. I felt haplessly southern—and haplessly white—having assumed that the community would appear wilder and more foreign to me. I felt even more colonial after coming across a wooden teepee assembled between two homes, exhaling as if to confirm my cultural and societal bias.

I rode past CKLB, the community's Tlicho radio station housed in a log cabin across from a float plane dock. I parked my bike and sat on the embankment watching five large smoking men try to load a refrigerator into a pontooned Plummer's Arctic Lodges aircraft that tipped and grumbled with the weight of the appliance. I could hear everything the men were saying: complaining about guests and bugs and the government, and talking about a guy named Ray (apparently, it's always a guy named Ray): how he'd ruined a stove after losing it in the water while trying to push it up a plank. Finally, the fridge landed with a thud in the hollow of the plane. The propellers spun and the engine gurgled and the plane shot into the sky, bound for one of the lodges run by a man named Chummy Plummer, who'd hosted George H.W. Bush and Wayne Gretzky on separate visits. I watched it disappear into the blue on the longest day of the year, after which everyone scattered: me on my bicycle and the men in their long silver-faced trucks.

I rolled back past CKLB. The Indigenous radio station had had its share of issues—mostly related to funding and management, the usual community station worries—but its importance in and around the Northwest Territories was pronounced broadcasting programs in as many dialects as they could accommodate. There was a Saturday afternoon open line show where people from around the Territories called in to request their favourite country and western songs (at least half of them were by George Jones, who, years ago, came to Yellowknife for a show because of the almost manic demand). Callers inevitably began by asking "Am I on the air?" before beginning their request, which never came without an Odyssean backstory. The person would pass the phone to other family members and the calls lasted until everyone had their turn. The announcer—a half-Gwich'in, half-South Asian woman named Nadira Begg—suffered through it, occasionally shouting down those who were offside. It was lively, hilarious, and culturally radiant broadcasting, exactly the kind you never hear anymore.

By the time I returned, I found CKLB consumed in a fog of dandelion spores: huge cottonesque snowflakes that engulfed the front porch like a Christmas globe. I fumbled in my pocket and took a photograph before noticing, behind layers of white, a person with long dark hair, slouched in a chair wearing blue jeans and a grey hoodie, waving around a hand with a cigarette at the end of it.

"Hey!" said the voice through the fog.

"Hey," I said back.

"Hey," he repeated.

"How's it going?"

"Going good," he said.

I parked my bike and passed through the spores to find Lawrence Nayally sitting on the porch of the radio station where he worked. Lawrence asked what I was doing in Yellowknife and I returned the favour. This prompted a long prologue from the young broadcaster and activist that was part testimonial, part sermon, and part lesson on the modern history of the Dene. By the time he was done, the dandelions were gone. He invited me to sit and so I did.

Despite being a slight figure—although married with a young family, Lawrence seemed as if not yet grown into the fullness of adulthood—he used the whole of his physical self while storytelling: throwing about his hands, arms, and legs and occasionally pantomiming to get a point across; pinching his fingers to suggest a narrow escape or distance between life and death; holding up his hands to slow down whatever presumption I was about to make; and poking the air to show the number of stars in the night sky above Wrigley, the small community where he was raised by his gramma—"They called her 'Gosiah' ('Thunderbird') because she was born during a storm," he said—and his grandpa, a nomadic hunter named K'i Yeli ("Fast Arrow") or Bonifaceto the non-Indigenous.

Lawrence was part of a new generation of Dene kids who—instead of sinking into a world of Coke and chips and *Grand Theft Auto*—applied themselves to an understanding of the land and the traditional ways of living. It started early for him, around twelve years of age, when his grandparents sent him alone on a vision quest into the bush. "They said: 'We want you to go over there,'" he announced, pointing to an imaginary forest in the distance. "They told me to build a lean-to, set a snare, find food, and survive as best I could. I did this for two nights, following a special protocol. I made a circle using the ashes from a fire, and didn't leave the circle, which is what I'd been told. I didn't eat, had only a little bit of water, and spent most of my time dreaming. This was my journey into manhood. I knew the concept of *Nah'dah'tseh'ti*—a word in Dene that describes a solemn request for help from all the energetic forces that make up life, such as the air, water, land, insects, animals, and trees—but I had no idea of the number of hours or days it would take. I came out after two days having experienced something, although I wasn't quite sure what it was.

"Later on in June, my elders sent me and three friends to Fish Lake. I was there for a month. We learned how to hunt properly and harvest fish, things we'd never done on our own before. I was with my friends, and it was fantastic. I felt closer to what I would become, but this sense didn't kick in until the following winter, when I went on a hunt to Deline, on the shores of Great Bear Lake. Shit, it was a real awakening for me," he said, closing his eyes for a moment, and then opening them wide to the daylight.

"We were out there hunting caribou," he said. "We'd herded them toward the harvesters and they knocked them down, skinned them, and threw the meat on the toboggan. I felt important and valued, but pretty soon everybody left and I was there by myself. The sun went down and the blizzard started. I got scared. Shit, I was stuck out there. I thought I might freeze. I knew that I could easily dump out the meat and sleep under the toboggans or sleep with the meat to keep myself warm, but I didn't want to do that. I made my offering of tobacco and took off. I packed my meat, started my Ski-Doo, and took my time finding my way home. But the blizzard got worse and my headlights could only see so far in that kind of weather. I had no idea where I was. I fell off the trails and couldn't find them again. I was on packed snow, then not-packed snow. I told myself, 'Just go straight,' but had no idea if it was the right way.

"Suddenly, a black wolf came out of nowhere. It stood in front of my Ski-Doo and looked at me, then it started running. The black wolf had bright yellow eyes and he started to pick up the pace. He looked back and I swear that he kind of nodded at me. At one point I wondered whether I could trust him and whether he was steering me to where his buddies were maybe waiting to kill me. I decided that I had no choice. I kept going."

"I chased him on the tundra and then, suddenly, he stopped. His face was illuminated from the lights of the Ski-Doo and I could see breath coming from his mouth. I felt like I knew him. Then I heard the thunder of hundreds of caribou, and, all of a sudden they were there right in front of me, their tongues sticking out as they charged past. When you get near a caribou you can hear it and smell it, and the sight of this group was like having cold water poured down the back of my neck. The hair on my arms stood up. It was incredible. I wanted to cry, laugh, smile, everything. I felt everything so clearly. I felt every little flake of snow landing on my face. The wolf stood there like a traffic officer. At the end of the herd there was a white wolf and a grey wolf chasing the caribou. As they passed, the white wolf looked at the black wolf as if to tell him, 'Okay, now it's time to work. You've got your friend to where he has to be, now come.' The black wolf nodded and took off.

"I turned off my Ski-Doo and I sat there. Even if I died, at least I'd had this moment, this connection. I started back up and continued going straight. Not even twenty metres away, I landed on solid ice. I was back on the ice road and I followed the snow burn into Deline. When the harvesters saw me, they couldn't believe it. They were talking about having to go out and find me."

After these experiences on the land and in the Sahtu (the northern-central part of the Territories), Lawrence lived in Yellowknife, where he was lost and conflicted. "People told me, 'You can't fish here,' and 'You need a permit to start a fire.' There were all of these rules, all of these boundaries, and I found it hard to reconcile where I was and what I was doing." He abandoned the wishes—or, at least, the aspirations—of his elders, who suggested that he become a leader, a sub-chief, an MLA or whatever important position came next. He kicked around town with his young wife and eventually got a job working for the mine. "It was a difficult thing to do," he said, "because I'd been taught to respect and value what was in the Earth, and there I was working for a company that was pulling things out. I'd spent all of my life in open places close to the land and now I was in a city living someone else's life. Everything just stopped. I got up for work, went to work, came home from work. I was in the wheel," he said, spinning his arm about the air. "I didn't know who I was or what I was doing.

"I remembered being told by the elders that when you needed to figure out which way to go, you took to the drum. I got it out and played it and sang one of our songs, asking for a different job. It was a rainy day, a sad day. I slept and had a dream that my cousin had been shot. I woke up crying. Two days later, my friend, Amos Scott, called and said, 'Hey, why don't you come and work for CKLB? I need a language communicator.' I accepted and pretty soon I realized that it was through the radio," he said, gesturing to the walls of the cabin behind us, "that I could reach great numbers of people. I started telling Dene stories and had other people come on and tell theirs. We had listeners everywhere. It awoke something in them and it triggered something in me. The station engaged a whole new consciousness among people of my generation, as well as older people, too, who thought that it might never come back."

When I asked Lawrence about his responsibilities as a young voice in the Indigenous community, he got up from his seat and kneeled on the porch, stabbing the ground with his forefinger. "I am just an ant," he said. "I am one ant among many. You need a group of people—a team—to carry through with this, and I cannot do it alone," he said, even though, by this point in our conversation, I believed that he could. "Whether it's Dene or Métis, or white people, we are all part of this. *All of us.* We all bleed the same blood," he said, pretending to cut his forearm.

Lawrence climbed to his feet and a door opened behind us. There was a man who was taller and thicker than Lawrence, as subdued as his friend was electric. His name was Jesse James Gon. Lawrence shouted, "Oh, hey: two musicians! Here, talk your musical talk!" before bolting into the station, where he was due to host an evening broadcast that I'd listen to later on my transistor radio, his voice rolling through the speakers like river water under a low bridge.

Jesse was a guitar player. He performed under his alias, Digawolf, whose third album—the Juno–nominated *Nake De (Two Worlds)*—was a rock and roll record sung almost entirely in Tlicho (Jesse didn't start speaking English until he was nine years old). I'd discover through his recordings that he was a visceral guitar player—fast on the neck, but with a layered sound—and his vocal manner was to roar through the choruses with low cage-shaking resonance that wasn't quite throat-singing, but came from the same chamber. If Digawolf had been, like many in the North, a folk or traditional product—money and availability had, for years, made full electric ensembles difficult to assemble—it would have been expected, but, after getting to know his records in the intimacy of my cabin, I was encouraged that the music sounded like where it had been made: towering rock built to match the height and breadth of the Shield.

If someone viewed the two of us from a distance, they might have imagined that Jesse and I were two men disgusted with the world, flailing our arms with every thought. But this was owing to a sudden storm of large deranged bugs, who arrived in dark clusters, dozens at a time. Having been raised Dogrib in Betchko, Jesse had mastered the talk-and-swipe, but I must have looked like I was waving semaphores. I told myself that the dive-bombing bugs were an aberration, but they only got worse as the summer lengthened, threatening to make my experience less about an understanding of the North and more about one man complaining about insects.

Jesse told me the story of how he got turned on to music. "My dad was a trapper, but he liked to play music: at home and sometimes at small parties. He spoke only Dogrib and the only times I ever heard him use the English language was when he'd sing Hank Williams songs on his guitar. He learned the words phonetically from the records, and because he played and sang, it's how me and my five brothers got into playing. My brothers were in bands, so that counted for a lot, too. They used to play records and jam through songs in the living room. They'd listen constantly to 'Honky Tonk Women' on the stereo, playing it over and over and working on it."

Jesse's musical life changed the day his brothers were clearing out their CD collection. He was twelve. "They had one disc that angered them, really pissed them off, you know? They threw it into the garbage and said it was unlistenable. I went to rescue it and when I put it on, it was so different, so strange. It was the hard blues, you know? And the singer growled. But it was beautiful, too. It was 'Rain Dogs' by Tom Waits. No one knew anything about him and so, for years, I walked around thinking that I was the only person who'd ever heard of Tom Waits. And maybe in the North that was even true."

A few years ago, Jesse was asked by a local Yellowknife promoter to open for the White Stripes on the Detroit combo's tour of the Canadian North, which stopped in Yellowknife for a show at the Multiplex. It seemed like the ideal gesture and the perfect bill—American independent superband facilitating exposure for an important local artist—but it didn't end up playing out that way. Jesse was joined by Mike Bryant on bass for the show. One day while sitting around the office, Mike revealed that "we showed up at the backdoor of the venue in the afternoon to do a sound check, walked in with our guitars, and the White Stripes were on stage rehearsing. Some guy wearing a big hat and a little red suit and tie—the crew and band's uniform for the tour—came marching over, grabbed us by the shoulders, and pushed us out the door. We appealed to him—'We're the opening band'—but he didn't care. We were out on the street. We met the White Stripes. They came in with their train of royalty and we stood there like servants, shaking the band's hands as they walked in. They put on their show and I thought they were really good. It was great that they came here. They even had a big N.W.T. flag that they waved around and people loved it.

"After the show, we went to get paid. We weren't there to do it for free. Jesse sought out the promoter, a local guy, to get our money. He said, 'No, you've gotta go to the White Stripes' manager to get paid.' It was the same guy who'd kicked us out before. Jesse chased him around and finally the guy said, 'Here,' and handed Jesse two hundred bucks from his pocket. Jesse took the cash and went looking for the band. He hunted Jack White down and knocked on his dressing room door. Because Jesse is so unassuming and such a sweetheart, they let him in—you just can't say no to Jesse; he's too good a guy—and he told them, 'Hey, Jack White. I just wanted to say thanks for the money but I wanna give it back to you and support the White Stripes because I believe in what you're doing. I want to donate to the band.' Of course, Jack White wouldn't take the money, but Jesse wouldn't leave. He kept offering it, and pretty soon, I think people got it: how obnoxiously low the amount was; two hundred dollars from a group who were selling out everywhere they went. Things got uncomfortable and the band left to get on the bus. Jesse went after them but they closed the doors to their coach and pissed off. He ended up leaving the cash inside the arena, walking away from it. I doubt that Jack White had any idea what was going on. But I like to think that every now and then he remembers Jesse, and that, one day he'll under-stand what was happening."

I said goodbye to Jesse and continued riding through N'dilo. My expe-riences with Lawrence and Jesse reminded me of a conversation I'd had the week before leaving for my trip. A friend of mine put me up against a wall in a bar and told me: "Lissen, when you write about Indians, don't fucking fuck things up." I responded by telling him: "I don't think people like to be called 'Indians' anymore" and "Who knows if I'll even meet any, um, Indians. So maybe I'll have nothing to fuck up." He wasn't amused.

"You can't write about the North without writing about whatever you want to call them," he said.

"I don't even think you can call them 'them,'" I said, making things even worse.

"Are you listening to me?" he said with six-beer petulance.

"Yes, I am," I said, with three-beer poise.

"You *will* hang out with Indians. I'm just calling them Indians, okay?" he said to me, taking a smoke out of his pocket even though we were indoors.

"Okay. I'll try not to fuck it up."

"That's the least you can do," he said, pulling out his lighter. "I mean, they've been fucked over enough. And what did we ever do? *Nothing!*" he said, putting back his lighter and walking away, the unlit smoke hanging from his mouth.

I thought of this conversation as I cycled through the community: a white southern goose in a baseball hat riding his ten speed across sacred land while suffering glares of contempt and looks of grit-toothed anger and frustration and hatred that never materialized. I'd arrived in Yellowknife at a time when sociopathic crimes inflicted upon Indigenous communities were finally being recognized, the legacy of residential schools having wrenched a generation, and a generation after that, from their land and culture by forces supported and facilitated by Canada's governing bodies. Had the residents of N'dilo lined me up while moving through their neighbourhood, I would have understood their rage, but like Akaitcho, it seemed as if they were more interested in living together than exacting revenge. Dëneze asked me, his beard arrowed in defiance: "Have you ever seen any First Nations take up arms and terrorize non-Indigenous people? Have you seen us mobilized by hate and revenge? No, you haven't. It's not our way. Is any of this celebrated by other Canadians? No. But that's okay, too. You're here. You're figuring it out."

I told him I was a long way from figuring anything out—the North, the Dene, Yellowknife, the land—but I was *up here*.

I would try.

7

≡

FUZZ AND DISTORTION

John McFadden was a large man in a smaller man's body: five foot something and asthmatic, having taken up smoking at forty despite a collapsed lung. "People tell me I have an honest face," he said, doing nothing with his eyes or mouth to disprove the point. John had a rousing laugh like a New Year's Eve party favour: the kind that you held in your hand and spun until it cackled to rest. He considered himself both above the mean at which his career had levelled while acknowledging that he probably deserved to be where he was: working for a small paper in a remote corner of the continent for half of what he'd made in the big city back home.

John was as close to hard-boiled and hard-drinking as anyone at the *Yellowknifer*. In many ways, he was the kind of subject I'd been hoping to find after walking into the newsroom: a lifer who couldn't help himself and who didn't know any better. He'd arrived in Yellowknife after working, and then not working, at every level of media in Toronto: fired or excused—John used the word "gassed"—from CBC, City TV, the Sun News Network (for whom he was its voice), and television stations around Peterborough, which is where he landed after leaving his hometown of Orangeville, Ontario. One of the last jobs he had was as the scribbler for the news crawl that appeared on CP 24. "It was mostly okay," he confessed, "and I only screwed up twice. One time, I called 50 Cent 'a raper,' and another I wrote:

69

'[Premier] McGuinty calls pit bull ban *pubic* safety issue.' My bosses asked me, 'What's your excuse this time?' I told them: 'That's where they bite you.'"

John had been thrown out of bars, kicked out of apartments. During his time as a bike courier on the streets of Toronto—a job he took between media gigs—he was apprehended at the courthouse twice while on delivery: once after a security guard discovered a bag of weed, and another time after he made a comment about the cops cracking skulls during the G20 summit. He'd gone to rehab, pinballed around Ontario, and was hired to work at a commercial radio station in Yellowknife—he was fired from that, too—before landing at the *Yellowknifer*, where he emerged as the type of dogged crime reporter that neither the *Yellowknifer*, nor Yellowknife, had ever seen. "John had so much energy, so much personality," one local told me, "that the town didn't know what to make of it. People crossed the street when they saw him because they didn't know what he had to offer. He was a fish out of water, but he was an enormous fish."

John wrote every story hard, in a gust of life. He was perfectly suited to be the paper's crime and court reporter, maybe because he was a reprobate with a straight job, but maybe not. When I asked Mike Bryant to name his favourite stories published in the paper, he recounted John's famous series about the sword murder that had occurred at the Sunridge apartment complex in which the reporter staked out a surviving witness whose name the RCMP wouldn't release, interviewing him for the newspaper. If some factions in the city found distaste in his work and blustering personality, he was the most-read writer at the *Yellowknifer*. His lead in the sword murder story:

> A man who survived horrendous injuries on a night in which his best friend was killed said he is fearful the person who beat and stabbed him will come back and finish the job.

It was a story you couldn't help but continue reading. The last bit— "finish the job"—was classic McFadden, reading the way he spoke: a disappearing kind of writing in a disappearing industry. McFadden was an ink-stained flag bearer no matter the condition of the pennant—tattered, barely hanging off the stick—the rest of the article guiding the reader to a hospital bed in Edmonton—"The victim regained consciousness [but] was still covered in blood"—and back to the subject's apartment, down the hall from a crack den where "everything was upside down and pushed against the wall."

To the young and unproven staff of the paper, John's garrulous nature and unself-consciousness registered as equal parts unprofessional and enviable. In their eyes, it was confounding that someone so deep into their journalism career could end up at a paper like the *Yellowknifer*, and for those who were just starting on their newspaper journey, he was both a road map and a puzzle. While most of the young writers were loath to make waves and end up in Bruce's office with the door shut, John created a wake wherever he moved. Still, if others got wet, few got soaked more than he. No one spent more time wrestling with management, either.

At work, he was either full force—savaging the phones trying to nail down the source for a story from his corner desk strewn with junk and a worn copy of the *Criminal Code*—or running on empty: exasperated at an editor's demand, fed up with his reporter's pittance, and wearied by the claustrophobic nature of the town. "There's Planet Earth and there's Planet Yellowknife," he said, sometimes laughing because the irony of being where he was, was funny, and sometimes not. He shared my concept of everything being stretched here: time, space, perspective. He knew he was somewhere different, a reality that played to his strengths as an inherently social person, but also fed his weaknesses as someone drifting through his career and life.

John was so broad-mannered—pacing on the spot and gesturing with his hands when he spoke—that when he sat in the windowed press gallery of the Legislative Assembly behind the MLAs, he offered better theatre than what was happening on the floor: barking on the phone, stabbing the air to make a point, and vigorously draining cups of coffee while the elected members said their piece in the chambers. After work, John bicycled around town—he didn't own a car, an almost preposterous notion in the North—going from bar to bar to bar before inevitably ending up at Harley's, Yellowknife's infamous peeler joint. Still, despite having the energy of a rolling hurricane, there were times when he moved about as if a storm had robbed him of whatever he carried on his back, which wasn't much, living, as he did, in a shack without plumbing, where, occasionally, miscreants showed up uninvited, waving flashlights and looking for whatever they could steal.

The first time John brought home a woman in Yellowknife, she immediately started cooking ("She was so hungry," he said). Wandering home one night from the bar, he pointed her out to me huddled in a bank kiosk on a cold evening and missing most of her teeth ("She had more teeth back then," he said, shrugging). John had seen a few other women over his three years in the Northwest Territories. Some had stolen from him, some had not. His tightest relationship was with a local entrepreneur named Sarah, whose closeness to John was platonic. John was devoted to her. No matter how hard his life got in the North, he made time to help with Sarah's kids, shepherding them to school when she was busy, taking them to appointments. "I've never had a family of my own," he told me outside the Gold Range. "So, you know, I'm borrowing one," he said, pushing out a smile.

The writer and I were the same age save for twenty-four hours and a year. Growing up, we'd passed identical touchstones: Maple Leaf hockey, Blue Jays baseball, and rock and roll teenage misadventure. When John was fifteen in 1978, he went to see the Rolling Stones at Rich Stadium in Buffalo (Foreigner, Journey, and the Atlanta Rhythm Section were the opening acts). "There was so much pot smoke on the bus," he said, while leaning over a tableful of beers at the Black Knight pub, "that the driver pulled over and told us to stop because he was getting stoned. As soon as we got over the border, I bumped into two kids from Brooklyn. They were the same age as me. We did acid—just the edge of the blotter—and watched the Stones from ten feet away, the greatest concert I've ever seen. I was stoned for sixteen hours, and when I showed up at home in Orangeville later that morning, I walked into a doughnut shop and saw my sister there. She didn't even recognize me.

"I asked the kids from Brooklyn what they did most of the time and they said, 'We get up, smoke a joint, do a line, and play basketball all day.' We exchanged addresses at the show and two weeks later they showed up at my house. My parents were away for two months, so they slept in their bed. I took them around—to Caledon, Belfountain, and the Halton Hills—and we had a great time. A few weeks later, I was in Niagara Falls for basketball camp—Leo Rautins, Enzo Spagnuolo, and all of the big Canadian basketball players of their generation were there—and, when it ended, I hitchhiked to New York City and found them because I wanted to keep playing. Every day, we'd smoke a joint, do a line, and shoot hoops. Buddy, it was phenomenal. We saw Ritchie Blackmore on Long Island, and an unknown band called AC/DC opened. They only had two albums at the time. I handed out pamphlets for some politicians in the worst end of Brooklyn, and made enough money to get home. My parents were back by then. When I got home, they didn't suspect a thing. My sister told them I was away at camp in Midland."

John told me that he'd seen my band, the Rheostatics, play at Artspace in Peterborough. "Buddy, I can't tell you how much it means to have someone born in the same century work here," he said. I wasn't sure whether we were buddies—at least not so soon in our relationship—but it didn't matter to John. "Buddy, I've got nothing to hide," he told me in the parking lot, hacking a dart bummed from another writer. "My life is an open book. I wouldn't recommend reading it," he said, laughing a gallows laugh, "but I'll tell you what's in it if you want to know."

After three years in Yellowknife, John emerged as a controversial figure, and folkloric, too. This came mostly at the expense of two of the city's main providers: the RCMP and the GNWT (Government of the Northwest Territories). Because Yellowknife was a young city still figuring out what it was, its most powerful institutions with large workforces weighted the script in their favour. Because of this, and because of the nascence of the community, their roles went largely unchallenged. There was a feeling among some that, despite the opportunities offered by these employers—GNWT jobs were easily the best-paid in the city—their presence worked to bottle ambition and free thinking and the entre-preneurial nature of the place. According to some, this was partly true when it concerned young Indigenous men and women, the brightest of whom inevitably ended up in the employ of the government working for, or working as, MLAs or Territorial representatives, some influen-tial, some not. One point of view suggested that keen minds were being lost, swallowed like Jonah into the whale.

John's landlord, Elijah, who worked at the Tourist Centre and had lived all his life in Yellowknife, said that "what's worse is the fact that once most people leave politics, they end up on the board of resource develop-ers. They don't put anything back into the community. They don't use their experience to build and improve their city. Instead, they move to one of the city's new condos. They get fat and rich. Most people here simply end up working for the government." Writer Mark Rendell—a friendly and earnest young reporter for the media rival *Edge YK* who also hap-pened to play in a few Woodyard bands—suggested a similar problem when it came to the greater workforce in the North. "One of the issues, not only at the *Yellowknifer* but at CBC, the RCMP, and in the justice system is that a lot of people come here, learn their trade, and then simply leave." To Dëneze's mind, "our education system and funding for training pro-grams are all geared toward the mining industry. There's no scholarships and there's no incentive for the community beyond this."

Elijah estimated that about 70 per cent of all people who lived in the Northwest Territories worked for the government, or arms of the government, including contracts given out by the state. Even more frus-trating to people who shared Elijah's opinions was the fact that, because Yellowknife was small, change could, ostensibly, be affected faster, making the squandering of positive influence even more frustrating. With many people doddering off to the halls of the civil service, the same blood was being recirculated and Yellowknife would be Yellowknife evermore; never the place of possibility and new horizons that Travis Mercredi and Dëneze had suggested. There would still be poison in Frame Lake—and other places, too; the Dene told stories of children and animals eating berries and snow around the Con and Giant mines and getting sick—and hundreds of hard cases with drug and alcohol issues would be left without any support, or vision of support. There was still no rehabilitation clinic in the Northwest Territories. People with addictions were shipped out long-distance to Edmonton for treatment, from where, because of the cost and distance, many never returned.

Because John had arrived from Toronto—and because he'd worked to report hard crime in the veins of a city where breaking news was a staple of the city's social and cultural diet—he treated Yellowknife as if it deserved the same attention. Some people perceived his work as confrontational and needlessly combative and a nuisance to those institutions that had glided across controversy in the North. But he was also affording the city respect, covering it the way he would any other place.

John's first job was at the Moose radio station, then called CJCD. "I was hired by the wife of Charles Dent (the 'CD' in CJCD) on the strength of my resumé. She never heard a tape, never heard my voice. She knew that, because of my experience, I'd be fine. She went from fifty thousand dollars to sixty thousand dollars over the phone when she sensed that I was serious about coming. I had some growing pains when I came here, no two ways about it. After the last of the Dents left in 2013 and CJCD was sold to Vista Media, the first thing new management asked me to do was to lay off the sports director even though our department was only three deep. I saw through the chain that they had no problem downsizing—letting disc jockeys read news stories and vice versa—but I knew from my early days in Lindsay, Ontario, in the 80s that those paths can't cross because the guy who is doing the remote from the car dealership can't report fraud at that same business. Eventually, I asked the management how safe my job was. There was no answer."

John stayed for a while longer, but things soured. "I led two Moose newscasts with a story about how the RCMP had refused to give information to the public about a two-year-old boy who'd been run over and killed by a pickup truck at an industrial yard," he said. "This was despite the fact that an RCMP officer had given a quote to the CBC. I called the cops and asked them to confirm what was in the CBC's story but they wouldn't, so I announced that the RCMP was continuing to withhold important info from Yellowknifers. It was the Tuesday after the long weekend. I was grumpy and probably a little hungover. Less than a week later, I was let go."

John was hired by the *Yellowknifer*—"Two hundred dollars a week, cash, as a freelance writer at first," he said—but as his profile grew, so did his entanglements with the police. "We get a lot of young cops here straight out of training," he told me, "and a lot who landed in the shit wherever they were before. It's not the cream of the crop by any stretch. I knew that something was wrong about a month after I got here. I was at an inquest into the fatal shooting of an Inuit woman and former *News/North* reporter, Karen Lander, which was as much a case of suicide-by-cop as anything I've seen. There were a lot of things that freaked me out, but the main one was that the cops fired several bullets through the neighbour's windows, as well as shooting her several times. Four hours into the standoff—the police had come to Lander's residence after she'd called threatening to harm the cops and herself—they never told the neighbours, not once: 'You know, you might wanna slip out the back door.' They didn't have an ambulance waiting, either. It was abysmal."

John remembered that "the commander that night—the lead officer—said that once the bullets left the chamber, it was done, over, finished. That was fucking outrageous. I wanted to say: 'Apparently, the only people who were causing risk to public safety that day were the RCMP,' but I didn't. Karen Lander came out of the apartment with a gun, but she was too drunk to load it. The guy whose apartment she was staying in told the cops that all of his ammunition was locked away and she couldn't get at it. When she came out of the house, they all knew the gun wasn't loaded. But she threatened them and once you threaten the cops and then you threaten to kill yourself, they'll help you with the latter."

No police were ever charged in the shooting, and John said that even though there were eight or ten recommendations in the Karen Lander report written by Medicine Hat police, the lead cop boasted of never having read it. Because violent crime persisted after the incident, the cycle widened rather than closed, and very few lessons were learned from that tragic day.

"Lissen," said John, shaking his head, "Karen Lander was a woman who'd lost her kids, and the person from health and social services department who'd made the decision to remove them from her was a total bitch. Karen Lander had been at Stanton [the local hospital] threatening to kill herself, but they let her out anyway. She went back to this guy's house and she started drinking. With each call to the cops, she got progressively more drunk, but the cops fucking egged her on. Buddy, they did. They kept firing her up. I slept in the basement of the Yellowknife Inn waiting for the verdict. I did my job but they didn't do theirs. They delivered the verdict at midnight. No charges. None. They killed her and they didn't have to."

If John's open criticism of the RCMP had antagonized the police, his subsequent reporting on an incident involving a sexual predator sent the dials wildly spinning. During his first year covering crime for the paper, John discovered that a man, Bobby Zoe, who'd been convicted of sexual assault, had been released from prison. When John brought this to the cops' attention, they refused to admit their oversight and withheld the details of Zoe's release from the public.

"After Bobby Zoe got out," he said, "the first thing I thought of was the incident with the balcony rapist in Toronto [in the mid-1980s]: how the police had used the person's release as bait [after four unreported incidents]. My headline in the *Yellowknifer* was RCMP FAIL TO WARN PUBLIC

ABOUT SEX ASSAULTS. If you warn people and that drives someone underground, well, that's the cops' problem. Besides, there's no such thing as underground up here so there's even less reason not to release his name. You either fly out or drive out one-way. They can find you. When I pressed them on this, they didn't like it one bit. They didn't like a reporter telling them what to do."

When Bobby Zoe re-offended two weeks later—the same crime for which he'd been arrested: breaking into an apartment and sexually assaulting a woman—the RCMP looked culpable in the assault of one of their citizens. "Listen, nobody likes to be called out," said John. "I get that. But two weeks later the cops held a news conference announcing that they were changing their policies so that this kind of thing would never happen again. I felt good that I was maybe the reason why this policy had changed. The two policy changes were that they would make it known to the public whenever a potentially dangerous offender got out of jail [the North Slave Correctional Centre or NSCC] and that they would tell the public, right when it happens, whenever sexual assault is committed. I left the announcement feeling good. I'd helped them make that change."

Even though John's writing had, in effect, improved life in Yellowknife, people—especially RCMP society, an enormous component of the town—started the usual whispers: John was a loose cannon, a vengeful writer, a cantankerous drunk, and unprofessional in his behaviour. One writer told me that, even after the changes to RCMP policy, "it was all John could talk about, how difficult they'd been to deal with. And, in a way, it's all he still talks about." Holding the cops accountable was at the heart of John's life in journalism, or at least its northern chapter. In the climate of modern newspapering, where reduced staff had compromised the media's ability to pour resources into important stories, John's relentlessness was encouraging, although he forced the editors—Bruce and Mike—to consider how comfortable they were in assuming such a defiant role in a city so small and fragile. John's work struck a nerve in the newsroom like an axe into a tree, and the *Yellowknifer* had never had a more amplified voice. Whether his bosses could deal with the fuzz and distortion was another matter entirely.

8

SLOPPY PUNCHES
ON SPAGHETTI LEGS

My workday mornings started with the sounds of the Allooloo huskies waking in their pen and a choir of birds singing beyond my cabin window, their melodies wild, beautiful, and new. One of the birds whistled a three-note rising figure that reminded me of a small child *wheeing* down a bannister, while another honked like a parent trying to hector me out of bed. Shaking my blankets to the ground—the cold still teased the night even though it was early June—I grabbed my toothbrush, toothpaste, towel, and empty coffee pot and walked across the chainsawed yard to the Narwal, where, inside, I exchanged passing glances with whomever was staying at the B&B: a dozen sandalled Italians grilling sausages in the kitchen's toaster oven; three severe German tourists in hats and shorts looking over a map; and a transplanted Scotsman, David, who lived in Nunavut, wore a too-short blue bathrobe, and spent most of his time in the small common area watching American daytime TV on the Allooloos' satellite dish. If there weren't people inside, they were scattered about in the shade of the rock face, being fitted for life jackets or shown how to handle a paddle before heading out for a morning scoop. Cathy, Tiffany, and a few young volunteers brought the tools of adventure down to the dock while school kids and their mums arrived for summer camp programs. One morning, I stood in the cabin in my underwear, rubbing sleep from my eyes, when a mother and young girl opened the door looking for their program, which, previous years, had been held indoors, a detail that the Allooloos had neglected to share with me. The mother blushed and covered the young girl's eyes—I blushed and covered my nards—and said she was sorry before walking backwards out of the cabin. I shouted that it was fine—"Canadian literature in its natural habitat," I may have suggested—before realizing I should probably get dressed.

Some mornings, I walked to the edge of Back Bay and stared into Great Slave Lake, partly because of its pure yawning beauty, and partly because, as a kid in geography class, it was one of the few map blots tapped by a stick held by my geography teacher that captured my imagination. This was mostly owing to its name, which provoked the same questions every time: "Were there slaves there?" "Actual slaves?" "What had the slaves done to be enslaved?" "Who were their captors?"Another reason I was curious about Great Slave Lake was because one of my friends had an uncle who knew a guy who'd had his penis shot off while hunting in the Northwest Territories. Whenever I looked out at Back Bay, I told myself two things: "Holy crap, that's Great Slave Lake, right there," and "If someone asks me to go hunting, turn them down immediately."

The lake was named after the Slavey, an Athabaskan tribe that lived on its southern shore, although it was two Chipewyans—Matonabbee and Idotlyazee—who drew the first known map of the lake. While Great Slave Lake was evocative to me as a sneakered white kid who'd never been anywhere beyond the crescent of our Etobicoke street, many young Dene wanted the name changed. Dëneze told me that "the name of the lake goes back to the late 1800s, when French fur traders had Cree guides. There were battles between the Cree and the Dene, and when the fur traders came, they asked their guides who these people were, and they said, basically, 'Those are people we battle and we make slaves out of them.'" Dëneze called "Slavey" "a colonial term, a very terrible and horrible name. It's a beautiful place—majestic and huge—and I don't think the current name on the map is fitting." I told John's housemate, Elijah, this, and he agreed: "In the twenty-first century, no place should have the word 'slave' in its name."

Dëneze reclaimed his ancestral name after watching the great militant African-American poet Amiri Baraka (formerly LeRoi Jones) read in a Chicago theatre. He'd gone to Northwestern by way of the University of Calgary, which he entered on an anthropology jag before taking a turn one night into the wrong lecture, where actor Gary Farmer was doing a talk about the stereotypical portrayal of Indigenous people in the media, "using clips from *Braveheart*, *Dances with Wolves*, and a lot of old westerns," Dëneze told me over coffee at the Dancing Moose café, whose back patio gave way to the Air Tindi float base, which sat like a giant snail shell on the shores of Yellowknife Bay. "The actor said that 'all of the information out there on native people comes from a non-native perspective; from books, TV shows, and movies; characters with long hair, and braids with feathers in the hair. People buy into it, and if that stereotype doesn't fit into your head, it's an inconvenience.' He said that our own people were part of it. His exact words were"—he told me, raising a finger—"'All of you native people out there, you've gotta get on the radio, you've gotta get on the television.' It was inspiring. I immediately applied to the Grant MacEwan Community College in Edmonton for the native communications program and worked at CKLB. I went from failing my classes to getting out there and doing it."

Dëneze's idea was to start with the names and move forward from there. "Taking back the names of the land and the water bodies," he said, "is directly tied into identity [Slave Lake's Dene name was *Tu Nedhe,* which he wanted people to use]. For us, coming to terms with having been colonized is almost like an addict realizing they have a problem. People break down and cry when they understand the connection, and I've heard some Dene people say, 'I just thought everything was okay.' My father worked at CBC in the 1970s [he was an announcer] and one day he found himself at a story meeting when, all of a sudden, the producer told him to 'shut the fuck up.'

The behaviour was normal and back then, you could call someone a native piece of shit on the street and no one would bat an eye," he said. "Some people stood up and said it was wrong and the red power movement— which came out of Black power—had a lot to do with it. Amiri Baraka coined the phrase 'Black is beautiful' at a time when Black people felt bad about themselves, the way a lot of Indigenous people do now. Things have to change," he said, stabbing a finger into the air, "and things *are* changing."

Even though something about Canada in the twenty-first century felt different—singer Gord Downie calling out Justin Trudeau on national television; the dozens of men and women I'd seen reading copies of *Indian Horse* on my journeys around the North and across Canada; Tanya Tagaq's Polaris Prize–winning album; and television features, essays, and long-form newspaper stories across a rainbow of Indigenous issues—most Canadians still have mountains to cross in raising their awareness of the presence of First Nations. "Education, education, education" was a chorus that Travis repeated to me a few times, and it could have been the rallying chant for the Dechinta Centre for Research and Learning, a newly accredited college-level "bush" campus supported by the University of Alberta and McGill, where thirty students (out of four hundred applicants, 72 per cent of them women) lived off the grid while studying a hybrid of traditional teachings as well as vital, modern subjects related to Dene life, guided by northern leaders in a variety of disciplines. "It's the first kick at the can at having a university up here," said Dëneze, "and hopefully we can start giving out degrees. What happens is, you're there for two months and you spend half the day maintaining camp—learning to hunt and clean and dress animals—and the other half you're with professors: studying political science, Indigenous rights, and northern development for two seasonal semesters a year. With the exception of the Dechinta, the only way you can get a degree in northern studies is to go to a school down south, but, like, what the fuck is that?"

Travis added, "If Dechinta can take off and can get funding, it would solve a lot of problems. For me, when we got out of high school and went to Edmonton, it was a total bloodbath. You'd go from a small place to a big city, and nobody would be ready. You're dying to have fun and when you get to the city, it's pretty easy. Looking back, they should have never sent us down there, let alone given us money. A lot of guys leave the communities and never come back. They got caught up in the accessibility of everything down south. It's bad. Everyone talks about education because it's true, but people should be able to go to school without having to leave the Territories. How we can become free of colonialism without this being one of the main parts going forward?"

Once coffee-ed and watered at the Narwal, I hopped on my bicycle and rolled through Old Town—the streets were quiet and empty at the early hour—before charging eagerly up the Franklin Avenue hill into down-town (or "Blunderville," which is what the early settlers called it after businesses migrated, en masse, out of Old Town in the 50s), only to slow to a tortured huffing pace trying to pedal up the slope. Knowing that it would be a few weeks before I could master, or not master, the hill, I eased into a more writerly rhythm of moving: studying the faces in the muddy all-terrain vehicles that passed me; greeting the occasional person stroll-ing down the hill; and staring into the window of the Sally Anne—50 cents a book—to see if anything had been added to the pile. There was also the Good Hope shelter, a few pawn shops that never seemed to be open, a Vietnamese restaurant across the street, and a handful of small art galleries with carvings and watercolours in their windows. Around the corner at 50th and 50th was the Book Cellar, a good bookstore whose presence in this small and remote place revealed, I think, something about the people who lived here (there was also a drugstore—Sutherland's—where you could buy the *New Yorker* and *Harper's* and *Ad Busters* and what-ever else a person might find at a cool dispensary on Toronto's trendy Queen West were there any cool dispensaries left, which, in this case, at least, made the score Yellowknife 1, Queen Street 0. Come to think of it, there were also more bookstores on the Yellowknife drag, a vital statistic that Northerners should be encouraged to use the next time a Southerner looks for the caribou shit at the end of their boots).

If Yellowknife had one bookstore, and if the *Yellowknifer* had one book column—the weekly "Spotlight on Books"—the city also had one of everything else: one Canadian Tire, one Staples, one True Value Hardware, one cinema (four screens), and, naturally, one Walmart, which had been in the news after announcing a decision to stop selling Purell due to frequent visits from the city's homeless population, who ingested the clear gel for its low-alcohol buzz (it was also difficult to buy hairspray and most likely accounted for the reason there was no bar at the Yellowknife airport). For people in the communities who struggled to order goods from local suppliers, visiting the Walmart was like a trip to Disneyland. Every few months, they came down from Fort Providence, Whati, Wekweeti, Gamèti, and other places—sometimes on snowmobiles—and shopped all day before staying the night in a motel next to the store, which had recently expanded to meet the demands of the travelling consumers. During a later stay in town, I tried getting on an elevator at a Days Inn, only to be blocked by ballooning shopping bags filled with packs of Hallowe'en candies carried by a young mother and her sister, who'd been sent by their village to shop for the families in town. The same excitement applied to the Yellowknife KFC, where out-of-towners bought dozens of chicken buckets for whatever social events were on the horizon. The KFC regularly put orders on float planes, bringing salty treats to the fly-in communities around the Northwest Territories. Some mining events went as high as a thousand to fifteen hundred pieces, and people ordered dozens of buckets that they would freeze and eat during the cold months.

A strange dichotomy existed on the corner of 50th and 50th. The Book Cellar—elegant and brightly windowed—sat at the elbow of the main post office: ground zero for Yellowknife's poor or homeless community, or at least those who socialized rather than hid in doors sucking plastic bottles of Smirnoff, the community's poison of choice and almost always consumed without the pretence of a brown bag. Because city benches had been removed to prevent congregation, homeless men and women sat on the lip of the flower beds. Sometimes there were laughs, conviviality, and in-jokes; sometimes people huddled in a numbing cloud of abuse; and sometimes men and women shouted and threw sloppy punches at each other on spaghetti legs, none of this hidden—at least in the blazing, full-light summertime—in the margins of darkness. After the RCMP decided to stop arresting people for public intoxication in 2014—this was good news for some, but bad news for those who needed the bed—the violence and anger had grown worse, at least according to people who worked in the neighbourhood. The city would like to have veiled the almost entirely Indigenous post-office community or pushed them to the fringes of the town, but it was untenable: the homeless were custodians of their own theatre, right there in the naked centre of the city.

Many of these people could be seen day-drinking at the post office before heading off to the Frame Lake trail, which they favoured for its grassy beds and shaded treetops, but also because it ran straight to the Stanton Hospital and, around the bend, the bottle return depot. One evening, I toured the trail with Lydia Bardak, executive director of the John Howard Society of Canada and former manager of the Dene Ko Day Shelter as well as co-chair of the Yellowknife Homeless Coalition. Lydia grew up in Alberta with a father who was, in her words, "the king of the rednecks," but "compared to what a lot of suffering families have here," she said, "it was paradise." Lydia worked out of a second-storey downtown walk-up with a foyer pamphlet rack containing comic-panel literature that had nothing to do with comedy, including "A New Day: For Men Who Have Used Violence in Their Relationship; Intimate Partner Violence and Abuse (It Can Be Stopped!)" and "44 Questions," an Alcoholics Anonymous billfold.

Lydia organized the Citizens on Patrol Service, a twice-weekly outreach program in which contact was kept between the inveterate homeless and those who lived domiciled in the city. Lydia was a Julia Roberts' biopic waiting to happen. She had a dutiful, and charming, weariness about her, and because the city lacked a public service dispatch van to monitor homeless life or serve the ranks of the dispossessed, she was all the city had for its eyes and ears.

Our tour was both beautiful and harrowing. The trail was mostly quiet, but we met clutches of people upon returning to the city. Lydia knew everyone by name. She knew where they were born, if they'd been in jail, who their parents were, and whether they had any brothers or sisters or cousins on the street. She also knew if they'd been victimized by sexual violence, or if they'd done the abusing. "Sexual assault and rape is a real problem on the street," she said. "Women who live out here are vulnerable. They're assaulted all the time."

Many of the people living on the streets had been in and out of child welfare in the early parts of their life and had fallen into addiction afterwards. "When you're sixteen and in the hands of the state," said Lydia, "they ask, 'Do you want to stay or do you want to go?' You're made to feel useless and unwanted. If that was what my life was like from the beginning, I would probably drink, too." Activist Emily Lawson's experience in addiction counselling pointed to a similar set of numbers: "Ninety per cent of the girls I've worked with have been sexually assaulted and the further north you go, the worse it gets."

Travis Mercredi had travelled to the circumpolar community of Paulatuk, where, he said, "the principal of the school told us that there wasn't a single woman in the community above the age of thirteen that hadn't been sexually abused. No one is charged and no one talks about it. When someone speaks out in the community, they get ostracized and there's a sense of shame. If you want to leave the community, a miracle has to happen. People end up thinking, 'I'll just get arrested and go to jail in Yellowknife. I'll get out and then I'll go stay in a shelter.'"

According to bassist Pat Braden, one of the tenured builders of Yellowknife's evolving music scene, the homeless population had thickened because "a lot of people come here for prison, and when they're released, they stay. They get into bad habits, they're on their own, and it's often too difficult to return to their communities; partly because it's logistically difficult, and partly because it's hard to go back in a personal sense. There's no preparation on the government's end to help them through transition and, because there's no drug or alcohol rehabilitation clinic, if you fall back, you just keep falling. There are a limited number of beds in the shelters, and there used to be a few halfway houses, but the last of them closed." Another roadblock was the fact that the Dene who sought treatment were sent to a place called Poundmaker Lodge, a Cree facility whose healing techniques were based on the traditional Cree experience. Columnist Roy Erasmus Sr. wrote in the *Yellowknifer* that the government "sending Dene people to Poundmaker is continuing the colonization that started years ago." Bruce Valpy added: "No matter where or how you're treated, you never end up with the best doctor. The best doctors leave, and in some cases, our health care services aren't up to it."

During my walk with Lydia, I met men and women from everywhere. I spent a few moments with a hulking man the size of a Coke machine with an enormous egg-sized bruise over his eye who wore a Chicago Blackhawks T-shirt. He told me that he used to play hockey in Fort Smith after taking purple micro-dots to "make things more interesting." I met glue-sniffing kids from Dettah on BMX bikes who pedalled in circles around us cackling like hyenas, as well as an Inuit man who spat at Lydia and called her "a skinhound," his crooked arms violently shadow-punching the air. We met a sad older couple from the Deh Cho—their faces and half-lidded eyes purpled by booze—who retreated into a dark entranceway with a bottle held tight to their chest.

Near the end of the walk, I was introduced to a small, wind-burnt woman with black hair named Grace. She scattered at first before sitting on the steps of the Midnight Sun art gallery, where she started crying. Lydia sat down and asked what had happened. She said that she was in love with a man but that he didn't love her anymore. Lydia told her that she knew how it felt and put an arm around her shoulder. Across the street, the boyfriend appeared, laughing and baiting. Grace yelled at him, fell on her side, and cried some more. Lydia tried to get her to sit up. The man called Grace a whore and disappeared down an alley, proving that assholes are assholes no matter where they sleep.

We ended our walk at the post office, where I met two men the size of compact cars—Bear and James Thrasher, both from Tuktoyaktuk—who, like many of the city's homeless, had come to Yellowknife because of greater access to services, housing, and booze (Tuktoyaktuk was a dry community on the shores of the Western Arctic where contraband vodka sold for one hundred dollars a mickey). When they found out I'd be visiting their hamlet later that summer, Bear asked for my book so he could write down the Inuvialuit word for "white person." I handed it to him—the hardbound writing book looked like a pamphlet in his great hands—and his tongue curved around his lip while engraving the word on the page: *Kabloonik*. He told me in a voice like a hammer on a drum: "Now, listen, you might hear this word, but it's not necessarily bad. It depends on how someone uses it. You got that?" I told him I did.

There were times during our walk when I worried about being attacked. You never knew when things might explode and go terribly wrong. Because of Lydia's close contact with the homeless community—the highest per capita in Canada—I asked her if she'd ever felt threatened or worried for her safety. Lydia answered me by saying, "Oh boy," then directed me to a park bench in Somba K'e near the RCMP detachment. I sat and listened to her story.

"When I used to run the day shelter [before becoming the full-time director at John Howard], our idea was that intoxicated people shouldn't be tying up police time. If we gave them a place to be, they wouldn't be getting into trouble; at least that was the idea. We had a different operating principle than other places, too. In some shelters, if you're doing something wrong, you're banned for days, weeks, but not us. If we couldn't talk somebody down, they were asked to take a walk and come back later. If it was the morning, come back in the afternoon. If it was the afternoon, come back in the evening. People were only asked to leave for a half day. We wanted them to come back and start fresh.

"I remember being at the Salvation Army one night. A young guy walked up smiling and whistling and the staff told him, 'You're barred for forty-eight hours.' He was so crestfallen, having forgotten what had happened the night before. You could just see him sink down. With us, if he showed up in good shape, we rewarded him by letting him in. If he wasn't in good shape, we told him to come back another day. By turning him away and not communicating, all you're doing is allowing him to go out and hurt somebody.

"In the early days of the shelter, I spent a lot of time after-hours, reviewing incident reports, doing extra cleaning. When we moved in, I had a new floor put in, so it was sparkly and nice. I wanted to keep it looking good so people would feel comfortable. Still, we were having break-ins and we couldn't figure out why. One morning, we found two couches pulled together: somebody had slept there. I thought that maybe one of the staff members had had a fight at home and had spent the night. Another time, the fluorescent covers on the emergency lights had been removed and the lights were twisted off. I called the police and they had no idea how people were getting in. The police took [lights] for fingerprinting and found the prints of the staff member who'd taken the lights out of the box, and the one who installed them.

"One night, I came in through the back door. I found a man—his name was Ian Zoe—sitting at the office computer looking at pornography. I was like: 'Dude, you can't be in here right now.' I could tell that he was high. I remember saying to him: 'If you hurry now, you can get into the Salvation Army.' About an hour later, I heard a tap at the back door. Thinking it was my boyfriend dropping by. I went and opened the door and it was the guy I'd found in the office, Ian. He pushed his way in. I said, 'What are you doing?' I went to stop him and that's when he grabbed my wrists. In those days, I wore lots of jewellery, but I don't wear jewellery anymore because of the bruises he gave me on my wrists. He pushed against me and I noticed that he hadn't closed the door. I tried screaming and nothing came out, like something out of a dream or nightmare. It was after 9 o'clock and we were downtown, so no one was around anyway. After I tried screaming, he let go of my hand and punched me in the face. He kept punching. I tried raising my knees to kick him, but I was against a wall and I couldn't get at him, couldn't get any force. I stuck my thumb inside his eye socket as far as it could go. He hit me again and I stuck my thumb in his other eye socket, way down. That's when he threw me to the floor.

"He choked me and tried to rip off my clothes. I could feel the weight of his body on mine while lying face down on the floor. He was crushing my chest and I thought I was going to have a heart attack. I couldn't breathe because of the blood clotting in my nose. I was traumatized by this more than the sexual assault, which involved him grabbing my breast, grabbing my buttocks, and trying to poke a finger in me. He was high on something. He was blacked out at the time, and I knew this because I wasn't getting through to him. When he was still on top of me, there was a moment when I really did think it was the end. I was trying to relieve the pressure and all I could think of was I did not want my mother to find me dead with my pants down in a pool of my own blood. I said the Lord's Prayer over and over again and he screamed 'Shut up!' That's when he came out of it. All of his weight was lifted and he went: 'What the fuck? Holy shit. What the fuck?'

"He picked me up by the throat and went to the kitchen drawer for a knife and that's when he let me go. He tried stabbing himself. He was saying, 'I have to hurt. I have to die,' because when the other people who use the day shelter found out what he did, they'd kill him, which was probably true. Eventually, he slid to the floor and I was beside him. I kept trying to hit his hand so that he would drop the knife. I had to get through to him because suicide is a permanent solution to a temporary problem. I asked him, 'If you die here now, how will I ever work here again?' and 'If you die here now, how will your dad ever come in here?' He screamed '*Fuck my father!*' and I started to go into shock. I asked him, 'Do you have first aid training if I lose consciousness? Do you know what to do? Do you know the number for the ambulance?' He didn't know any of that. He was worried about the blood and he said, 'You have to get cleaned up,' reaching for my face. I was shaking. There was ringing in my ears and I was worried that my jaw was broken. My left eye was swollen shut. I asked him for help getting to the phone and he supported me walking to the office. I asked him to push open the front door so that when the ambulance arrived they could get in. He did that. He paced, holding the knife. The ambulance attendant kept me on the line. When Ian saw the police coming, he ran out the back door and ditched the knife. The cops came in, scooped me up, and went out looking for him. They started to process the crime scene and I went to the hospital. Within twenty minutes they told me that Ian had turned himself in. He showed them where he ditched the knife.

"When you put it all together, this guy is not a bad guy. I knew that a drug high doesn't last very long and I knew he would come out of it. I knew that I only had to survive until it was just alcohol I was dealing with. I told myself, 'Stay here until the drugs wear off,' because drunks are easy to deal with. I was in hospital until five in the morning. I went home, crawled into the tub to soak the blood out of my hair. I phoned my board chair and the national director of John Howard Canada to let them know what had happened. They couldn't open the day shelter that morning because it was being photographed. My two staff members ended up cleaning up my blood, even though we should have hired someone. Everyone was worried about me, but I was worried about them. I was fine. My staff needed support.

"Ian was charged with sexual assault causing bodily harm, break and enter, choking, breaking probation. He got three years and three months in the federal pen. It was amazing how quickly it went. Judge Malakoe had just been appointed to the bench. After sentencing, I phoned the warden to tell him that he was a suicide risk and at risk from other inmates. I called the chaplain and asked him to look in on him because he had no one. And then I called his father. I told him that he was going to jail for a while. I told him, 'Now I have to back off.' I got phone calls from friends and told everyone I was fine. No one believed me, but I knew about the occupational hazards going on. I work with mentally ill addicts. I chose to do this work because I'm good at it.

"Ian was given three years and three months and he served right to warrant expiry. Ian is a young man who, as suspected, was sexually molested as a child by his father, who was sexually molested as a child in residential school. It started with some sick teachers and priests and the residential school supervisors—they sent some of the worst offenders to the North—and then it continued through a generation of uncles and grandfathers, and now their grandsons are at risk. It's grown so large that we should all be interested in making things right. We don't want a disenfranchised angry young man out there. We need to bring him home and tell him it's okay. He can't read, but I've been told he's a good carpenter. We need to get him the skills he needs so he can have a meaningful job, and so that the tortured child in him doesn't continue to destroy his life.

"It's only my story. There are so many more out there. Most victims don't have the strength that I have. Most victims have major destruction in their lives. If I go nuts, people will make sure that I get help, but a lot of people don't have that. A lot of people, especially those on the streets, are alone. For me, it's just sad that we can't do better."

9

GLORIOUSLY AND GLORIOUSER

My first week at the *Yellowknifer* was a revelation, but you'll need to stop me—or perhaps flip ahead—if I come across as a floating-through-life artist layabout who ends up being surprised by their experiences while hanging from society's workday clock hands. For the first time since I was employed at a men's wear store as a teenager, I was hitched to a 9-to-5 grind in a conventional workplace, if one in which, rather than stacking piles of cargo pants at the Princeton Shop—I was pecking words into an old Dell computer, words that ended up becoming newspaper stories.

The writers, editors, copy editors, and proofreaders kept regular hours; drank coffee out of monogrammed coffee mugs; and wheeled themselves in office chairs to the edges of their desks, where they chased stories that filled the pages of the *Yellowknifer*. While pondering my column, I affected, as best I could, a manner of a reporter, making the occasional phone call to one of the local businesses ("What day is wing night? Is it Tuesday? Because I love wings"), tapping out emails to sources in potential destinations ("Can you tell me if your hotel in Fort Simpson has Wi-Fi?"), and, occasionally, burying my head in my hands as if deep in thought ("Did I leave the coffee maker on this morning? Do those things catch fire? I wonder if Loren will go turn it off for me? Better call Loren").

Even though the newsroom was a creative place where writers aspired to a higher craft, it was also an office filled with office types who tacked ironic office things to office corkboards as a way of reminding staff of that funny thing that person said that one time, remember? There was a picture of a nun staring gravely into the camera; a shot of a Buddhist temple with a child praying before it (nobody could remember what was funny about it or why it was there); a coloured photocopy of Edvard Munch's *The Scream* with Ewan's face superimposed; and a Spice Girl in a Union Jack skirt with Grant's face pasted atop her shoulders. Grant was the *Yellowknifer* sports reporter. He was large and goateed—although not quite as eggish as the drummer in Colt 45—and spoke commandingly as if pushing his voice out from his belt buckle. Although I couldn't prove this, he looked like the kind of fellow born to wear shorts in the cold weather, although in Yellowknife's cold weather, it seemed a stretch. Grant spat every time he took a drag of his cigarette, and rocked back and forth on his haunches whenever he made a point. I might have viewed him as an intimidating figure had I not known hundreds more like him: men who feel they must be more manly than the rest of us because they cover other men who play games for a living. Once, he wrote that a player had to "bend over and take it like a man," and another time he suggested that a certain whinging athlete "be taken out and pissed on." Over a photo of the sprinter Oscar Pistorius, Grant wrote, "In happier times, when he wasn't killing people," and in another column he included, "Watching Peter Mansbridge cover the federal election . . . I was waiting for the moment when he would pull out a photo of Justin Trudeau and begin making out with it." Still, because Grant and I shared a love of sports, we had an immediate shorthand, and even though he tried to school me about what was happening with teams that I followed and had known my entire life—he was especially scornful of the Leafs—I sat there and took it like a man. I was there for a good time, not a long time, and it was easier just to agree with him than pick a fight over whether Tyler Bozak was any good.

The *Yellowknifer* possessed other office-place archetypes. A quiet woman named Randi Beers sat near the back of the room editing and laying out the northern presses, and her desk was impressive in that it was the only station that wasn't a disaster. Everything was neatly ordered, including stacks of blank paper; a Strunk and White style book; a souvenir from the Snowshoe Inn in Fort Providence; the agenda for "Ministerial Travel for the Period July to Sept 2013"; a pink-jewelled ring; 35 cents in change neatly arrayed across the top of her computer; a box of Celestial Seasonings tea; a banana; and a baggie filled with all the raisins and nuts that John wouldn't be caught dead eating.

Beyond Randi's shoulder—the second row of desks and the next behind mine—sat Julius, a friendly young copy editor who'd previously worked at a medical journal and whose role in the social dynamic of the room was, as far as I could tell, to know more about anything than everyone else while not knowing exactly how to express it, at least in the short amount of time when, collectively, everyone leaned back from their computers, put their hands behind their heads, and made fun of Ewan's pants before Mike yelled at them to get back to work. A shy woman named Kathy sat next to Julius—the only time we spoke, she told me in furtive tones about how she was learning to use a broadsword, which I found only mildly terrifying—and a woman named Elaine sat next to her. There was a balance between men and women, straight and LGBT. The only glaring absence was the lack of a Dene staffer, although there were Indigenous contributors to the *News/North* editions. When I asked Bruce about this, he said, "If anyone from the community wants to work here, I would never stand in their way," leaving out a few points that critics of the paper tended to dwell on: the absence of its native outreach or an Indigenous journalism program they hadn't yet established.

My first column started fitfully, not knowing what to call those who lived in Yellowknife—were they Yellowknivians? YKers? Territoriers?— or how to open the run sheet, a computer program where the day's assigned stories, and their progress, were tracked. I'd also forgotten that writing in a newsroom meant having to create in the presence of other humming minds, to say nothing of the whistle of conversation and buzz of machines. But it was a lively group, and for that I was grateful. After someone introduced a subject, it would get batted about like a shuttle-cock, inevitably landing with John, who held, twirled, then stuffed it under the weight of his ass.

After John was fired from the Moose, the station replaced him with a fellow named Ollie, an effervescent Brit who affected the posture of a working journalist while hyping Super Bowl Jell-O parties and contests to win tickets to fly to Edmonton to see the Eagles in concert. He imme-diately opened two Twitter accounts to promote his work and, because the Moose was short-staffed, he was on the radio pretty much all the time. Because John resented Ollie, the newsroom went out its way to talk about what a great journalist he was, further chafing John's ass. Whenever John struggled with a piece, someone, usually Mike, wondered aloud how Ollie would handle it.

"Like a mongoose handling a snake," John said, rising to the bait.

"I think you mean 'gecko,'" said Julius.

"Yeah, there's a blind spot in your gecko knowledge there, Johnny," said Mike.

"Well, I know it's good luck to have a gecko in your house in Hawaii. I think I have a fair bit of gecko knowledge."

"I hear that Ollie's got a nice place," said Mike. "A friend of mine was over there the other day."

"Yeah, well, good for him," groused John.

"They were partying with Giselle Forget," said Mike, bringing up the name of the woman who owned John's cabin.

"Giselle," grumbled John. "When I met her, she said that she could tell by looking at me that I was a heavy drinker. But the way I see it, I'm more on the heavy side of moderate."

"You ever have a party at your place, John?" asked Mike. "You got room in that shack?"

"It's not a shack," he protested. "A shack is where Bubbles [from *Trailer Park Boys*] lives. Mine is a cabin."

"He lives like Alexander Solzhenitsyn," said Mike, turning to me. "In the winter, his boots are frozen to the floor. There's borscht on the table. It's like a gulag."

"Buddy, don't you worry about me," said John. "Where I live is the least of my fucking problems."

Shawn arrived in the late afternoon, rubbing his face then slumping in his chair. The young writer pushed out a sigh and rolled up his sleeves, settling at the keyboard.

"Everything okay there, big guy?" asked John.

"The John Franklin high school graduation," he said, speaking as if he'd just returned from dental surgery.

"Got any photos?" asked John.

"I only fell asleep twice."

"You're a warrior," I said, nearly punching him in the arm before drawing my hand back.

"That's me," he said, quietly unwrapping his sad lunch from Subway. "Total warrior."

Shawn covered most aspects of city life. One day, he would write about a shooting in N'dilo, the next he'd be covering news of the first ATM in Inuvik. Like everyone else, he was required to be on the job at all hours, even on off-days. Karen said, "Once, I had to meet a few sources for a story and the only day they could do this was Saturday. So, of course, I met them. I didn't like it—I was burned out the way a lot of the writers are—but if I wanted to get the story I had to do it. That's the way it is for all of us. You do everything here. It's both the best and worst thing about working at the *Yellowknifer*."

John was less charitable: "There's a lot of thankless jobs in journalism, but this is the most thankless. You could have a really good story on a Wednesday, but on Thursday morning get fucking cracking because we have a paper coming out on Friday. *Open the run sheet, open the run sheet.*

It's like there's a parrot in the room. You don't get to enjoy your story for two minutes. Once, I was having an asthma attack and they said to me, 'You can go to the hospital as soon as you have your stories on the run sheet.' Bruce and Mike aren't rah-rah guys, but if it was me I'd tell my writers when they were doing good work."

Shawn uploaded his photos and started on his story. Everybody was busy writing something, having to close the paper at the end of the day for an overnight print run. Behind me, a middle-aged woman named Ellen, who had a stylish grey-black spiked haircut and a tattoo across her sternum that read "I Exist As I Am That Is Enough" was on her feet every few moments talking to the writers while trying to order a sequence of stories that she feathered on the frame of her computer with multicoloured Post-it notes. She ran traffic for the paper as well as the assignment desk and she was the main cog in the whirling dial of stories. I was compelled to walk over—or rather, wheel over in my chair; the staff did lots of wheeling—to tell her that I was ready to step in wherever needed, but didn't want to overstep any boundaries so soon in my stay. But after what, I suspect, was a long while scrolling up and down the *Yellowknifer*'s staff roster before finding my name scribbled at the bottom, Ellen politely asked if I might have the time to write the paper's Buzz feature and the weather round-up—both front-page items—suggesting that I "make it fun." I expressed what must have seemed like a silly amount of enthusiasm before walking back to my desk as if I were retired slugger and pinch hitter Matt Stairs approaching the plate. Hockey, music, world travel are all things I've written about before. But making the weather seem fun? That shit was right in my wheelhouse.

I settled in front of my computer, finally not pretending to be a reporter. In a hot moment of fantasy, I saw myself as Walter Winchell, W.J. Heinz, and Bob Woodward (okay, maybe Carl Bernstein) scribbling out copy. I slashed and hacked at my keyboard with the intensity of an Iron Chef, driven by the opportunity to give people the straight Scotch that *Saturday night's Northstars Youth Club bingo will start at 5 o'clock at the*

Multiplex and proceeds will benefit two softball teams travelling to the Yukon for a tournament. I wrote three items—the complement was usually five— then stopped to breathe.

"Slow down there, buddy. You're making us look bad," said John, which made me feel good.

Once I'd finished the Buzz feature, I scanned every weather site I could find. A few times, Ellen asked if she could add the piece to the run sheet, making the whole process seem more electric. I tracked cold and warm fronts moving south from the Arctic Circle. I compared median temperatures from years past. I looked at weather websites and Twitter feeds, all in an effort to tell Yellowknifers that, no matter what they were planning for their weekend, they would probably do it at 20 degrees Celsius with some cloudy skies on Friday and a possible thunderstorm in the late afternoon on Saturday, but that, mostly, "the weather will start gloriously, and end gloriouser." If that didn't win the *Yellowknifer* another Better Newspapers Competition Certificate of Excellence, I didn't know what would.

After filing, me and a few of the writers adjourned to the Gold Range tavern, sucking back seven-dollar 50s like the reporters we were or weren't. Between the third and fourth bottle, I realized that I had to return to the paper, if only to close a bracket that had been opened years before. I left the Range and fobbed my way into the *Yellowknifer*, walking through the empty half-lit newsroom *zzzrrrrring* with sleeping computers. I made my way back to the printing press and, catching my eye, Jewala produced what I wanted to see. He held the paper in front of me, but as I reached for it, he wagged a finger, rolled the newsprint up with both hands, and pitched it into a nearby bin. I tried not to take the gesture personally.

"Not ready," he said.

After a few more passes, the front page was approved, and not long after that, the paper was ready. I chicken-winged it under my arm, mounted my bike, and headed down the Franklin Hill back to the cabin. By the time I'd exhausted my copy and flung it on the pleather ready for another read in the morning, the workers had tied the bundles together, stuffed the trucks and delivered the papers into the city, where they waited on store doorsteps warm and fat, telling the story of yet another day in the bright North.

≡

10

STAY OFF THE BOOZE
AND OUT OF THE NEWS

To say that John McFadden didn't dominate the newsroom would be to suggest that Keith Moon wasn't a very busy drummer. This was partly because, having worked as an announcer, he projected at great volume, and partly because John's idea of "personal space" and the sanctity of thoughtful quietude were antithetical to his nature. The writers had come to accept this, even though they had little choice in the matter, but because he wasn't boastful—his stories often ended in situations of personal compromise: John picking up two young hitchhikers in N'dilo and bringing them back to his apartment to get warm, only to have his cellphone stolen; John getting locked out of his shack (again); and John breaking his collarbone after cycling head first into the sign in front of the Arnica Inn on his way home from spending Good Friday at Harley's—people tolerated the peccadilloes.

John had once written a story in which the accused—a young woman—was reprimanded at a trial for wearing a Playboy T-shirt on the stand. The woman's boyfriend confronted her after reading the story—she'd been trying to keep her conviction a secret—and she turned up outside the *Yellowknifer* offices with a half-dozen of her largest friends leaning against the fender of her truck, arms crossed, baseball caps tipped low over their eyes. "If one of the guys had got me, it would have been game over," said John, "but I managed to get back inside. I was as white as a ghost, these guys here will tell you," he said, waving an arm about the room. "Before I left her, though, I told her: 'Stay off the booze and out of the news.' It's the kind of thing we say around here now. We use the term," he told me, having crafted a *Yellowknifer* slogan used by no one but himself.

Because John was a crime reporter—and because he did drugs and had his own pot dealer, a Newfoundlander who wheeled weed to pay for testicular cancer treatment—he knew what was happening in Yellowknife from the ground up, perhaps even below that. He'd spent enough time in the Raven pub—the bar closest to the paper—that the owners surprised him on his fifty-first birthday by decorating the bar with balloons and streamers. He wrote starkly about Yellowknife's underworld, yet he found humour wherever he could, writing, for instance, about the guy who tried breaking into the local prison to sell dime bags of weed, or the inmate who had a handful of pot delivered to him at the airport just as he was about to leave with an RCMP attendant on a three-day pass. But this was the soft end of the crime beat. More often, it was a dark and harrowing.

John let me follow him to the courts. He appreciated the company, he said. We left the office one morning and hopped on our bikes, heading across town to the courthouse—this took five minutes—which was directly across from the Black Knight, where lawyers and their clients softened the day with a pint. "At the Black Knight, you can find a guy who's just out of jail sitting next to an MLA sitting next to a guy who's going to jail sitting next to the mayor," Bruce told me as a way of illuminating Yellowknife's social latitudes.

The courthouse—some people called it "the sardine can" for its silver-ribbed façade—had a look of pure utility, the kind of place where you'd go to either pay a parking ticket or change your name from "Dave Bidini" to "Dan Bodono" (or "Ben Dandini" or "Bob Bobono," both of which have nice rings to them). Until my visits with John, the only court I'd ever been to was traffic court, and we all know how that goes: you forget about your appointment until a few days before; grab whatever suit jacket and tie is lying crushed under a pile of even less-worn clothes; and hurry down to the most official-looking building in town hoping the jerk cop who wrote your eating-while-driving ticket won't attend. But he always does and so you say nice things to the judge that you don't mean before you drag your ass to the teller where you pay someone $140. You forget the episode until you're caught speeding again, which inevitably happens.

The courtrooms had small galleries with benches at the back; a resolute sheriff checking bags; showroom clocks and desks and Stepford lawyers that seemed, at first, interchangeable; a terrarium where the accused sat during their bail hearing or sentencing; and a rising wooden construction at the front of the room—the bench—where the magistrate pored over court literature and listened to barristers argue for clients. John knew everyone and they knew him. He knew the lawyers and he knew the judges and he knew some of the accused. He also knew the cops, sometimes for the wrong reasons, and sometimes not.

I appreciated the courts for their subdued and chaperoned atmosphere: no blinking cellphones, no cameras, no tape recorders. Provided you weren't working or on trial, they were meditative places where only the thrumming of the barrister's voice and the occasional gallery murmur busied the ear. The magistrates meted out their words carefully, with long drifting pauses in between to ebb the pace of whatever dramatic and life-affecting circumstances might emerge.

After we arrived at the courthouse, the door closed and hit John in the shoulder. "Fuckin' place," he said, rubbing his arm. For him, coming here was to return to the scene of yet another episode that had stalked him during his time in Yellowknife, having been rousted and thrown to the ground by police after being refused a seat in the courtroom.

"It was a bail hearing for a seventeen-year-old girl who was charged with second-degree murder," he told me as we sat waiting for another set of charges to be heard. "She was at a party at her friend's house and this guy wouldn't leave, so she grabbed a knife. The guy said, 'Go ahead,' so she did. The guy died. The sheriff at the courthouse was a prick. At the hearing, he said, 'You can't bring your bag in here,' and I said, 'Hey, it's got the tools of my trade in there.' He said, 'No, I don't care, you can't.' Julius was there working for CKLB and he was good enough to put my bag in his car. I came back and got a seat in the front row. It went on for about an hour and a half and after a while I had to go to the washroom. I came back and the sheriff said, 'We gave your seat away.' I said, 'Well, I'm gonna need the name of your boss.' The guy knew I was media; he knew I was working. He grabbed me, and I thought, 'What the fuck?' I could hear my shirt rip and so I planted my feet. He started running me to the front door like a football drill. An RCMP officer happened to be there and saw what was happening. He jumped on and they were both on top of me. I was face down in cuffs, shirt and pants ripped, kneecap torn open and cut. Finally, they let me get up. The RCMP guy said, 'You shouldn't really be here. She's only seventeen.' Now, fuck, I know what the Youth Criminal Justice Act says. We can't print her name, but she's been charged with a serious offence. It doesn't matter that she's seventeen; I'm going to report on it. Besides, there were other media there. Another writer, Dan Campbell, overheard a cop say to the sheriff: 'If you do that again, I'm gonna have to charge you with assault,' or words to that effect. I just went away. I didn't want to stir up shit. I didn't know what to do; I figured I'd done something wrong.

"Later, I was out with a few MLAs and they said, 'You have to report this, because he could be doing it every day; we don't know.' I had a meeting set up with some high-level justice department people and I asked for $120 for my shirt and pants. I should have asked for five grand. I would have got it. I don't think I ever got an apology. I had to sign a thing saying I wouldn't go after them anymore, but I got the money.

"Buddy, they did this to a *reporter*," said John, slowing his cadence to express the weight of that last word. "Can you imagine something like that happening in Toronto or Vancouver or Montreal? Can you imagine a reporter getting thrown to the ground outside a courthouse; what it would all mean? But here, no. There's no oversight. The RCMP does what they want and nobody—well, almost nobody—thinks anything about it."

John's story had been repeated to me by others, although no one else had seen John assaulted by the cops. A few people scrunched their shoulders and said, "Well, that's John," and a few others, including Mark Rendell of the *Edge YK*, said, "John may have his issues, and he's not perfect, but nobody gives the cops the right to do that." Another writer, who asked that I leave out their name, was less charitable, saying, "Who the fuck leaves their seat in the courtroom and wants back in? It's not reserved seating. I think he went outside for a smoke; that's what I think. John started asking the sheriff, 'Who's your boss? What's your boss's name?' He was challenging authority and all of that. It's the sheriff's courthouse and he calls the shots. His job is to control people in the gallery and John was out of control. The sheriff isn't answerable to John. He didn't have to tell him who his boss was. In his mind, he thought: 'If you're gonna push me, I'm gonna throw you down to the fucking carpet and drag your fucking ass out of here,' and that's what he did. Fucking cops lie all of the time. What John doesn't understand is that it's a court of justice. The judge is gonna side with the police every time because it's the cops who uphold the laws of justice. Cops over-exaggerate all of the time and they'll never admit guilt. The takeaway for me is don't fucking leave the courtroom. If he doesn't leave, none of this happens."

The RCMP tried to ban McFadden from attending police news conferences, even though he was the *Yellowknifer*'s lone presence on the cop beat. It was the beginning of what would end up being a fractious relationship between the paper and the police, further stressed the harder John worked and the deeper he probed the RCMP's alleged inadequacies.

A few months after this, John wrote a story about a set of firearms that the police had reported stolen: an AR-15 assault rifle, a Glock, and two thousand rounds of ammunition. John told me: "They put out a one-page news release reporting that the firearms had been stolen, and that from another residence, some hockey equipment and laundry tubs were taken, as if it were all one and the same, which it wasn't. I interviewed Elenore Sturko, the RCMP media liaison, about this, and she said, 'We treat all break-ins the same,' which I thought was ridiculous. My lead sentence to the story was 'There are serious concerns in Yellowknife after the theft of firearms.' I know that's too nebulous a lead and Mike admits that he should have caught it, but I didn't say that the RCMP had serious concerns. Still, because Elenore Sturko was the only person quoted in the story, she was upset. She wouldn't respond to my emails or phone calls for a month and a half. This is the *media liaison*. People in the newsroom didn't think anything about it at first. They said, 'You're still getting news releases, so do you really need her?' I said, 'I guess not,' but it was still pretty frustrating. I mean, I dealt with it, but still . . ."

The RCMP announced that they would be holding a news conference about a drug bust. Sturko phoned Bruce Valpy and, apparently, told him: "We want you to send somebody other than John McFadden." Bruce told her, "Not until you tell us why," but the RCMP refused. The *Yellowknifer* sent McFadden, and that's when the shit hit the fan.

"When I got there," said McFadden, "Elenore stopped me at the door in front of the CBC videographer and said, 'You're not coming in; we've already told your boss.' I said, 'Why not?' and she said, 'Because of your disrespectful and unprofessional conduct.' I just walked away. I went back and I told Bruce. He flew out of the office and went to the RCMP to meet with her boss, Frank Gallagher, who told him, 'He's been writing inaccurate stories and we don't like the tone of his emails and his phone calls.' Bruce said, 'Well, let's see these sources; let's see these emails,' but of course there were no stories. There was one email and Bruce looked at it. Not only was there no smoking gun, there was no gun, period. Then *Canadaland* [the expository Canadian web journal] got wind of this and it ended up becoming a national story."

The RCMP lifted the preposterous ban, but if Bruce bandaged one wound, another needed attention. This time, it concerned the paper itself, from which someone—a staffer—had fed *Canadaland* the company's emails. No one knew who it was—and no one confessed—although most people thought it was Karen because of her connections to Toronto media (when I asked her, she denied leaking them). Still, the leak—and the attention it brought to the issue—forced Bruce to gather the writers and demand that they close ranks to protect, rather than expose, the paper and their fellow reporters. "It was the single most professional thing the paper has ever done," said John, but it was also a little like trying to hide an elephant by putting a doily on its head. The storm had many fronts: the RCMP attempting to dictate who in the press covered what and how—a situation that only worsened after it was exposed nationally— and questions about the fealty of the *Yellowknifer* staff and the identity of the mole. This is to say nothing of John's small victory in his battle with Elenore Sturko, which he treated with immodesty. Two weeks later he was doing a phone interview with her about something completely unrelated, when "he threw the whole Bobby Zoe thing in her face," according to another writer. Once he brought it up, she ended the call.

John sighed when I told him what I'd heard. "Lissen, I keep being described as rude, but all I'm doing is asking questions," he argued. "Honestly, I'd had good times with Elenore Sturko. I'd gone on ride-alongs with her. We'd looked for a drowned man on Back Bay in minus 40 temperatures. We were fine. She was kidding with me about me farting in her car while following the sewage truck. Everybody thought we had a strong, funky relationship. I know she's a lesbian and has kids and lives with another woman, and I love that. I'm from Toronto, for fuck's sake. I'm open to anything. After the incident with Elenore, my bosses advised me to keep it professional, so I did. I thought everything would be fine. But it wasn't fine. I really wondered, like, what the fuck?" he asked, tipping back his head, exasperated. "It's crazier than a tomcat in a bag full of weasels. Like, what the fuck do they have planned for me?"

Because Yellowknife is a small place, its storylines were obvious to anyone who spent time here. But it was through the courts that its pathos and complications were laid bare. John coached me through the docket days and sentencing. Nobody looked good in this setting—they were either behind glass or broadcast from a room in another city with a desk phone in a community jail—but the women prisoners looked especially ragged and despairing. The area in the depths of the RCMP headquarters where they were kept—a pen with a concrete floor with no pillows—was lit all hours of the day, and because, in 2015, there was no women's prison in Yellowknife—the biggest city in the Northwest Territories—many were sent to Fort Smith, an old wooden relic that was out of range of most inmates' parents or support groups, more than eight hours to the south.

"This woman," whispered John, gesturing to a girl not much older than my daughter, with heavy-lidded eyes, long dark hair, and a grey sweat top, "was caught drunk driving with open liquor. She was with a guy who was brought up on murder charges, so the cops hauled her in. It's pretty sad," he said. The girl buried her head in her hands while the Justice of the Peace asked her to recount the details of the night she'd been arrested. Sleep-deprived and off her medication, she barely managed to communicate her feelings to the judge. She spoke about the pervasive light and the endless clamour, the result of the women's cells being next to the drunk tank, which howled with noise most hours of the day.

The girl was given a two-week sentence and brought back downstairs. She was replaced by an Indigenous man with a broken doll face—swollen eyes, scraggled features, and a bloody wound on his forehead—who lit up like a dark house illuminated at the holidays after the judge ordered him to spend another month in jail. "Oh, right on," he said, nodding his head. There was some tittering in the gallery. The judge looked severely at us and we fell silent.

"Three hots and a cot," John told me, counting the number on his hand. "I know a couple of people who went to jail and fattened right up. Look at the bastard," he whispered. "The bastard is happy. How fucked up is that?" A few weeks later, John and I were standing outside the Raven when the broken doll man came around the corner, asking for a smoke. He did this politely—his face shone as it had during sentencing—but his wound had yet to heal. The sudden presence of the man sent John into paroxysms of laughter. "How fucked is this place? *How fucked?*" he asked, his head shaking back and forth.

The procession of the accused included a seemingly friendly, bright-faced woman who'd stabbed another woman at a party; a fellow whose last name was "Canadian" and who'd assaulted a couple after an argument on the street; a hand-biter who'd chomped off the end of her boyfriend's finger; and a bad dude with a face like a cored pear who'd beaten up a cab driver minutes after leaving the home of his girlfriend, whom he'd also beaten up.

A middle-aged man in a faded-logo T-shirt and jeans—he was a contractor and water-truck driver—took the stand before lunch. He was accused of hitting his wife during an argument. The man told the story of how he'd tried staying dry for his wife and child, but had slipped on Father's Day. "I thought, 'Well, I did good not drinking,'" he said, rubbing the back of his neck. "'Maybe I could celebrate just a little.' But I went down the drain again." The man wept, doubling over on the stand. The bench gave him some time to compose himself—it took a minute—and when he looked up, his common-law wife was mouthing the words "It's okay" from the gallery. He lost it again, and we waited a second time.

Among these sad narratives came the saddest yet: a twenty-year-old man accused of domestic violence who, at six years old, had seen his father assault his mother. A lawyer who'd been assigned to one of his prior cases told me that the boy had tried to stop the fight but was thrown to the wall and battered by his dad, who was raging drunk at the time. "It was his earliest memory," the lawyer said, "and it will haunt him forever." The case echoed something that Lydia Bardak had told me: at least ten inmates at the North Slave Correctional Centre had told her that, as kids, they'd cleaned up their mother's blood after she'd been beaten by their father. These stories were told on the hour at the courthouse.

The majority of the men and women who appeared in court were Indigenous, but it wasn't the entirety. Some of the accused were tank-topped white dudes with tattooed sleeves—members of the 856 gang—who'd come to Yellowknife from British Columbia selling weed and chemicals. "The last thing this community needs is harder drugs," said John. "Especially on top of the booze, and everything else." At their hearings, gang members behaved exactly as you would imagine: cocky, arrogant, trying to act hard. Many would end up hightailing it back to British Columbia waiting to be defended—often successfully—by an Edmonton lawyer who dined out on this clientele. They were replaced by other kids, the drugs continued to flow. Because the pain of young, Indigenous—and some young, non-Indigenous—men and women was constant, the strength of street drugs—crack, pills, opiates—had risen to meet the suffering. You could see why smoking a joint didn't do it anymore.

According to Bardak and others, many of the young people who appeared in court had fetal alcohol spectrum syndrome, a condition that lawyer Peter Harte told me had mutated to the point that medical diagnosis hadn't yet caught up to its changes. "Some kids go in to be tested, and they're graded one way—a traditional way—that doesn't necessarily apply. The medication and treatment is wrong. People are misdiagnosed and it's a nightmare for everyone, especially Indigenous kids adopted by white families who don't know what they're walking into." Another of Peter's concerns was the lack of mental health treatment in the community as well as in prison, and how an opportunity was being lost to try to rehabilitate people who'd been caught in the cycle of abuse. "They get to this point with a myriad of issues. Lots of anxiety, schizophrenia, bipolar, and addiction-related problems. We have to do a better job of supporting these cases, of trying to improve lives rather than solely punishing them." Lydia Bardak's view was that the system lacked a sense of restorative justice. "We have to admit that we have no idea of the extent of the suffering that has affected people's lives."

Another young woman appeared in court near the end of the day. While her charges were equally severe—she'd been charged as an accessory to an assault—her parents were in attendance: a couple dressed as if for church, hiding their faces into each other's shoulders as the girl was booked for extended prison time. After the hearing, I found her mother standing outside the courtroom. She told me: "It just been a real mess. We've tried to help. We really have." Then she broke down. Her husband stubbed out his smoke and came over, giving me the kind of hard awful look that people who ask questions of despairing men and women are given every day. While it wasn't a pleasant feeling, the exchange made me feel more like a reporter. John came over and pulled me away, asking: "Wanna go for a ride?"

"Where?" I asked him.

"Well," he told me, cupping his hands to light a smoke, "a woman is trying to get back into her home in N'dilo. Someone murdered her brother in there and the place is empty. Come on," he said, squinting through sunlight. "It'll, you know, lighten the mood a little."

11

THE FIRST FEMALE FISHING GUIDE ON GREAT SLAVE LAKE

Trading up our bikes for the *Yellowknifer* company car, John and I headed to an apartment complex close to the newspaper. Even though the downtown core showed its edges almost everywhere—a product of the punishing weather and the challenging economic conditions—the complex was located in an area that seemed rougher than most, especially on a cool grey day, with boarded-up homes and weathered tenements on either side. John telephoned the person whose brother had been murdered in N'dilo—a sixty-something woman named Susan Chaffee—and, after a few moments, she came out of the building wearing a flowery blouse and long earrings, her purse pinned between her arm and her side.

She climbed into the back seat and we drove across Latham Island into N'dilo. Susan was tall with long dark hair tied into a ponytail and large-framed glasses, over which she gazed at us with a frozen scowl, hiding whatever light appeared to be shining behind her eyes. John asked how she was doing. She crossed her arms and said: "Well, I'm angry."

"Considering all you've been through," he said, "I'd say that's a natural reaction."

"Natural, I don't know," she said. "But I can get angry as good as anyone. Don't tempt me," she warned us.

"Don't worry," said John. "I'm just here to tell your story."

"Don't get me mad!" she said, lurching forward in her floral print, grabbing at the middle arm rest with two hands.

"Not a problem," said John, trying to keep his eyes on the road.

"You don't wanna know what happened to the last person who got me mad!" she said. "You wanna know? I put him in the hospital. Oh, I can fight. I can fight good!"

"What's your technique for fighting?" I asked her, trying to guide the conversation into a less explosive place.

"My technique. Okay," she said, holding out her hands. "What I do first is, I punch them in the neck; maybe in the throat, if I can. I take away their air!" she exclaimed. "Then I grab them around here," she told us, reaching out to a set of invisible shoulders, "and I twist them and push them down. And then I stomp all over them!" she said. "*Don't get me mad!*"

"What if you miss?" I asked, both wanting and not wanting to know.

"Well," she said, sitting back in her seat, a little winded after her demonstration. "That's the first rule of fighting."

"What's the first rule?"

Susan paused.

"*Don't miss!*" she told us, surging forward again. "Especially don't miss when you're fighting a man."

"What if you're fighting a woman?"

"I used to fight women, but I don't anymore," she said, shrugging. "It's too easy. I feel too bad after the fights. I hurt a lot of them. It was pretty bad. I didn't like doing it, no matter if they deserved it or not."

After a few minutes of being both terrified and charmed by Susan, we pulled up to her brother's house in N'dilo. Archie Paulette had been killed by his common-law wife, who was later charged with second-degree murder. In the aftermath, local kids had smashed windows and destroyed parts of the building, although the place was in disrepair before the killing.

"When I used to come over with friends, I'd send them next door to use the bathroom instead of using Archie's. Everything in there was spoiled. It was in an awful shape. There was mould and smoke everywhere. It was bad, a real mess. When Archie was still alive, he used to tell me that if anything ever happened to him, he wanted me, and me alone, to move into the place. I'd take care of it."

The house was in limbo because of ownership concerns, and it's why John was writing the story. There were issues with the home being potentially condemned, and no one was sure about the N'dilo chief's role in its protection. "Chief Ernie [Ernest Betsina] told me that he'd help when the time comes, so I'm counting on that," said Susan, although Kevin Brezinski, the director of public safety for the Territorial government's Department of Municipal and Community Affairs told the newspaper that, "somewhere in the mix, there's an owner and the owner is ultimately responsible for ensuring security and safety of the structure from unlawful or inappropriate access." Still, I thought the salient—and terribly sad—point was that Susan's options for residence were so limited that choosing to live in the decrepit home of a murdered family member seemed a decent prospect. With rent being disproportionately high and affordable housing at a premium, people had few choices, fewer still if you were an older Indigenous person.

John took Susan's picture in front of the house—she smiled for the first time while holding up a photo of Archie—and finished his interview with her. On the drive back into town, I tried to get her to tell me more about fighting, but she lacked the spirit for it. She talked about Archie—how he'd been a father figure to people in the community, and a good guy to his family—and how he'd supported Susan during her time on the streets—eight years living in the bush around the city—after which she'd met her husband, with whom she still lived. I asked Susan how they'd met and she said, "At the Arctic Star fishing lodge."

"What were you doing at the lodge?"

"I was guiding."

"Guiding what?" I asked, sounding more like a doofus from the south than I had at any point during my trip.

"Guiding on the lake!"

"Oh."

"I was the first female fishing guide on Slave Lake," she told me, glowing with pride.

"How did that happen?" I asked her.

"It's a long story," she said.

She and I ended up at the Gold Range Bistro, where Susan talked about her time on the water. The raggedness of her voice softened and the light in her eyes washed across her sharpened features. Suddenly, the woman who'd punched at shadows in the back seat of the car grew calm and reflective, slowing the pace of her words as she drank coffee with honey and ate scrambled eggs. The diner emptied out after midday, leaving the two of us at the table.

"I grew up on the Barren Lands," she told me, stirring her coffee. "There was nothing out there, maybe a few shrubs. There were no villages, just lots of empty space, and we moved around. That was my life growing up. That's how it was. I was too young to know any beauty, really. Because it was so hard on the Barren Lands, my grandma and grandpa, who raised me, sent me out with my uncles to the East Arm of the lake, near Snowdrift. When I first saw it, I couldn't believe my eyes: green everywhere, and all of this gorgeous water in the middle of it.

"First, they brought me in to do laundry. They had a ringer, an old-time washing machine. Nobody knew how to run it, but I figured it out; it was easy. They introduced me to the cook and the rest of the girls in the laundry room and we got along fine. No fighting. It was the first time I'd ever been part of this kind of group. It opened my eyes, that's what it did.

"I wanted go to on the lake bad. The guides wouldn't take me because they were out all day from 8 in morning till 5 o'clock, and they wanted to be on shore for the rest of their time. I asked one of the boys to teach me how to run the motor, but they were touchy about their stuff. If something broke, you couldn't just run to the store to fix it, so they had to be careful. I asked a man named Alfred Abel if he'd take me out and he said he would. He brought me to the middle of the lake and shut the motor off. He said, 'You wanna learn how to drive, right?' I started the motor and we took off. I just missed hitting a rock, and made it back to the shore. I told myself: 'That's it. I don't wanna do no laundry anymore.'

"I wanted to be on the lake, but I didn't know anything about fishing. One day, I was down at the dock with my rod and I couldn't catch nothing. I threw my rod down and started crying. Nobody would teach me. Al Simon—he was the head guy at the lodge—saw me crying and asked what was wrong. I told him, and he said, 'You're not going to learn how to guide by sitting here crying. Wipe your tears and come down to the motor shack.' I went down there, and he said: 'You see this motor here? This motor here is going to be yours. It might look funny, but it's going to be fast. It's going to be your baby.'

"He put it on a big twenty-foot boat and took me out on lake. He took my hand and said: 'Pretty soon, you're going to know every part of the lake and every reef like you know the palm of your hand. They'll blindfold you and you'll still be able to get around. I'm gonna make you my number one guide.' He treated me like a younger sister. He taught me how to flay, bake, and fry and how to make fish chowder. I learned all of that. I learned how to guide.

"I took the rest of the girls out. They'd finish their chores and we'd go. I'd carry my twenty-horse-power Mercury motor by hand, by myself, and I'd bring it to the boat. I'd get the steel shore lunch boxes with me and fill them with salt, pepper, butter, and potatoes, and when we caught a fish, I'd cook it over a fire using spruce willows, laying the trout right there in the boughs. There were some guides who thought that just because I was a girl, I couldn't do it. They thought women should stay home and look after kids, but I could do anything. I laughed at them, and so did my guests. I was bringing back twenty-two-pound catches and winning trophies. I was in my glory.

"I respected the water, the lake. My uncles had taught me this back when we were on the Barren Lands. When you're going on the water, you pay your respects with tobacco. You talk to the water and you tell it: 'With this tobacco, I'm gonna show my respect because I'm gonna be on you for half the summer. Thank you for everything you are gonna give me.'

"I thought a lot about my mum and my grandma when I was out there. I thought, 'If only they could see me on the lake.' Grandma didn't know that I was guiding, and when she found out, she was ready to murder my uncles. When she got mad, she got really mad, oh boy. She was a midwife and she used to go with her dog teams to do the work. She had no vehicle, no Ski-Doo. When the diseases came—chickenpox and measles—she helped take the kids away from their homes into the city; 250 of them, but only eighty survived. The old women told her: 'Take all of the clothes you have and get rid of them. Take the kids and wash them, too. Try and save them.' She ended up burying the ones who died. She covered them in dirt and put a cross there and a sign that said 'Don't come here for a long time.' My grandma and my grandpa taught me everything. And then one day, my so-called brother-in-law went into their home and killed them. He murdered them. He's somewhere in a mental hospital now and they write me letters every few months to tell me how he is doing, but I can't bring myself to read them. My husband reads them to me. I have a daughter and I don't want my brother-in-law to know about her. I might not know how to read or write but I'm still responsible for my daughter. I'm still her mother."

Susan had to stop guiding after her daughter was born. It's a decision she didn't regret, but it still hurt being away from the water. "It was the only thing I ever knew how to do," she said. "I cried for three days when it ended. I still look at the old pictures."

We finished our breakfast, with Susan's plate only half-finished. She asked our server to wrap it up. We went outside into the warm daylight and I thanked her for the chat. She told me it was no problem before approaching a grey-faced man collapsed in one of the Gold Range alcoves:

clothes like torn skin, lips bitten, eyes blotched and purple. Susan leaned down and said, "Hey buddy, here you go," laying the take-out container at his feet. The fellow raised his hand and waved in appreciation before letting it fall with all its weight.

"I hope he's hungry," said the first female fishing guide on Slave Lake. "They was pretty good eggs."

12

≡

BEATLESQUE

Despite the terrestrial wonders of living in Old Town—the stone, the water, the bitten shoreline—I spent a lot of time staring into the northern sky, which, most summer days, was a tightly stretched canvas of blue and white before transforming later in the evening into cotton-candy pinks and Tim Burton mauves that seeped overhead as if a hand were tilting vials of paint from the edge of the frame. On long July nights, a golden ring-like glow gathered around the city as the sun dipped to hide its head below the covers, only to pop up moments later like a person deciding they weren't very tired after all. Sometimes when the brightness of the glow made it impossible to sleep, I stayed awake doing cabinesque things: listening to weather reports on the radio for places with long clacking names: Kugluktuk, Tsiigehtchic, Kakisa; texting my wife at home while being careful to sound as if I were doing serious work when I was mostly reclining on the pleather listening to Bonaparte gulls flurrying in the cheeping marsh; keying into the sounds of a softball game being played at Fritz Theil Park, which sat behind the Allooloo grounds and hosted play deep into the evenings under the deathless light; and studying long tracts of geological compendia in an effort to write a not-boring chapter about rocks (and fishing). All of this ended, however, once I noticed a wriggle of new coloured light on the plywood walls, at which point I threw my book to the ground and ran out to the edge of the dock, watching the sky do its thing.

There were many strata of life above Old Town. Conventions of birds flew about constantly, and while I rifled through texts on northern natural life trying to identify species, I was best assisted by a set of large woodcuts by local artist Diane Boudreau bolted to a wall downtown, recognizing the common redpoll, Harris's sparrow, northern flicker, belted kingfisher, lesser yellowlegs, and bald eagle, among others. Beside the birds was a series of indigenous flora—gooseberry, soapberry, crowberry, dewberry, cloudberry, et al.—their names translated into seven languages, including Tlicho, North Slavey, Gwich'in, Chipewyan, Inuktitut, Inuinnaqtun, Inuvialuktun, and South Slavey. The paintings provided further insight, I thought, of how the community measured the importance of animals and the land, putting images of birds and berries on a great open plank where, in most places, they would have hanged portraits of famous sons and daughters, or builders and politicians. One Hollywoodian who had emerged from the neighbourhoods was Margot Kidder, known for her role as Lois Lane in the *Superman* films, although the veracity and duration of her northern childhood was in question (Kidder's father, Ken, was responsible for Yellowknife getting its first telephone system). The dirt road in Peace River Flats—Lois Lane—wasn't named after her, but, rather, her character, and some historians insisted that it wasn't even Kidder who inspired the road, but rather a local woman named Lois Little, who lived there longer than Margot ever did.

Another element of Old Town's aerial life were the men and women standing on rooftops, scaffolds, and peaks calling out to one another, waving hammers and slinging canisters of water. Since it was impossible to build in the winter, people used June to August to obsessively work on their homes and businesses, echoing the longstanding yuk about there being two seasons in the North: winter and construction. This was especially true of the Old Town Glassworks and Bike Rental—the only source of two-wheeled transport in Yellowknife—which seemed to grow wider and more baroque with each passing season. One small building—an original Hudson's Bay shack from the 40s—was engulfed by a bicycle repair shop domed in a Quonset hut with a geodesic roof built out of tire rims and wrapped in canvas. This gave way to a set of ladders climbing from one stone plateau to another, ending at a rocky lookout filled with two-wheelers, their tires and frames kicking at the sky. This stuttered pace of construction made everywhere in Old Town look like an archi- tectural broken telephone, and the same was true of the Narwal, where elegantly designed lake-view rooms with monogrammed towels and fancy shower gel were but a hallway removed from the pale skeletal frame of a half-built addition going up beside the kennel, a project that, Cathy said, would take "however long it would take," which seemed to be a common measurement of time for anything in the North. Every now and then, a truck arrived with parcels of wood that Cathy staked or cross-wove into a support, the excess lumber finding its way into yet another pile stored in one of the yard's vinyl tents.

More than any of these visual elements, however, it's what happened above the rooftops that left the deepest, most fantastic impression: a Yellow Submarine-era Beatlesque carnival of float planes that filled the air in the nearly twenty-four-hour light. They arrived in Back Bay announced by a distant propellered flutter followed by their cool shadow—Skyvans, Norsemans, Buffaloes—painted butterscotch and mint green and cruising low enough that it seemed as if I could poke them with a paddle. My sense of childlike glee while watching these long-shoed mechanical raptors skid to rest on the water proved limitless, my imagination piquing whenever the planes were from Wolverine Air, whose airline, I thought, couldn't have sounded more northern (except, I suppose, Canadian North). The planes moved both weightlessly and with an enormous sense of force and power—Back Bay was at the heart of an aerodrome—before landing merrily pontooned on the lake, their noses bobbing in self-satisfaction while moving toward the wharf. The toaster oven, composite hockey stick, and Internet are all fine inven- tions, but whoever dreamed up the pontoon—or "float"—should be celebrated on a coin or festive pennant.

Yellowknife's longstanding culture of air travel and transport was a huge part of its history, from Wop May to Marten Hartwell to other important figures not written about by Stompin' Tom Connors. The Dene even had a word for travelling by float plane: *endaruwi*. When the first planes arrived in the 1920s and 30s—piloted with open cockpits by Punch Dickins, Max Ward, Whiskey Papa, Weldy Phipps, Daddy Ho Ho, and other men whose names sounded as if invented by an eight-year-old— people living in bush communities were startled after hearing what they called "thunder in March," and terrified at the sight of the hulking metal birds. Soon, however, the aircraft provided mail service—all of this in treacherously unmapped parts of the land—and communication quickened between people across the North.

Flying in the Territories was a take-your-pick kind of adventure legacy, although I was partial to Hartwell's terrifying and brave story, in which the pilot attempted to fly three passengers—Neemee Nulliayok, nurse Judy Hill, and fourteen-year-old David Pisurayak Kootook—from Cambridge Bay to Yellowknife for medical care in November 1972. Nulliayok was having issues with a late-term pregnancy at eight months; Kootook suffered from appendicitis; and Hill was accompanying the pair from their remote community of Taloyoak. According to a story written by the *Yellowknifer*'s Svjetlana Mlinarevic, "Hartwell began to worry after failing to pick up the Contwoyto beacon halfway to Yellowknife. A sudden break in the clouds gave him momentary relief as he recognized signals from Fort Reliance and Deline—700 km away—but Hartwell's luck changed when clouds began to amass and the wind picked up speed." When ice crystals formed over the aircraft's exterior, Hartwell lowered the altitude of the plane, also hoping to get better radio reception. He unleafed a map across his lap and turned on an overhead light, but the plane's right wing clipped a tree on a suddenly rising hill, sending the Beechwood cartwheeling into the bush. "Hartwell [was] knocked unconscious," writes Mlinarevic, "but he soon awoke to the horror surrounding him as the cold air rushed into the broken cabin of his plane."

Nurse Hill lay prone across Hartwell, half of her body sticking out of the pilot's window. The other three passengers, however, were alive, if fleetingly. Kootook, the rubbery young teenager, was the least affected; Hartwell's ankles and knee were broken; and Nulliayok and her unborn child would die within hours. The unlikely remaining pair kept starvation at bay by eating rations, lichen, and sugar pills, and, as Mlinarevic writes, "Kootook built a lean-to, gathered firewood, and tried several times to go fishing at a nearby lake but had to turn back each time after going part way," the weather and distance proving untenable. Hartwell, a vegetarian, realized that the only way of surviving would be to cannibalize one of the bodies, and so he ate meat cut from Hill's thighs. Kootook tried getting by on bark and lichen. Eventually, the boy's heart fell to the hopelessness of their situation—they were living under the lean-to in minus 38 degree Celsius weather—and he died after the plane's Dart signaller failed to catch the attention of a passing aircraft. Hartwell came to terms with his almost certain mortality, writing a letter to his son and telling him that he loved him and that, "in my heart, I was not all that bad." The fifty-seven-year-old lay down to die, but, on his thirty-first day at the crash site, he was rescued by a Canadian Forces team responding to a faint distress beacon from the downed plane. When the soldiers found him, Hartwell announced: "Welcome to the camp of the cannibal."

He was taken to Yellowknife where he was nursed back to health. A coroner's inquiry showed that some of the plane's instruments had been in failing condition—Hartwell's relative inexperience, they said, also con-tributed to the crash—and it was recommended that Kootook be cited for his bravery. What is perhaps most astonishing is that, when Hartwell decided two years later that he felt good enough to work again, he resumed a normal flying routine with planes full of passengers neither wary that he'd brought down an aircraft nor terrified that he'd resorted to cannibalism to stay alive. In the end, he was just another northern pilot, getting people from one part of the territory to another, "not shunned by any means," according to former Yellowknife mayor Dave Lovell. It said a lot about the attitude of people living in the North. Because of the land and its conditions—and because of the region's remoteness—most Northerners had stared down their mortality at one time or another, or were close to someone who had. This informed the average Yellowknifer's sense of humility, as well as priority. Affecting self-important was less, well, important in a place where the elements could either knock you out of the sky or gnaw you to pieces in an instant.

Bravado can't begin to describe the nature of those who flew in the early days of the settled North. The author Dick Turner, who is famous for two regional page-turners—*Nahanni* and *Wings of the North*—possessed an almost absurd amount of élan as someone who flew during the formative years of the Northwest Territories. *Wings of the North* opens, almost instanteneously, like a Michael Bay film, with a terrible crash destroying a plane. When Turner makes his way home after landing his Taylorcraft—a yellow fabric airplane with wooden spars—on its back, his wife, Vera, reasons, "Be glad no one was hurt," but the author is outraged: "Not hurt. Not hurt? Christ Almighty, the AIRPLANE [*sic*] is hurt, that's what's hurt." Turner describes stamping "around almost out of my mind with grief and fury" before eventually returning to the air. The entire book clops along with more of the same—crash, recovery, crash, majestic flight, crash, recovery, majestic flight—and the only question left unanswered is whether Turner was a good or terrible pilot, or whether a person can be both at the same time.

After a day spent searching the *Yellowknifer* archives using the key phrase "Twin Otter Crash 2010–2015"—an Air Tindi Cessna 208B crashing into a cliff on the Pethei Peninsula outside of Lutsel K'e; Max Ward's venerable Twin Otter slamming into the Back Bay waters while landing; pilots Martin Bouvier and James Batten destroying their First Air Twin Otter during a fuel run between Iqaluit and Markham Bay; a Perimeter Aviation Flight 993 going down in Sanikiluaq and killing young Isaac Appaqaq, who died while being held in his mother's arms; a float plane crash blamed on an ill pilot; an aircraft careening into a lake near Rat River Pass after the pilot attempted landing near a herd of caribou; a flight from Yellowknife to Resolute Bay that killed fifteen people; a retired American businessman who died in the wreckage of a Beaver somewhere south of Norman Wells; a Twin Otter near Good Fort Hope that slammed into a hidden mountainside, its passengers incinerated at once; and a deadly crash that took the life of Lawrence Neyalley's father, the Twin Otter hitting a telecommunications tower while piloted by a captain who, two months earlier, had been terminated by another regional airline for his "inability to make operational decisions." After all of this, another kind of story popped on the screen. It centred on a different kind of flying thing: the Soviet Kosmos 954 satellite, which, on January 24, 1978, sank from the sky and riddled fifty kilos of enriched uranium—only slightly less than the *Enola Gay*'s payload—across a six-hundred-kilometre area from Great Slave Lake east to Baker Lake. Soviet space technicians had originally intended to bring the orbiting vessel—a surveillance device that monitored North American military activity—to the Earth without its radioactive core, but a malfunctioning internal mechanism compromised the ejection, sending the satellite's full complement of nuclear materials, much of which still remains at large, into the waters.

At first, the Russians claimed that the satellite had disintegrated upon re-entry—a note that should be placed in a terrible-news-but-not-horrible-news file—but the Canadian and American military, using the code name Operation Morning Light (an operative organized in case the radioactive material landed in Yellowknife), found twelve enormous pieces of debris in the water, although the radioactive core failed to be recovered, a note that should be placed in the horrible-and-very-possibly-worse-than-horrible news file. The military was assisted in its clean-up— covering about eighty thousand square kilometres—by a group of six canoeists who were hoping to spend eight months travelling the North in relative seclusion. During their time on the land, they found strange materials embedded in the surrounding ice, and after communicating their find to the Atmospheric Environmental Service in Yellowknife, they were surprised, one morning, to find an invasion of military personnel in radiation suits appearing out of nowhere as if born from some kind of Stanley Kubrick hoser jam. The paddlers were airlifted immediately to Edmonton and Yellowknife for testing, going from "a very quiet, simple existence to being fed pizza and getting back rubs from the nurses," according to one of the canoeists, Chris Norment.

Around Yellowknife, stuff was in the sky and out of the sky, and it was hard to walk around feeling as if, at any moment, you might have to duck. Old Town itself had suffered one of the most dramatic float plane crashes in Territorial history in 2011: an Arctic Sunwest Twin Otter arriving from Thor Lake—one hundred kilometres southeast of Yellowknife—that struck a set of power lines and flung into the street, miraculously landing in an empty lot between a busy Aurora Geosciences office and a condo dwelling, while also missing a summer waterway busy with paddlers and surrounding houseboats. A woman named Debbie Doody was in the kitchen cooking for four customers at the Dancing Moose Café across the street from the crash site when she heard a roaring sound swell from above. "The plane came from the lake and skirted the building, skirted our house, and crashed right across the street," she said. "It looked like it did a bellyflop and flipped over."

The Old Town Glassworks' proprietor, Matthew Grogono, was working when the plane went down outside his door. The episode rang all kinds of bells for the glass-cutting artist and entrepreneur. Matthew— ragged workman's pants, a beard that seemed as if tended by a Swiss Army knife, and a body like the long trunk of a thin oak—was one of Yellowknife's eccentric guardians and a totem of Old Town. He'd run for mayor and lost by four votes ("You could hear the chambers erupt in laughter when my name was nominated for submission," he told me); battled the city to allow houseboats to remain beyond governance in the Yellowknife Bay waters; and had a dog named Mimby, a formerly impounded vagabond border collie mix who lived a romantic existence on the Yellowknife streets, never once leashed. All of this was leavened by

Grogono's experiences while living in Nova Scotia, where he'd been present during the Swissair Flight 111 crash in 1998, which landed seven hundred metres from his daughter's schoolhouse. He couldn't know that, seventeen years later, his life would be swiped by yet another encounter with a descending aircraft.

Grogono was first on the scene of the Old Town crash. He attempted to rescue the nine people aboard the flight, who were returning from a site tour and day trip.

"The adrenalin was flowing and my mind was very present and pragmatic," he told me from a bench under a cherry tree on the Glassworks grounds, where Grogono chain-smoked Drum tobacco while rubbing his grey beard. "The first person that came to my mind was Stan Rogers," he said, summoning a memory of the barrel-chested Canadian folksinger, who perished in an airplane fire back in 1983. "I'd heard two stories: one that he died while re-entering the blazing aircraft, and another that he was the last one off the plane. Nonetheless, it occurred to me that I was about to climb into a vessel with fuel flowing underneath it and smoke coming from the engine, and because Stan Rogers had died in these circumstances . . ." he said, trying to fit the jigsaw of the memory together, ". . . I thought to myself: 'Okay, who's got a fire extinguisher?' Then I said those same words, loudly: '*Who's got a fire extinguisher!*' This was about a hundred to two hundred seconds after the crash, and yet my mind was clear. I thought several things simultaneously—polycognitively, they call it—but the one thing I knew was that, at the end of the day, I was going to be famous. I just didn't know if I would be dead or alive."

The plane crashed in the full light of day in the only empty pocket of Old Town's busiest street, although "busy" is a relative term in the North. High winds had tossed the aircraft around, and there were reports that the plane had attempted to land but was swooped back into the air as if an unseen hand had batted it from behind. Because of a float plane's unique weight and ballast—and because a pontoon landing on water doesn't necessarily mean it will stay on water—the Twin Otter was carried beyond the bay and into the lot. Apart from the plane's damage, there wasn't any carnage—human or otherwise—to speak of.

"Having been close to the Swissair crash in 1998, the shock impact of what happened outside my door was lessened. I was desensitized, I think, in terms of crisis management, but there was no blood. The pilot and the co-pilot died, but they were stationary. They weren't deformed. Visually, there wasn't anything that evoked horror. They were just no longer there. I was thinking, 'Well, you know, we all have to go sometime,' and these two people died doing what they love. Within a few seconds, they were no longer an active working body," he said, closing then opening his fist to enforce his point. "Another thing: there was no collateral damage. There was no destruction. It was one of those things . . ." he said, taking a long drag from his own-rolled cigarette, "that maybe was meant to be."

While Matthew might have naturally bent toward a philosophical and metaphysical understanding of life, I wanted to know about the circumstances of the flight, trying to square up the relative good fortune of the landing and the fact that the plane coming down on the only empty patch of Old Town was the equivalent of an elephant passing through the eye of a needle. He cocked his arm as if pumping the muscle of a thought and told me: "We are a mining town. We are a frontier town. The cold and extremes filter out the ambiguity, the animosity, and mediocrity. Very little that is normal or standard occurs here. It is a strange place. There's nowhere else like it. And that's not bullshit," he said, standing up and looking out to where the plane had descended.

I waited for him to continue, but there wasn't any more. I think what he was trying to tell me was this: while the North could bat about your life from the water and through the wind and cold it could also take you from above. It could descend out of nowhere, suddenly, engulfing your world in flames and smoke. Learning this—and knowing that, over the course of my stay, I'd be flying in Otters and Beavers and D-8s all around the North—I was aware of all that was happening around and above me. Maybe that's what made every day so affecting: my eyes were on everything all the time; they had to be. It was impossible not to devour the Northwest Territories whole.

13

YELLOWKNIFE IS BURNING

My journey into and out of the city for work was the same every day: up the Franklin Hill, down the Franklin Hill. It was the busiest stretch of road where I met the most interesting people. One morning, I walked my bike into town with a linebacker-sized, long-haired Dene fellow in sweatpants named Thom, who carried a wolf hind in either hand. "Gonna bring 'em to the museum," he told me, plucking fur from the bone. "See, you've got to boil the wolf traps in spruce boughs if you wanna get one," he continued, "and put sticks covered in oil-of-beaver musk to trap 'em. The wolves go crazy for them!" After telling me about his life on the land, Thom said that, as a teenager, he'd run away with the circus, working the Tilt-A-Whirl in the deep south; places like Arkansas, Mississippi, and Columbia, South Carolina. "You ever been to Jock-O's?" he asked me, panting as we crested the hill. I asked him what Jock-O's was, and he said: "A club, man. A great club. Oh, man, the women they got there . . ."

Another time, I came upon a scratch-faced Dene fellow as thin as a banjo string sitting cross-legged by the side of the road, having been shut out from an overnight bed at the Sally Anne, which was rooted about halfway up the Franklin Hill. He listened to music from his iPod through a pair of small speakers playing a kind of electronic dance music I couldn't possibly identify. I coasted toward him, and the fellow's eyes raised to meet mine.

"You want to listen? Here, I have headphones," he said, standing up and reaching into the pockets of a torn windbreaker.

"No, I'm good," I said. "I like having music in the air. I'm not much of a listen-on-your-own kind of guy."

"Nope, me neither," he said, stuffing the headphones away and breaking into a heavy cough. This lasted for a while until he finally gathered himself.

"The music sounds nice playing in the streets," I said, because it did.

"Yes!" he said, raising a hand and swaying a little. "This," he said, pointing at his iPod, "this was my brother's rig, but you want to know a secret?" he asked.

I told him I did.

"Okay," he said, looking over his shoulders. "When I got this thing, it was all New Country," he said, pretending to gag. "I like different music," he told me. "This kind. You sure you don't want the headphones?"

"Yeah, I'm sure," I said.

"Where are you from?" he asked, looking at his iPod, then at me, then back at his iPod. "My name's Derek," he said, turning the volume to its maximum setting so that it distorted the music.

"My name's Dave," I said, shouting over the song. "I'm here from Toronto."

"Toronto?" he shouted back. "Nice city. But remember: we have a lot of multiculturalism here, too."

"Really?"

"Oh yeah: people from everywhere. People from Simpson," he said, counting on his hand. "People from Tuk. From Great Bear. I even met a guy from China."

"Cool," I said.

"Well, he wasn't cool," he said.

"Oh that's too bad."

"No, I don't mean he was bad or anything. Just not cool."

"Right."

"I mean, we're cool," he said, parting his arms, which I thought were meant to embrace me, but were really just a way of expressing the expanse of our coolness. He held them there a moment before falling to rest.

"You know what they say?" he asked me.

"What's that?"

"It's all relative."

"Yeah, I guess it is."

"We could be in Edmonton! Now that would be cool," he said, probably the first time those sentences had followed one another.

The song faded—so did the distortion—and a different one started. It was "Mambo Number 5" by Lou Bega.

Derek closed his eyes. "Whoooaa. This," he said, thumbing at the volume control, trying to make it louder.

"Right on. Listen, I have to head off," I told him.

"Okay. Happy mushroom picking," he said through closed eyes. I assumed that his send-off was a traditional northern phrase, so I wished him the same. For some reason, Derek found this hilarious. He started coughing, sounding as bad as the first time. He held his ribs and bent over. His iPod fell to the pavement and it skidded across the ground, the music still playing. I picked it up and handed it back to him. Through his hacking cough, Derek looked up and raised a thumb, showing me he was okay. He carefully bundled his iPod into his coat and, thumb still raised in the air, turned and headed around the corner, the song's horns muted in the recess of his jacket.

It wasn't until I got into the office the next day that I discovered that mushroom pickers were a thing: dreadlocked young men and women with bush camp armpits who drove stickered vans from Western Canada and headed north to pick morels (the small button fungi) for a hundred to two hundred dollars a day. The mushrooms had bloomed in the charred loam of the apocalyptic wildfires that swept across the Northwest Territories in 2014, the smoke devouring Yellowknife skies at midday in charcoal grey and black with every breath tasting of burnt wood, "the sky raining ash," according to Mark Rendell, the writer with *Edge YK*. Because I was neither dreadlocked nor Birkenstocked and hadn't worn long shorts since an ill-considered period of stage wear in the early 90s, I was confused that Derek had called me a mushroom picker, but didn't dwell on the matter. A handful of other street people also called me this, and so did a bushel-haired woman with aquamarine eyeliner at the Gold Range. That she used the term affectionately made me feel sorry that she hadn't hit on an actual rope-armed picker, having to settle, instead, for the fake journalist for whom travelling to distant regions and hunting fungal delights was equal to following Hoobastank on tour or listening to Hoobastank or knowing a song by Hoobastank.

Sitting at my desk, I thumbed through the latest copy of the *Kivalliq News*, the *News/North* Nunavut edition out of Rankin Inlet (circulation 1,165) and its surrounding communities, including Baker Lake, Whale Cove, Arviat, and Chesterfield Inlet (the most comfortable of all inlets). The paper possessed a rare beauty in that it was printed half in English and half in Inuktitut, with its arrows and semicircles and fish-hook lettering. The paper itself was loaded with delights: stories about a makeshift paintball court on the tundra; a visit by three justice students from Calgary studying the Nunavut courts; and a regular column—"The Latest from Around the Kiv"—in which the writer, Joyce Ayaruak, sent out best wishes from readers to friends around Canada ("Happy birthday to my wife. We'll celebrate on our trip to Winnipeg, love your cuppie-cake, Joachim"). It was a reminder of the value of the weekly newspaper in a region where the climate made it difficult for groups of people to be together; digital communication was not a given; and postal delivery was challenging because of the unpredictable weather. It was also a throwback to the *Native News*, a Yellowknife paper filled with personal messages sent between readers, my favourite being post-party missives where lost wallets were reported and guests were called out for owing beer money.

The morels phenomenon caused staffing gaps at the paper, with a few writers dispatched to cover the story. This, in turn, saw me assume the duties of other writers. Ellen asked if I wanted to do one of Ewan's streeters—I immediately announced that I would, forcing him to sound a small cheer from his desk—and that's how I became the reporter-who-did-the-kinds-of-assignments-that-other-reporters-didn't-want-to-do. I was sent to visit Walter at the photo desk, who told me what was required of the story: "small headshots, name of subject, and a one-sentence answer to a question of my choice." My imagination fired with ideas about what to ask—"Did the Illuminati exist?" "Did Oswald act alone?" "Was Oswald controlled by the Illuminati?"—until Walter broke the news that it would have to be Yellowknife-specific, immediately dampening my fun.

Before I left the newsroom for my assignment, Mike called me to his desk and handed me a stack of white cards with *Yellowknifer* script across the front. "Take these," he said, rather unceremoniously. "I dunno if you'll need them, but maybe you can use a few. It has the paper's phone number on it, at least." They read: "Customer Service Representative: Yellowknifer," which seemed about right.

I hit the streets with my cards and camera and stopped people with a question vetted by Bruce and Mike: "What do you think Yellowknife can do to better attract tourists?" It was the *Yellowknifer*'s equivalent of "There are people here!" but it was okay. People were nice and their answers were gleeful—"More bars!" "A monorail!" "A waterslide!" "A brothel!" "A street with just bars on it!"—and only once did a woman ask me if I was who she thought I was and what was I doing asking people about tourism on 50th Street? I explained politely that I wanted to come to Yellowknife to find out about the North, and she replied the way most people do when they find someone from a bigger place visiting their smaller place:

"Why would you want to do that?"

The eager sweetness of the people I met while doing my streeter might have had been tied to the overall lack of media in town. John said, "People aren't used to it. They aren't cynical about the media, yet. It's not like in Toronto, where you can't walk down the street without seeing someone with a camera." For Yellowknifers, it wasn't until the mid-1970s that anything close to regular television programming appeared in the area. Exclusively taped programs were aired four hours a night in the late 60s (the radio went off the air just past midnight), and locals remember being tortured with three hours of random TV programming—some weeks, it could be wall-to-wall billiards; other times *Hymn Sing*—collected by a disinterested wonk from the south. On the YK Memories Facebook page, contributors remembered taking holidays in Edmonton to watch colour TV and it wasn't until 1974 that *Hockey Night in Canada* was broadcast live (before then, games were taped and then put on a plane and flown to Yellowknife for rebroadcast). The arrival of the Anik satellite service helped expand multi-channel programming, although this didn't ensure consistent programming. A fellow named Ron Williams posted about being in the TV studio one night when "two of our late night programming staff wanted to watch pornography together in the master control room [of] Mackenzie Media. They accidentally flipped the wrong switch and sent the blue movie to all Yellowknife viewers. There were no complaints until the VHS machine jammed. . . ."

My next assignment for Ellen involved being dispatched to Fred Henne Park—the site of Folk on the Rocks and campgrounds for locals as well as tourists visiting in their RVs and campervans—to shoot people sunbathing and splashing about in the water. I felt like a creepazoid skulking around taking pictures of children in their rubber rings and people in their bathing outfits, but I got my shots, wrote everyone's name down in my book, and returned to the office to file—that I was "filing" made me feel on the verge of legitimacy—only to discover that I'd mixed up a few names, confusing Anne Carmichael for Julie Carmichael. I knew this because, after Mike looked over the piece, he said, "Wait, that's not

Anne Carmichael. That's her sister, Julie." Here, again, was the benefit of working at a small paper in a small place: if you got a name wrong, chances were that someone knew someone who knew the person, and this was the case with Mike, who called a friend to confirm his doubts. Even better, he gave me Julie's number, who told me that her kids weren't named Tom and Emily, either, but Tony and Emma. Then she asked, "So what are you doing in Yellowknife?" I told her what I told the woman on the street.

"Why would you want to do that?"

That same day, I found time to finish my second column for the paper in which, through paragraphs three and four, I lamented the state of the city's coffee. This was brought on by a frustrating experience at the Narwal, where I mowed through a series of coffee makers that nearly ruined a series of summer mornings. After my first machine died in the cabin, I found another in the Narwal kitchen: an old Melitta, which, when I popped open the used filter carrying ancient coffee grounds, looked as if someone had opened the top and shat in it. Carrying it forlornly to the cabin, I vigorously extracted the coffee poop, only to have it, on first try, produce a coffee volcano spewing over the top. Cathy told me to punt it, so I did, but the situation only barely improved with a series of other machines, leading me into the city looking for a caffeine fix.

In my column, I offered that it wouldn't be until Yellowknife could make a decent macchiato that the town would finally come into its own, a thought that probably made me sound like a person from a bigger place visiting a smaller place—and, more than likely, a bit of a dick—but I wrote it anyway. I started with the fact that, in a recent poll, the Esso gas station was ranked the fifth best place in town to get a cup, then moved on to Javaroma. The "café"—I use the term lightly—sold a latte and an Americano, but the place was to boutique coffee what Finger Eleven are to punk rock. A lot of their coffee was slave to the process by which modern caffeinitia suffers: giant utility urns with level guides on the outside that remind you of the last funeral you attended, as well as jugs of milk that sit in the sun longer than George Hamilton. These mistakes were partly owing to Javaroma's staff: post-pubescent girls and boys who'd come from Japan and Korea to work in Yellowknife on longer-term stays because of the café's difficulty staffing the operation with itinerants, and the general shortage of labour in a city of twenty thousand. I tried not to be too hard on the place. The "baristas" were friendly and they seemed to work with a kind of verve, but I decided to call it the way I saw it. The column was passed on by Ellen to Mike, who passed it to Bruce. Moments later, Bruce's office door opened, making everyone look over their shoulders. He stepped out, and I wondered what Karen or John had done this time. Pivoting on the floor, he turned to face me.

"Dave? Got a minute?"

I passed my eyes around the newsroom wondering if the person along the far wall whom I hadn't met yet might be named Dave—turned out his name was Anton and he was about to be farmed out to Inuvik—before understanding that Bruce was asking for me. I straightened the tie I didn't wear and smoothed back the hair I didn't have and gathered myself before walking into his office.

Bruce sat in a large padded chair. Because he did, it wasn't hard to know what was about to go down, or rather, who was would be administering the go-downing. Bruce tented his fingers, untented them, then grabbed a piece of paper from his desk, which he waved around.

"I've just got to say," he said, biting his lip and sucking back a breath, "I don't really like your column."

My reaction didn't make me feel upset as much as it made me feel proud, and certainly more like a reporter. I sat there and took it. He told me that he didn't feel that a town should be judged by whether its coffee was any good and, "besides," he said, "it's a bit of a cheap shot, isn't it?" I formed counter-arguments in my mind about why the opposite was true before deciding that if this was as strong as the medicine would get, it was okay. When I emerged from the office, the staff looked up at me, partly out of pity and partly relieved that it wasn't them. Shawn furtively drew his hand from under his desk, shaped it into the barrel of a gun using two fingers, and jammed it into the softness of his temple. John wheeled around his chair and commanded: "Smoke." I followed him outside and Ewan joined.

"So what was that about?" asked John.

"They axed my column. Well, Bruce did," I told him.

"What was the subject?" asked Ewan.

"The coffee in Yellowknife. How it's . . . not good."

Ewan rolled his eyes. "The coffee's terrible."

"You know why they killed it?" asked John.

"Bruce told me it was a cheap shot," I said.

"Well, the truth is that someone in *Yellowknifer* upper management—the head salesperson—is married to someone who owns half of Javaroma."

"You think I should file a grievance?" I asked.

"Sure, buddy," he said, punching the air. "You go right ahead and do that."

Ewan snorted, and then John did, too.

"Stick it to 'em, buddy!" he said, now punching with both hands. "Stick it to 'em hard!"

I rewrote my column to appease Bruce, but he never got around to reading it because of what happened a few hours after the *Yellowknifer* office closed for the day. Shawn was awakened at around 5 a.m. by the sound of his police dispatcher squawking madly. When he turned an ear from his pillow to listen, he discovered that a houseboat was on fire in Yellowknife Bay. The young reporter leapt out of bed, threw on his clothes, shouldered his camera bag, and cycled down Franklin Hill in the yellow of the morning, the flames visible from the top. Shawn skidded his bike to the edge of the government wharf, where he found the fire department retreating after their pump failed to express water (because there were no fire hydrants in the granite foundations of Old Town, officials were left to use a single water tank to contain the blaze.

If it ran out, so did the fire department's ability to put out a fire). One man, the houseboater Gary Vaillancourt—an original resident on the bay—stepped into the breach, bringing his small Boston Whaler to the edge of the fire and spraying it with a working pump of his own despite calls from the wharf by RCMP officials to stand down (the fire started because a leaky propane tank had been ignited by a citronella candle, and officials feared it might spread to another boat). Across "the gut"—the area of water between the shore and Jolliffe Island—a motor boat with two one-hundred-pound bottles of propane caught fire next and became untethered, but sank itself before erupting in flames. Around the same time, both Matthew Grogono—the city's default disaster expert—and a Dene woman named Charlotte Overvolt arrived to contain the blaze, a scene that, if ineffective in stemming the flames, represented a kind of northern gallantry: a white dude from Nova Scotia and a woman whose family had been in the area for thousands of years working to help a friend, Kimberly Fuller, who escaped from the fire unharmed by swimming across the water.

The event presented a few narratives, one of which addressed the fire department's ambitions—or lack thereof—to assist the houseboater who lived, like thirty-three others on the bay, tax-free and beyond the auspices of the government (this accusation was refuted by city services, who pointed to the faulty pump as the reason for the firefighters' abandoning the burning boat). The same freedoms held true for the beyond-the-law Woodyard—the settlement of shacks near Ragged Ass Road, where, in 1990, citizens posed with unloaded rifles to express the encampment's vigilance—whose status produced divisive opinions about why people were allowed to live free from governance and yet expect the same kinds of services provided to the rest of the city (that the houseboat had been partly built using a flammable poly-styrene material was also debated). It was an issue made even more poignant after the area was reappropriated from Commissioner's Land into the hands of the city proper. Some people believed that the fire had ultimately given the city the thrust it needed to designate Woodyard shacks as detached secondary suites, allowing it greater control of the area, and, they feared, the ability to shape the plots of land into more legislated residential zones. If anything, the episode pointed to the fragile nature of Old Town. Fire hydrants equalled progress which equalled a different kind of place. At some point, you wondered whether Yellowknife would have to decide to either be functional and safe or continue to simply be itself.

After the fire, Shawn's story sat on the shelf for two days, waiting for the next issue of the paper. Because of the *Yellowknifer's* twice-a-week print schedule, and owing to the fact that it had no immediate digital presence, the most dramatic story of the summer was written days after all the other competing news outlets—the CBC, *EdgeYK,* and the Moose—had covered it soup to nuts. Even though Shawn was the first reporter on the scene, it didn't do him or the paper any good. Not only that, but because of the *Yellowknifer's* stance against first-person writing, his adventure was absent in the storytelling. "Getting scooped is killing me," said Karen, "but nothing is changing. I worry that, over the next few years in media, where reach is everything, the paper is going to be left behind. People like Walter, the photo editor of the *Yellowknifer,* to do great work, but nobody gets to see it. There are so many opportunities business-wise to license his photos, publish exclusive stories by the writer, get the word out there." The reporter ended her inventory, but both of us knew she could have kept going.

Over the next week, Shawn sighed a lot and slumped in his chair, occasionally thumping his fists on his desk in frustration in a patrician expression of angst. Even taking him out to the bar did him no good. "They're burning the poor kid out," John said, after Shawn left the bar earlier than anyone else. "I mean lookit," he announced waving around his friend's half-drunk pint, "he didn't even finish his goddamned drink," those last few words pregnant with the melancholy of some-one for whom abandoning a drink was a matter more regretful than others.

Another missed chance for the *Yellowknifer* happened awhile later during another fire at a home under construction in Niven Lake. I'd been with John and a few friends earlier in the evening before cycling down to a shack in The Woodyard for the neighbourhood's Thursday Scrabble night, although, other than the fact that there was a Scrabble board on the wooden table, it was more about being in a small place filled with smoke and a bottle in everyone's hand as opposed to who could spell "oxyphenbutazone." Later in the evening, I called John and he answered by telling me: "There's a fire, a huge fire, happening at Niven Lake. I'm heading there now." Mark Rendell of *Edge YK* was with me in the shack and I told him what John had said. We drove to the fire, but when we got there, firefighters told us that John was the first on the scene, taking photos and getting information. Mark got what he could—a few pictures of the hazmat team and some RCMP cruisers and an interview with a neigh-bour—and immediately checked his Twitter feed to discover that no one from the *Yellowknifer* had posted the story (John certainly wouldn't have; he wasn't on Twitter). Mark got on the case, laying his handheld device on the trunk of his car and typing his 140-character report with an accompanying photo. Because the Wi-Fi was patchy, he had to wait on it, but, after a few moments, it was clear Mark had scooped the *Yellowknifer* even though he'd been second on the scene. "We all get along," he told me, tapping the screen of his iPhone, "but journalism is competitive. It's part of what makes it exciting." Because John wasn't digitally savvy or wired to twenty-first-century media—he didn't even own a home com-puter—it didn't matter much to him that Mark had broken the story, but being the most recognizable, and controversial, journalist in town, it was perplexing, and why the paper hadn't capitalized on his ability to draw readers to their paper by hooking him up with a Twitter account or cultivating a presence beyond newsprint (John also had a national profile after the *Canadaland* story). After Rendell's tweets, and after they were shared and reshared and reshared some more, you wondered how long the *Yellowknifer* could bury its head in the sand before people stopped going to it for news.

I was conflicted over the *Yellowknifer's* stubbornness, remembering a time when journalism wasn't about a writer's multi-platform presence or their ability to tweet stories. I'd always been encouraged that good journalism mattered less about how one appeared, as opposed to how one wrote, although this was changing before our eyes. Journalists in the twenty-first century—although not *Yellowknifer* journalists—were encouraged to stump their brand on social media and provide visibility in the rush to sustain readers, spending most of their day online. In sports and arts reporting, for instance, writers who worked on television and radio were valued more than those who preferred working in a vacuum, and the same was true in publishing, where celebrities and writers with a media presence were embraced. Alas, the scourge of entertainment had infected all prose families, providing less room for the introverted author slouched behind a desk sweating to get the story right. Now more than ever, it was about how you looked doing what you did rather than what you did. I wanted the *Yellowknifer* to hold steady to show that it could be done its way, but I also feared it would be lost to the ages if it didn't concede on a few fronts, changing a little to maintain a lot. Then again, the North was the North was the North. Change came slow, and the print dinosaur still roamed.

In the aftermath of the houseboat story, the paper trudged along: tight deadlines, crazy story turnover, lengthening hours, and the person who-I-thought-was-named-Dave-but-was-actually-named-Anton leaving for Inuvik. Through this routine, Karen could barely sit still at her station after finding out that her magazine story for *Toronto Life* was due to arrive at the Yellowknife Walmart over the next few days. It was a monster piece—some five thousand words—which she'd constructed during late sessions at the paper after everyone had left, or at home in the absence of difficult roommates. Even when she was alone writing in her fourplex, the situation proved challenging. "I'd write at the end of my bed, my laptop propped up on my TV tray. Sometimes people in the building would override the router and our allotment of data, so the apartment manager would turn it off. I'd head to Shawn's to borrow data so I could do research and download stuff and submit it to my editor. Afterwards, I'd go and see the guy I was dating, and I'd lie on his lap talking about my job. He said, 'You love everything else you're doing, but you hate your job.' I'd say that it wasn't that bad, and then go and write for two or three more hours. And then go to work. That was my life."

When the *Toronto Life* issue finally arrived in Yellowknife and was brought into the newsroom, Karen kept it close to her station. Some writers came over to look through it; others not so much. If most of the staffers dreamed where they might end up next—it was a muddy dream considering the nature of the business—Karen was already in the doorway of her fantasy. That big-city magazine success had found her in Yellowknife was also profoundly singular, because if other Southerners had come to the North to start over and escape to a new place, Karen was lunging in the opposite direction. Being surprised by the success made it even sweeter and more surreal.

In private, Karen talked a lot about the piece, and how it was being received in certain corners of journalism. There were times when I found this tedious, but mostly I was excited for her despite my frustrations about where I was in my writing life and what the whole nature of the craft meant anymore. Each day, a new voice shouted to her from the digiverse: this important person had retweeted it, that important person had reviewed it. Soon, she was slipping out of the office during lunch hour to be interviewed on the phone by BBC World and the *Washington*

Post and other media outlets around the world, a matter that, Mike Bryant told me, rubbed him and other people at the paper the wrong way. Weeks later, New York City called: a television executive wanted to meet her with an eye to developing her story for the screen. Karen kept filing for the *Yellowknifer*, but if you stood close enough to her, you could feel the swoosh of another door swinging open. The dream was chasing her down.

14

≡

A NOT BORING SECTION
ABOUT ROCKS (AND FISHING)

O ne of the things about the North that I learned almost immediately—from the display cases at the city airport to great cairns fixed
with historical plaques leading into the city to a view of the old
mining headframes at opposite ends of the city—was that rock—or at
least the discovery of its minerals—was essential to understanding the
region and its role in helping grow Yellowknife from a tiny map dot into
a capital region (what was also immediate was the realization that I would
have to write about this subject—inherently dull, or so I thought—in a
way that wouldn't make you decide to flip over to the part where I leave
Yellowknife for a journey farther north, which you should regard as a
reward for reading a not boring chapter about rocks [and fishing]).

Even in the twenty-first century, with mining booms having come
and gone and the headframes both abandoned, the discovery of rock (or
its minerals) was still a common topic of conversation in the city. Minerals
were a concern as early as 1934, when two men named Johnny Baker and
Herb Dixon paddled down the Yellowknife River while on a sojourn from
mineral prospecting at Great Bear Lake. Baker found rich gold on the
east side of Yellowknife Bay—the site of the short-lived Burwash Mine—
and, soon after that, Con Mine began production, Old Town was settled,

and the city thrived as money poured in, in unprecedented quantity. Like any boom, however, it eventually busted, dooming Con Mine's commanding seventy-six-metre-high Robertson headframe, which, during my summer in Yellowknife, remained butted into the earth blazing orange at its tip like Zeus's Navy Cut. Despite providing a distinctive city landmark—dozens of people lost on the lake had stories about navigating home after finding its blinking tower—it was demolished in 2017, moving the city further away from its industrial roots and closer to the bureaucratic focus that provided the bulk of work.

In 1991, there was a second mineral boom, this time coming after a vast sea of diamonds was found gleaming in kimberlite pipes on the Barren Lands, three hundred kilometres north of the city. The Barren Lands is home to, arguably, the oldest rock formation known to man— the Acasta Gneiss within the Slave Craton—estimated at around four billion years old (some have suggested that the Jack Hills in Australia date at 4.4 billion years, a subject disputed among geologists). I remembered learning this in slow-moving school geography class, where the study of rock was never much like the study of Rock, and where the romance of mineral discovery—the wild chase for unfathomable wealth, the danger of prospecting, the struggle between humanity and nature—was somehow absent from the curriculum. It wasn't until I came north that I was compelled by rock the way I was with Rock, understanding how close I was to the essence of the Big Bang. History tells us about the infancy of time as it relates to the pyramids, Mesopotamia, and the primordial seas producing life, but it's in the Canadian North where the first lands were ostensibly formed. Perhaps it's a function of age or the slow appreciation for a subject that my younger self would have eagerly zoomed past, but staring into the roaring Canadian Shield, and its mythic bodies of water, I felt lucky being so close to such raw history.

The diamond boom of the 1990s had a series of moving parts, but there was one man—a young geologist and fanatical mineral collector from Kelowna, British Columbia, named Charles "Chuck" Fipke—who was largely responsible for the city being reborn in post-gold-mining times. Fipke is described by Kevin Krajick in his outstanding book, *Barren Lands: An Epic Search for Diamonds in the North American Arctic*, as overwhelmingly friendly and usually "attired in a bright red field vest; its many pockets jam-packed with notebooks and other objects, several crammed backpacks, and assorted compasses and cameras [swinging] chaotically from his neck." Fipke's mind clicked like a ticker-tape and his mouth went even faster. He possessed a savant's curiosity for geology, and if half of prospecting is about the dogged and sustained pursuit of minerals over uncertain periods of time, Fipke's boyish energies kept him careering into the chase. During a difficult episode in the field in which a blizzard once hemmed in a team of fellow researchers, Krajick wrote: "Things looked bad as they got to the last jar of peanut butter, but Chuck just kept laughing."

Fipke came to mineral exploration in Canada after travelling as a geologist to Papua New Guinea, an experience that toughened the twenty-four-year-old for whatever lay ahead. He was helicoptered into hazardous jungles by Vietnam war veterans, where, according to Krajick, "monsoons, bugs, hostile locals and leeches" failed to abate his search for copper minerals. He was guided by spear-carrying tribesmen who ate live frogs for lunch and had "two-foot squash gourds strapped upright to their penises." After a time, Fipke, out of respect for his hosts, stripped naked and adorned himself with jewellery, but a terrible bout of malaria had him shipped out to a hospital in Australia, where doctors told his wife, Marlene, that he would almost certainly die (Fipke found no copper but, years later, mining companies staked the land and pulled up the bounty he had sensed was there). He suffered through a semi-coma until one day, while supposedly on his death bed at home, he opened his eyes and spoke to his wife.

Chuck got better, eventually returning with Marlene to Kelowna, where Chuck's once-abusive father had quit drinking, become a Jehovah's Witness, and helped build a patched-together mineral shaker/shifter that

Marlene also used as a slow cooker. In 1979, Fipke was sampling minerals near Golden, British Columbia, when Marlene found chrome diopside—regarded as a diamond indicator—in a nearby stream. The young prospector passed this information on to Hugo Dummett, a senior geologist at Superior Oil for whom Fipke worked, and he agreed to pay for further exploration in exchange for an interest in any discovery. According to author Matthew Hart, whose book *Diamond* is indispensable reading on the subject, Fipke phoned an acquaintance, geologist Stewart Blusson, and they prospected together before coming across a set of kimberlite pipes—a trace rock to diamonds—which, while ultimately barren, saw Blusson quit his government job to join the greater diamond hunt. During an offhand conversation with a helicopter pilot while searching alongside Fipke and Blusson in the northern Rockies, Hugo Dummett learned that the mining giant De Beers were exploring a site east of the Mackenzie River, near Norman Wells, in the Sahtu region of the Northwest Territories. The men set up a nearby camp at Blackwater Lake and studied found samples—a glacial till with large garnets, ilmenites, and chrome diopsides—at which point Blusson hired a workforce to chainsaw 240 miles of wilderness, over which they used magnetometers to look for kimberlite, also snipping spruce twigs and sealing them in envelopes in hopes of finding root traces of nickel, cesium, strontium, and other key minerals. During a flight from camp, Fipke laid eyes on the massive De Beers operation where, according to Hart, "a figure rushed from a tent and trained binoculars on them." Fipke and Blusson darted into the clouds and were never found out.

Eventually, the prospectors discovered a mineral presence older than the indigenous rock, hinting at a trail with new possibilities for gold. Having studied the path of glaciers across the greater northwest, Blusson guessed that the source of the material was the Slave Craton, so he informed his bosses at Superior Oil, who disregarded the information and suggested he abandon his search, the Craton area proving too expensive and time-consuming to drill. Without support from the company, Dummett checked

ve Fipke and Blusson his field data before the pair headed north-
e least hospitable chunk of land on the continent.

two prospectors worked for a handful of years, tracking indica-
led nowhere while continuing to raise money through unlikely
Fipke's barber, his mechanic, a local gunsmith, an upholstery
pool of orthodontists who raised fifty thousand dollars, an Air
ilot with whom Marlene worked, and the owner of a Greek
t in Fipke's hometown of Kelowna. Chuck's brother, Wayne, told
hat, when looking for investors, he "took pains to paint his
s a mad genius. The more obtuse and helpless Chuck appeared,
honest people assumed him to be." Wayne harped on Chuck's
ness, his tendency to mumble to himself, and his propensity for
. On occasion, he gave potential investors tours of the shit-
-everywhere home mineral lab to further emphasize Fipke's
dicated genius. They raised several hundred thousand dollars at
d kept on looking.

tually, Blusson moved his interests elsewhere, leaving Fipke to
and devotedly carry on. He peddled shares in a company he
Dia Met Minerals, for seventeen cents a hit, while remaining
ely secret" in his work. Yellowknife legend has him dining at the
ge Bistro and giving the wrong information to local prospectors
of shading his endeavours. He also paid his float plane pilots in
ey rotated taking him out so that no one would know his exact
n the area—and he insisted that all names be kept off receipts.
o conversing in public with his hand over his mouth, fearing lip
nd other surveillance devices.

seven defiant years of exploration, Fipke zoned in on one spot
aton, just north of Lac de Gras, a fifty-mile tundra lake. There
ered diamond indicator G10 garnets, staking a huge block of
ng an alias to disguise his identity. Chris Jennings, an employee
tional Corona, a gold producer, found out about Fipke's work
tched to the deep North a young woman named Leni Keough,

who moved through small Indigenous Barren Lands settlements and camped on the tundra while taking rudimentary tests on a huge swatch of land from Great Slave Lake to central Northwest Territories. She found diamond indicators so abundant that she could see them by staring at raw samples. In some cases, they yielded microdiamonds. The discovery propelled her on.

Fipke and Keough/Jennings raced to find the bounty. Fipke registered his stakes as nearly preposterous gold claims, raising little interest or suspicion at mineral offices in Yellowknife. One afternoon, while flying over his claimed land—about 385,000 acres, or six hundred square miles—he noticed a small, round lake, and it was here that the penny dropped: the lake was shaped exactly like a kimberlite pipe. The diamonds, he reasoned, were in the land. The pipe was beneath the water.

Two things happened next. First, Fipke sent some samples to a lab in Cape Town for assessment and then he phoned Hugo Dummett, who'd since become the exploration chief for BHP Minerals. The report from the lab suggested that the materials were "the best for diamond potential that we have seen anywhere in the world." Dummett signed on to commit five hundred million dollars to develop a diamond mine. According to Hart, "they drew a curtain of secrecy around the little lake and began to expand their camp."

Dummett drilled twenty-four hours a day, naming the body of water "Point Lake" as a misdirection, since another Point Lake existed nearby. They hired a local Yellowknife geologist and prospector, Ed Schiller, who, to his amazement, identified a diamond-riddled 130-pound sample of kimberlite drilled at a depth of 950 feet from the lake. Conducting further airborne studies, Fipke identified an entire field of pipes, and within a year, Dia Met's seventeen-cent shares had reached eight dollars. They climbed well beyond that, and, eventually, Fipke would know wealth beyond comprehension, earning upwards of seven hundred thousand dollars a day. Soon, the Barrens were writhing with prospectors and mineral companies, with trucks charging along ice roads for as far as the eye could see.

Other prospectors, big and small, followed Fipke, including De Beers, whose operation could have them on the ground drilling within weeks. One woman, Eira Thomas, a young geologist who worked for her father, Gren, at Aber Resources (later Diavik), led a Barren Lands drill team, who raced against the elements—and the short spring window—to pull up logs of split core before sending them to Toronto for testing. Hart described the diggers' conundrum at the site: how warming weather threatened to pull the entire operation into the frigid waters. He wrote: "The drillers balked. Water was already forming on the ice. They did not want to drill at all, let alone with a heavier rig [required to take a larger sample]. Thomas was adamant, and no doubt understood that it would have been difficult for men with such a roughneck, swashbuckling demeanour as drillers to turn down a woman whose request was nothing less than a challenge. The crew chief consented . . . [but] they missed [hitting the spot]. Thomas faced the decision of whether to try a second hole [but] by this time, the drill shack was awash. The pool around it would not drain away. Water was knee deep around the drill and the ice was dangerously soft under the surface water."

They kept drilling, but the conditions worsened. The drill produced clouds of black smoke and the weight of the machinery was pulling down the ice, threatening to drag the equipment under, "in an oily depression," according to Hart. Open water appeared under the shore and a great fog descended on the site.

Thomas's comrade-in-arms, a geologist named Robin Hopkins, arrived during a change in shift and inspected whatever core boxes had already been pulled from the site. He discovered they were full of kimberlite. "I kept taking samples and filling my pockets," he said. When he found Thomas alone and disconsolate, sipping tea in the camp's kitchen, he started "dumping core out from under my shirt piece by piece [and] with each piece Eira's face got brighter and brighter until she was practically bouncing around." After closer inspection of the core, they saw it gleaming back at them through the rock: a 2-carat diamond "bouncing light from its crystal face."

Thomas slept with the core beneath her pillow, and the geologists swore to keep the find private until they alerted Gren Thomas. Thomas had discovered the highest-grade cluster of diamond pipes in the world, containing some 138 million carats. According to Hart, it would "support the mine for twenty years and supply the market with an annual 400 million dollars' worth of rough." This would prove true, although, in 2015, the reserves were nearly exhausted. It behooved Yellowknife to figure out new ways to sustain itself unless more diamonds, or comparable minerals, were found, but often the prediction came down to this: the city would grow if they were, yet remain in stasis if they were not.

If the history of minerals helped tell the story of Yellowknife, the surrounding waters—Yellowknife Bay and Back Bay, and the activities on them—were also essential in understanding the psychology of the city. No matter how much Yellowknife changed through development, the land always released itself to the yawning lake. With buildings going up and, in some cases, rising along ridge rock that overlooked the bays, people were even more fanatical about being on the water: by canoe with the Allooloos; by tugboat with the Snowking, Tony Foliot, whose towering winter ice castle on Yellowknife Bay was the majestic focus of the early spring; by rowboat to the houseboats; and by Mike Bryant, who, one day, asked if I wanted to go fishing.

I accepted for a number of reasons. Since Mike was a veteran angler, I sensed it would be different than my other experiences in small boats staring at the water while trying to set the record for number-of-Bud Lites-consumed-vs.-the-number-of-fish-caught, which was, inevitably, a ratio greater than zero. Mike also wrote a column in the *Yellowknifer* called "The Fishin' Technician" and was on a personal quest, along with a handful of others whom I can only describe, affectionately, as angling freaks, to identify, in person, as many species of fish as possible (Mike had reached

104, partly owing to Slave Lake's reputation as "the Galapagos of fish biology," according to ichthyologist Paul Vecsei). Another reason I felt I should go was that he was, effectively, my boss, and the third concerned the fact that I'd only just learned that the editor, father, and angler wasn't entirely who he claimed to be.

Before coming to Yellowknife, John Samson, the former singer and songwriter for the Weakerthans, told me that I should look up an old acquaintance of his, whom he thought might have settled in the Northwest Territories. The person's name was "Stinky Mike."

"He's a fishing guide, I think. I replaced him in Propaghandi [John's pre-Weakerthans' band]. He was pretty wild then and he's probably pretty wild now. You should try to find him. He'd be pretty entertaining, I think." I thanked John for the tip, but he told me another thing: "If Stinky Mike asks if you want to see the cigarette trick, tell him you don't. I can't say why, just don't, okay?" I promised him I would not.

One afternoon, Mike Bryant was talking music from his work station in the middle of the newsroom. The discussion began after a plea from John to turn on the giant TV screen hanging on one of the walls.

"Can't you put on Much Music or something?" asked John.

"Maybe you can build a time machine and we can go back to 1986," said Mike.

"That would be good. I had a good time in 1986," said John. "There was this one girl: she was smokin' hot," he said, drawing groans from the room.

"Was it Cyndi Lauper?" asked Mike, starting the carousel.

"Alannah Myles?"

"Gloria Estevan?"

"Suzanne Somers?"

"Was it Alf?"

"Can't a guy say a girl is smoking hot?" asked John, indignantly. "It's a compliment."

"Well, it's kind of offensive and judgmental and——" said Karen, before John cut her off.

"Yes, I am judging. I am judging that this chick was smoking hot," he said.

I told Karen that I'd explain later to John why it was wrong, telling him, "John, I'll explain to you later why it's wrong."

"It isn't wrong," he said under his breath before returning to his keyboard, which he stabbed at with the pointer fingers of both hands.

Someone, maybe Ewan, continued on the Much Music jag—how it had once been a decent thing but was now an awful thing—and, eventually, Mike started talking about playing music in Winnipeg, doing gigs at the same places I used to play when I was crossing the country.

At that point, I knew.

"You're 'Stinky Mike'!" I shouted. I may have stood up and flung about my arms and said it a second time.

He confessed that he was.

While on his fishing boat, I asked Mike about Propagandhi—how they used to do shows naked while touring the punk circuit across North America and Europe—before telling him what John Samson had told me. The editor didn't flinch at the mention of the cigarette trick. He said: "My foreskin. It has a hole in it. Something went a little wrong when they did the procedure, I guess. I used to put a cigarette in there. That's pretty much the story."

I thanked him for telling me.

"You don't wanna see it, I'm guessing?"

I told him he guessed right.

Eventually, we anchored near a rocky cove, the small waves drumrolling against the side of the boat. It was a grey day, with temperatures dipping into the teens. My hoodie was pulled tight to my head and I shivered a little in the rising wind, which came hard across the lake. Mike handed me a fishing rod, which I cast awkwardly into the dark waters.

In my life I will never be confused for an active angler, although it's something I like to do whenever I find myself doing it. Staring into the opaque depths of the lake, the complications of the newspaper and my writing life fell away, which, I remembered, was exactly how this sort of thing was supposed to work. If Yellowknife had been a storm of sound and colour—everything new and interesting and different—now it was calm without a single figure—no trees, birds, bars, or other people; no John; no Franklin Hill—in sight.

The reverie lasted a moment before my line shook violently. The rod bowed like a question mark and its spinner made a hissing sound. Mike shouted things like "Steady!" and "Hold it!" and "Ease off; now stop easing!" but I was already too consumed by the drama of what was happening: raising a strange creature out of the unknown, which, in that instant, I understood to be one of the great things about angling. Butterflies netted and geese shot and chickens chased across a yard are okay. But pulling a creature from darkness is something else entirely.

The line hiccupped a few times—I fought with the fish for a few minutes—and then Mike helped me pull it out of the water: a ten-pound monster of a northern pike (the Northerners call them "jacks"). It was mysterious, prehistoric, oily, and easily the biggest and most impressive fish I'd ever caught. Mike unbarbed the hook and then handed the jack to me. It lay heavy across my arms and I giggled like a child.

Canoes outside the Narwal B&B.

Welcome sign at N'Dilo.

Great Slave Lake.

John McFadden, smoke in hand, beside the ball diamond at Fred Henne park.

Pilot Ted Grant in Fort Simpson.

Papers off the press in the *Yellowknifer* building.

The *Yellowknifer* printing press.

Sign recognizing the Prophet Aiyah in Deline.

The Cirque of the Unclimbables in Nahanni National Park.

Virginia Falls in Nahanni National Park.

Susan Chaffee at the Gold Range Bistro in Yellowknife.

Painting of the four prophets in Deline, in the cabin where the Prophet Ayah had died.

Me on the Deh Cho
(the Mackenzie River).

A whaling camp
at Tuk.

Edward Pokiak in front of
the DEW station.

Smoking whitefish on the shores of the Beaufort Sea.

Indio Saravanja (left) and me.

John on the phone on Elijah's rooftop.

Me in front of the wooden welcome sign at Tuktoyaktuk.

15

HERE COME THE WARM JETS

Growing up in the Toronto suburbs, we headed south for the holidays—Florida, North Carolina, Las Vegas—chasing the warmth and sparkle of the U.S.A. People still do this today, but it was an even more profound quest in the 1970s, when American culture—film, television, music—dominated Canada with its thunderous mass of noise and colour. We ran to Disneyworld, we ran to Myrtle Beach, we ran to Universal Studios, drawn by sun, money, and fame. My family nearly ran over actor Cloris Leachman on Rodeo Drive with our rented car, one of the highlights of our vacationing lives.

In *Playing Dead*, Rudy Wiebe writes that "we [Canadians] will always go whoring after the mocking palm trees and beaches. . . ." For me, it's a little harsh, because, apart from the insecurities that come with being a stranger travelling through that lurching beast of a nation, our southern journeys also yielded a trip to a Major League Baseball game for the first time (pre-Blue Jays; Angels vs. the Rangers) and Roy Clark on stage at Circus Circus in Vegas, the first time I'd ever seen a performer of his calibre live. Later on, while touring through Scandinavia, I was grateful for my American influences: a boldness of expression, a freeing of character. Still, Canadians have traditionally been more inclined to define ourselves *down there* instead of *up here*, measured against how we're perceived by others rather than how we perceive ourselves. When the Rheostatics began, we were about looking in rather than looking out, an aesthetic developed after long and thrilling summer tours of Canada. For us, visiting Regina and Winnipeg was like going to Paris and London, partly because we knew very little about those places—having suffered through a dry (and colonial) scholastic impression of our culture and history—and partly because it was the first time we'd travelled anywhere on our own, exploring a new place that also happened to be our country. We wrote our entire second album on our first tour, a wild trip that carried us across northern Ontario to the Rocky Mountains, taking almost three months to complete. We became adults, and we became artists, on the road in Canada. It produced a career and a life.

Still, those trips saw us mostly hugging Highway One, a band of road that, more or less, glues itself to the border. This points to another quote from Rudy Wiebe: "Canadians have so little comprehension of our own *nordicity*, that . . . until we grasp imaginatively, and realize imaginatively in word, song, image and consciousness that North is . . . the true nature of our world . . . we will always be wishing ourselves something we aren't." Because I still had little true sense of my own nordicity—or rather, my nordicity was informed having visited northern places that, in the end, weren't so northern at all—I came to it after spending time in other cold, remote cities around the world. I went to Harbin, China; Ulaanbaatar, Mongolia; and Omsk, Russia, for hockey work: a triangle of top-of-the-map cities that revealed the experiences of warm people in cold places. Every time I went to these locations, I told myself how "Canadian" they seemed without ever having visited their latitudinal cousins. My sense of remote Canada had come at a distance, even though I considered myself—had made a career of considering myself—a person with a seasoned view of the country. That view included a northern sense developed anywhere but here.

While planning my summer in Yellowknife, I knew that, in order to get an idea of life in the white band across the top of the country—a place that my geography teacher's pointer could barely reach at the top of the classroom's pull-down map—I had to move around the North. After asking to see Bruce in his office and sharing my concerns with him, he said, a little too jokingly for my tastes: "You could go on assignment!" I told him that's exactly what I planned on doing, pretending not to hear him chuckle as I closed the door and returned to my desk.

"Ducha" is the Dene word for "heading out of town"—as a measure of balance, *"araduthla"* is the word for returning—and it's what I did, throwing two small bags in the *Yellowknifer*'s hatchback and heading to the airport with John, who refused to allow me to go any other way. "It's what friends do for friends," he insisted, but when we arrived, he disappeared into the far end of the airport parking lot. I sat on a bench and waited, and when he returned, I asked if he was okay. "Yeah, yeah," he said, waving a hand around. "Just had to take the edge off, you know," he said, putting two fingers to his mouth and pantomiming smoking a joint.

"It's me who's flying, not you," I said.

"Oh, Christ. Did you want some?" he said. "Buddy, I'm sorry. I should have asked. I feel like a heel."

"No, no," I said. "I can't fly stoned. That would be awful."

"Oh, okay," he said, pacing about.

"You okay?" I asked him.

"Yeah, yeah, fine," he told me.

"I don't have to worry, do I?" I asked him.

"Christ, no," he replied. "It's fine. I mean, it's not really," he said, hacking out a laugh. "But, you know . . ."

I almost missed my thirty-minute flight to Fort Simpson, a town five hundred kilometres west of Yellowknife located at the confluence of the Liard and Mackenzie rivers. It took me awhile to find the gate because it wasn't so much a gate as an unmarked white closet door. A man with a clipboard poked his head out and asked if any more passengers were bound for Simpson, the quiet of his voice implying that he hoped there weren't. I leapt out of my bucket chair and asked to be pointed toward security, but he told me, voicing three words I thought I'd never hear at an airport—"No security check"—while holding open the closet door.

Flights to Simpson and other communities around the Northwest Territories eschewed conventional security measures. This was partly because it was commonplace for men and women coming and going to carry knives, guns, and other hunting paraphernalia on the aircraft; partly because getting planes in the air without security hang-ups was essential in unpredictable weather conditions that wreaked havoc with flight schedules; and partly because the empty North was among the last places on Earth where terrorist threats were a real concern. After a few trips around the Territories, I became grateful for the stressless boarding procedure—it maximized my time in places I might never return to— while only a little concerned after hearing large weapons rolling around in the compartments above me.

I was collected from the small Simpson airport—it was no bigger than a suburban rec room—in a van driven by a great-bellied, moustached Nova Scotian named Reg, who had an apple crate head and skillets for hands, with cooked sausage fingers. Reg spoke excitedly and with great import; every thought spiked with exclamation. He had a lot to say about lots, but he mostly talked about bugs, whose great numbers swirled about the insides of the van like something from the TV show *Fear Factor*. I spent most of our trip to town batting about my hands like someone trying to divert a disconsolate child's attention away from whatever had made them disconsolate, while Reg talked about the time a wasp stung him on the bag.

"I was driving, see," he said, eating an apple with one hand and driving with the other. "And there were wasps everywhere. It was really bad! They were like these things," he said, pointing around the van at the bugs. "Only they were wasps! Jesus, I couldn't keep up. Right then, I felt something down here," he said, pointing between his legs with his apple. "And Jesus it hurt! Like a spike going in me, you know? Christ, I was in agony! Sheer agony!"

I asked Reg what happened next, even though I knew he would tell me anyway.

"Well, I stopped the van and I climbed out, right there on the highway. And I pulled down my pants," he said, waving the apple about. "A few people saw me out there and they didn't know what I was doing. But I shouted to 'em: 'My bag! A wasp stung me on the bag!'"

I could have listened to Reg talk about his bag all day, but his story, and our ride, ended after he deposited me at the three-storey Mackenzie Inn, where I spent the next few nights reacquainting myself with the conveniences of bathrooms you didn't have to march across a chainsawed field to get to. If Yellowknife was a city proper, Simpson was more of a small town: flat and Shieldless with a long dusty main street and only two or three places to eat, including the Nahanni Inn and Pandaville (the worst Jimmy Buffett album ever), the latter a Chinese restaurant annexed to the Ice Breaker Lounge, whose lettered sign at the edge of the road encouraged passers-by to CME A HIDE AT T ICEBREAKERS. This was bad enough, but if you played *Wheel of Fortune* with the letters, you arrived at COME AND HIDE AT THE ICEBREAKERS, leading me to conclude that the place was frequented by fugitives in fake beards and broad hats.

While walking the streets—or, rather, the street—of Fort Simpson, I discovered that when all the bugs in the Deh Cho ("big river" in Dene and pronounced "Day-Cho") weren't hanging out in Reg's van, they were amassed along the riverside with their annoyed cousins: flies the size of licorice Nibs that locals called "bulldogs." The bulldogs' organized a relentless and vengeful attack, pelting my face and chest like small helmeted thugs, and because forest fires were currently burning as near as thirty kilometres away—my flight had been filled with firefighters from Saskatchewan and Ontario coming to the Northwest Territories to battle a record number of blazes—the combination of the insects and the acrid smoke made walking in Simpson feel like ambulatory Hell, which may have explained the relative emptiness in town. Simpson was peopled—or, I suppose, unpeopled—by the occasional kid racing a bike or skateboard down the sidewalk or a few old men standing on either side of the street carrying on loud Beckettian conversations that were always variations of:

"How you doin'?"

"Doin' good!"

"Okay!"

"Where are you goin'?"

"Nowhere!"

"Okay!"

The men continued on to wherever they weren't going and then, eventually, another two men took their place.

I slept well on the night before my trip into the Nahanni National Park even though it took a moment for my body to stop shaking after salting it with handfuls of MSG found in Pandaville's noodles. Still, I laid on my duvet and stared between my feet at the muddy river outside, noticing a few float planes bobbing, tethered to their docks and wondering which one would take me into the park, my main reason for visiting Fort Simpson. The river—renamed the "Mackenzie" after explorer Alexander Mackenzie, who traversed it in 1793 in an attempt to reach China—covered 1.8 million square kilometres. It was the second-biggest river system in North America—the Mississippi being the first—its watershed panning over 20 per cent of Canada. It was a huge roaring force in the land, and vital to the anatomy of the natural world, providing nearly 11 per cent of the fresh water flowing into the Arctic Ocean.

Mackenzie had failed to reach China on his journey, evermore referring to the Deh Cho as "the River of Disappointment," something that exasperated locals who wanted to return the Mackenzie to its ancestral name ("And we've been disappointed ever since" was the Slavey rejoinder to the explorer's expression). The Gwich'in perspective was such that, in a young adult book called *Mom, We've Been Discovered!*, the uncredited author wrote: "We, as a people, do not perceive Alexander Mackenzie as a great person. He was to our people rather insignificant at the time. His significance to us today lays within the fact that our reality has changed because of him and others that shared his interest. We are no longer the independent and self-sufficient people we once were."

The next morning, I showered, dressed, ate a modest breakfast with an eye to the unpredictability of short-haul air travel, and walked down the grounds of the inn toward the dock at the bottom of a brown riverbank slope, where I identified our vessel for travelling into the park: a 1956 Beaver float plane shimmying in the rippled waters. Six passengers were scheduled to fly: two from Ottawa, three from Yellowknife, and me. The plane was piloted, and owned, by a sixty-six-year-old legend of the Deh Cho named Ted Grant. Ted had flown thirty thousand miles and made three thousand trips for his company, Simpson Air. If you narrowed your eyes, he cut the figure of a dashing airman from time beyond, smoking a cigarette with an aviator's cap tipped rakishly to the side. Ted had a thin dark moustache and a lean posture as straight as an asparagus sprig, and his running shoes, baseball hat, and what can only be described as dad jeans seemed wasted when a pilot's uniform would have suited him perfectly. After I "Oooooohed!" audibly at the mention of his impressive flying record—he'd voiced the numbers while standing beside the plane and patting its flank as if it were a stabled thoroughbred—the pilot reacted by saying, "And those were all real flying hours. None of this," he added, pretending to play with the joystick on a flight simulator.

Ted's first flight was in 1976. He came to Fort Simpson after his tenure with the RCMP, which he joined on his nineteenth birthday. "When I was a kid growing up in Oak Hills [Saskatchewan], my dad brought an old fighter plane [a bomber] to the farm. I used to sit in the cockpit and pretend, so I guess it's always been in here," he said, tapping at his temple. Ted's life in the skies was part of his family's greater legacy. His grandfather's cousin was the famous World War I and bush pilot Wop May—one of the first people to deliver mail to the North—and his bloodlines included Frederick Banting, who invented insulin, as well as decorated CFL and NFL coaching legend Bud Grant. "We used to have Bud out to Little Doctor Lake [the Nahanni property owned by Grant], and he'd come out and fish and have a good time. I'd like to spend more time there myself," he said, sighing, "but it seems I'm always in the air.

Because of his years flying in and out of the park, Ted saw himself as a kind of guardian for the Nahanni, and a dyed-in-the-wool citizen of the Territories. He was the N.W.T.'s lone representative during a recent national tourism gathering in Ottawa, where he presented his case to then Prime Minister Stephen Harper about supporting the region. "I told the prime minister that our land mass, between Yukon, Northwest Territories, and Iqaluit, represents 45 per cent of our country, and yet we have the poorest infrastructure in all the western hemisphere. I told him about the roads—the Dempster, the Liard, and the Mackenzie—all of which were closed at one point or another before our meeting. Two weeks later, I got a call from the minister of northern affairs, who told me, 'You certainly made an impression on the prime minister.' Eventually, they pledged $78 million more to us, and over the last few years, where do you think that money has gone? Not here," he said, gesturing around him. "But I'll keep trying. One of these days they've got to listen to me."

Because I was the first to arrive for the flight, Ted offered me a seat in the cockpit. I accepted. He cranked open the heavy door to the plane and, one by one, we climbed into the close, warm cabin of the Beaver, the grey, factory-issue controls and old De Havilland nameplate staring at me from my seat. He passed headphones to us to muffle the roar of the propellers and the thunderous rattling of the plane, which started once he engaged it for takeoff. My eyes passed across a dashboard switch that read FM/VHF, and I half-expected to hear Foreigner's "Cold as Ice" or "Radar Love" by Golden Earring, or, even better, "Jet Airliner" by the Steve Miller Band flooding into my headphones. Alas, this was not the case, and as we skied on pontoons down the South Nahanni River—home to the Dolly Varden trout, I learned—before being hoisted into the air, the water disappeared and the banks thinned and we flew over postcard patches of forest and small lakes toward the park. Although Ted possessed the kind of capable, steady-handed touch and demeanour that would make even the most nervous flyer feel okay, I considered whether being airborne with a veteran pilot in his old warhorse of a plane was a good or bad thing before drawing up a list. On one hand, Ted Grant was a legend who had flown for years without incident, while, on the other, *Ted Grant was a legend who had flown for years without incident.* Because the plane was such a relic, I wondered whether it was destined to have something fall off, but reasoned that it was probably better than being in something that had been downed many times over. I also asked myself whether it was the smartest thing for my nerves to have searched "Twin Otter Crash 2010–2015" at the *Yellowknifer* before coming to Fort Simpson.

The first part of our journey was a tipless ride. Ted worked the controls using two hands as if he had twelve: punching numbers into his GPS, easing the throttle, steering a great metal arm that grew out of the floor of the cockpit, and flicking switches and spinning dials like the Great Oz. My mortality was the last thing on my mind as the most astonishing landscape came into view: enormous green canyons giving way to towering charcoal ranges giving way to a changing moonscape where huge cylindrical hills, known as "tufas," blasted out of nowhere. I gazed upon a set of granite towers with ridges running down the side like an enormous set of knuckles pushed into the earth before gazing farther down at the supine South Nahanni River, which wound about the terrain like an azure necklace. It was as if the creator—or whoever—had scribbled designs on one page before tearing that page and starting another, only to use all the pages, including whatever had been thrown to the floor. Unlike the Rockies, whose numbing and ferocious thunder is mostly uniform in its beauty, the landscape was an ever-changing jumble of forms, like a board game using pieces from every other game. As I made notes, I wanted to employ the word "epic" to describe the view, but I resisted for fear of confusing my experience with a *Walking Dead* episode or that road trip to Bonnaroo. Still, it's what it was, and after ninety minutes in the air, there was something more: the view of the enormous forest fire that we'd tasted in town, its beehives of smoke rising twenty thousand feet in the air with flames spidering over the scorched ground.

Ted busied the throttle and worked the controls as we dove around the tufas. My stomach held fine, bouncing like a small child on their parents' lap as opposed to a soccer ball kicked around the intestines. Ted barked something into our headphones—the clamshells were as old as the aircraft, and for most of the trip, I couldn't hear anything other than the grinding of the plane—and pointed the nose of the Beaver toward the waters of the Nahanni. We settled there as smoothly as a placemat frisbeed across a table and taxied to a nearby wharf, our landing point in the Nahanni National Park.

The Nahanni park is a UNESCO Heritage Site—the *first* UNESCO World Heritage Site, named along with three others in an inaugural set in 1978—and was designated for protection after a canoe trip by the buck-skinned Pierre Elliott Trudeau. Coming up from the wharf, we followed a pair of guides—two women in Parks Canada dun green and beige—across a log path into the depths of a forest, where we settled on a landing above the Sluice Box Rapids running into Virginia Falls (Nailicho in Dene), a cascading waterfall twice the depth of Niagara Falls, and, perhaps, the most poignant natural symbol of the Northwest Territories: awesome, enormous, and barely reachable in the middle of the entrancing nowhere.

The falls roared and the mist billowed and everything was blue and gold. It was a warm day, but the great rising spray of the water made us feel refreshed and cool, more so considering how dry and hot it had been in the plane's cabin. One of the guides told us how many people travel into the park—about four hundred annually, she said—and then nobody said anything. We just stood there feeling grateful to be where we were.

One of the guides was Diane Andre, a small woman with a meditative way about her. Diane was from a village called Deline, on Great Bear Lake. I asked her about it and she described a place that sounded more like an

invention or, possibly, a dream: home to a Dene spiritualism that followed the teachings of four prophets, including a man called Aiyah,
who, she said, had foretold many of the world's events. Deline was also
the first successful town in North America to adopt Indigenous self-
government, and, according to elders of elders, the true birthplace of
hockey, having witnessed people "drift across the ice in winter," said
Diane, "as if they were skating." She also told me about something that
happened during the 30s and 40s: how local Dene men were hired as
labourers at the Port Radium mine to excavate raw uranium for the
Manhattan Project, resulting in mass cancer deaths that nearly robbed
the village of an entire generation. I made a note to, first, find Deline
on the map, and then scheme a way to get there.

We hiked for a while longer, the forest pad crunching under our
feet. The guides told stories about how the Nahanni region got to be the
way it was; how, two hundred million years ago, the North American and
Pacific plates pushed together to force layers of rock to the surface, bending and breaking and cutting away the stone into eccentric forms. Because
the last glaciers (about eighty-five thousand to ten thousand years ago)
missed the Nahanni, wild formations were left to stand and develop, as
opposed to being pressed into a more singular design, weighted with the
same creeping mass of ice.

Historians have measured the first signs of human life in the
Nahanni at around ten thousand years ago, old enough to be considered
pre-history. The first people—the Naha—disappeared cryptically,
replaced by the nineteenth-century Mountains Indians, who, each
spring, travelled down the river with families, cargo, and pack dogs in
forty-foot-long moose skin trading boats, only to dismantle the boats
upon arrival and trade everything—the wood, their supplies, and the
moose skin—for goods. They returned to their settlement with whatever the pack dogs could carry—the river currents prevented them
from going back the same way—coursing through treacherous land to
get home.

The interaction between traders and Indigenous people led to (unfounded) rumours of gold in the area, which led to invaders from the south risking their lives to seek their fortune. The corpses of two men, the Métis prospectors Willie and Frank McLeod, were found headless around 1908, and many features in the park were named for those who came after: Deadmen Valley, Headless Creek, Headless Range, the Funeral Range. Later, in 1964, the explorer and parachutist Jean Poire jumped into the heart of the park, making four consecutive expeditions where he discovered at least 250 caverns containing Dall sheep's skeletons dating back to 2500 BC.

We stayed in the Nahanni—listening and hiking, then listening some more—for a few hours and I wondered at which point the guides would bring out lunch, fantasizing over the Nahanni equivalent of what Cathy Allooloo had served during her canoe trips around Back Bay. Instead, we were led dutifully back to the wharf, where Ted immediately fired up the plane. Soon, we were back in the air, due to fly another forty minutes to a different spot in the park.

We landed at Glacier Lake in the granite shadows of the Cirque of the Unclimbables (worst Cirque du Soleil show ever), staring up at the Lotus Flower Tower and, in the distance, the Vampire Spires, among the most daunting and fearsome-looking peaks in the world. The view was beautiful and terrifying, but I found myself looking over my shoulder wondering when a team dressed in culinary whites would emerge from the forest to produce our meal, only to realize they would not. I rechecked my itinerary and discovered no mention of stew or bannock, and after finding the other passengers unpacking knapsacks and gorging themselves on snacks, I understood that I would probably be starving for the next three hours until we returned to Simpson. Panicking, I approached one of the passengers: a woman named Heather Marshall, who kindly gave me, in order of consumption, a pepperet, a Quaker Oats Chewy bar, and an apple. I scarfed them in haste, pushing them into my mouth before Ted called us back into the plane. At this point, you may or may not know where this story is going.

We flew over another forest fire, and as we did, the plane was caught in a terrible, and terribly smoky, crosswind, tossing the cabin about like a bad amusement park ride. It was then that a cage match began in my guts to determine which clod of food might escape first, coming up as quickly as it had gone down. I closed my eyes and tried to dream away the nausea, the smell of the fire battling the dry heat of the cabin like Mothra vs. Godzilla. For some reason, I concentrated on what I was hearing in my headphones as a way of training my thoughts away from how sick I felt. Through the awful grinding—among the least comforting textures to hear while in the throes of pre-nausea—I thought that Ted had engaged the FM/VHS shortwave toggle because, for some reason, I could hear the opening guitar chord sequence to Toto's "Hold the Line," which, it turns out, is the second-least comforting texture. The wind continued to knock the plane about like a giant elbowing their way down a supermarket aisle, and I began sweating before realizing that the guitar chords were a product of the plane's industrial disharmony, the grinding of gears mimicking the song's rhythm and key, adding "What Toto would sound like if played by angry primitive robots" to my list of airborne experiences. The Beaver dropped a few feet and that was all it took. Ted's expression held throughout all of this—focused and unflappable while trying to escape the gusting wind—and I flailed at the seat pouch, finding the sickness bag. Barfing in private is no fun, but barfing in an airless, pitching float plane cabin presents a new kind of humility. It makes the rest of the passengers feel both good ("Hey, at least I'm not barfing!") and not good ("Hey, a guy is barfing right beside me!"). Heather patted my back and told me it was okay. For those keeping score, the pepperet won.

16

A BOY AND HIS DOG

I spent the next day riding around Fort Simpson in a slow-moving truck, which was about all I was good for. I rode with Gerry Antoine, the fifty-something Dene chief of the Liidlii Kue First Nation, and Dëneze's uncle. The reason I know this, and the reason why the name of his community is spelled correctly, is because whenever Gerry dropped a word that left me searching, he asked that I hand him my notebook. He laid it across the dashboard of his F-350—rather, his wife's F-350; she had the day off from her cleaning business and we were using her car—and, with my V Point pen, he carefully wrote the words on the page. The purring of the truck's engine and the soft scratching of the pen proved a comforting sound, more so after my trials in the air the previous afternoon.

You could tell that Gerry was a good guy. While I know that's not a description to challenge the writings of Proust or Nabokov, I don't care: with some people, you just know. Gerry had smoky features with friendly eyes and a laugh pushed out from his stomach. He spoke slowly and deliberately and the pace of his speech had a fugue-like rhythm, never hurrying to get to the next note. The truck moved at slow speeds to match the calm of his storytelling, and sometimes we simply stopped, idling, on the highway, sitting for minutes at a time while the chief continued his narrative.

I asked Gerry how a recent gathering of Dene chiefs had turned out, and he said: "Well. We drummed for nine days," proving that those who measure the nature of their success by hours-of-music-played inevitably find one another. Gerry was warm-spirited, but his storytelling was direct—the faintest trace of bullshit seemed beyond him—particularly when talking about residential school classrooms and the oppressive residential home where his heart was held captive and where his identity as an Indigenous person was systematically knifed away.

Gerry spoke about his anger—that he talked about this in a calm, almost arrested, manner made his feelings more impactful—after having been wrenched from his home when he was two years old and forced into residential school until the year he turned fifteen. At school, instructors refused to allow him to see his sister, even though she studied in the same building. Things were just as bad where he lived, his foster parents forbidding him to speak Dene or see his family, who lived on Rabbitskin River, twenty-four kilometres from Fort Simpson. "Everything that happened in that house—knocking on the wrong door, dropping a plate—was cause for punishment, which, for me, meant the strap and getting pulled around by the ears. They took away my confidence and self-esteem," he said. "I felt like I was always doing something wrong. They gouged me clean."

Gerry tried to make himself invisible, as any kid would, but his retreat into the interior to protect whatever was left of his identity—there wasn't much, he admits—produced a sense of awareness about the world, his world, their world.

"I decided to use this time as a time of observation," he said, "taking in the big picture and learning to read people. I grew quiet and I barely spoke. I just watched. It was enough to help me get through, but there were times when I wondered whether I would."

When he was only nine years old, his foster parents ordered him to cross the river late one evening in the springtime to fetch mail from the nearby airport. Because of the season, the ice had thinned across the river, but despite the dangers, Gerry went anyway, not wanting to face the consequences. The boy was joined by his dog, Upok, who pulled him on a toboggan. When he got to the airport, the wife of the postmaster was aghast that Gerry's foster parents—he never once mentioned them to me by name—let him cross the river. The postmaster's wife helped him get warm. She was very motherly to him. Gerry stayed with her for a while and tried to understand the nature of this contact after years being kept at a distance by his foster parents, who communicated only to hurt him.

"The time finally came for me to go," he remembered. "Me and Upok headed back across the ice, which had grown even thinner and wetter after only a few hours. The sky was bright with stars. I could hear the wolves howling. The moon was bright, too, and it was peaceful, in a way, so I sat there awhile thinking about my life. I was young, sure, but I felt old, too. I asked myself why my life was the way it was. I was nine. I was just a boy. And yet so much of my life had already been played out."

Gerry wondered whether he would—whether he should—simply go through the ice and die. He asked himself whether he might ever see his parents or his sister or his grandparents ever again. The boy started to cry.

"After I was done, I looked across to my home. I could see that the ice had shifted again. There was nothing but water between me and the shore and so I looked at Upok. Upok looked back, and, after a moment, the dog jumped in and pulled me across. By the time we got to the other side, I felt as if I knew who I was within the sprawling land and the vast universe. I can't remember what happened next."

When he finally got into high school, Gerry sought guidance from the elders. "I returned to my earliest memories, like watching my grandpa come back to us after being on a hunt, and floating down the river on a raft with all the food of the land: fish, moose, berries." Gerry had to relearn everything about where he came from: the language, the ways of the land. "It was a long, long road," he said, upticking at the end of the phrase. Along with all of this, he was awarded an International

Baccalaureate scholarship at a school twenty miles west of Victoria, British Columbia. "I remember someone asking me, 'How are you doing?' It was the first time in so long that anyone had asked me about my feelings. It really choked me up. It choked me up a lot."

Coming out of this, Gerry went hard doing field work for the Truth and Reconciliation Commission, spending days listening to stories of what other Dene people had to suffer through during their times at residential school. "Slowly—very slowly—people opened up," he said, unclasping the fingers of his hand like petals opening with the sunrise. "People started to feel less alone about the whole ordeal. We had suffered, yes, but we had suffered together, and there was something in that!" he said, his eyes brightening. "The way I think of it is this," he said. "One person cannot take down a caribou by themselves. You need many hands, many helpers. This is what we have to figure out moving forward: how, out of all of this sharing, we can use this energy to build something great together." At the end of his last thought, the chief paused. He straightened his baseball cap and toggled the truck into reverse. Along the way back to the Mackenzie Rest Inn, he showed me where all the residential schools were, pointing through the bug-flecked windshield: there and there and there and there. I sat for the rest of the ride and said nothing, reminding myself to also look for the ghosts of the North while I was busy looking at everything else.

17

MAMA GRIZZLY

I flew back to Yellowknife in the morning. After landing, I headed to the Gold Range Bistro, hoping to get some food into me for the first time in two days. The diner was busy, scented with cut potatoes sizzling on a grill. The bistro—a fancy term that flattered the greasy spoon—was owned by a cancer survivor from Truro, Nova Scotia, named Mary, who waited on tables dressed in gold and silver evening wear, no matter the hour. I said hello to her while she sorted handwritten waybills behind a countertop, and she replied—"Hello darlin'"—her eyes trained on her sorting.

An old television hanging on chains above the room and macraméed with dust blinked in a corner, going from the CTV News Network to a blue panel warning of an impending removal of service without the settling of cable fees. Whatever news was being communicated—or not communicated—on the TV paled in comparison to the gossip being shared among equal measures of Dene and non-Indigenous men and women eating breakfast chosen from laminated menus at small tables, with an extra dining room in the back. The gossip came in modest parcels: a fire started here, a fish caught there; a truck broken down and fixed by cousins; and *How come the boy was in court? Was it because of that other kid, Otis? I don't think you can trust Otis. He's all kinds of bad news.*

Despite being thousands of miles to the Far North, the bistro was still a national centre point. It collected every type of person, both men and women: fishing guides with curve-brimmed baseball hats from the East Arm of Slave Lake; long-necked pilots from Saskatchewan; sunburnt builders from Nova Scotia with dory accents; bun-haired Manitoban surveyors; spritzed MLAs from N'dilo; young briefcased lawyers from Alberta; clods of stud-faced B.C. hempheads; and one Ontario writer, none of this counting the diner's short-order cooks, who wore triangled hats and white smocks, and whose families had emigrated from Southern China. This relative peace and cohabitation—stuck with the glue of winter, people in small, cold places are forced to get along lest a greater solitude consume the one that naturally exists—was also reflected in the N.W.T.'s political structure, where four governments—federal, territorial, municipal, and Indigenous—worked closely together, particularly in the matters of devolution, an initiative in which federal responsibilities were being downloaded to the territorial level. In the words of the musician Pat Braden, "You have to find a middle ground when it comes to government, and this trickles down, I think. We're all different, but we're all the same. We're all *up here.*"

The Territories' elected officials had zero party representation and they espoused no tribal platform beyond the concerns of their communities. With most of the MLAs coming from outside Yellowknife, a Dene majority—a.k.a. "consensus"—was guaranteed, allowing for "Indians to run the government, while whites run the industries," in the words of a mildly racist mining worker I'd met on the way home from Simpson. One of the government's other quirks was that, after every election, twelve officials sequestered themselves in a star chamber and debated who among them would be premier. It was a cloaked and mysterious process, sometimes taking days to resolve. John said it was more like choosing a Pope than a premier ("There might as well be a puff of white smoke coming out of a chimney," he grumbled), but the process forced the group to work together. The premier, who led an executive arm of the assembly, its de facto cabinet, was a man from Fort Providence named Bob McLeod. At the opening session of the legislature, he quoted Stompin' Tom Connors, and later that day, he kibitzed with John in the press gallery, telling him that if the reporter ever ended up in jail, he'd come to the NSCC and deliver his writing to the newspaper.

"I'll tie it to a rock and throw it to you from over the fence," John told him. "I'll call it 'Tales from the Jail,'" he said, which would have been funny if you couldn't actually imagine it happening.

As with the Territorial government, a Dene majority prevailed at the bistro. You had to be actively anti-social not to walk into the guts of a story. If I were in a position of federal power, I would decree that groups of Canadians be required to visit the diner as way of crash-coursing a study in Indigenous life—or, at least, Indigenous breakfast—as it existed at that moment in time. While government symposia can be useful, something seems to happen over pancakes and coffee, and at the bistro, it was hard to find the seams between people. Northern writer Tim Querengesser said that "Yellowknife just kinda just works. Indigenous people come here because they're respected. They aren't segregated the way they are else-where. It felt so detached when I lived in Whitehorse, where I had to work to make connections. But in Yellowknife, it's so accessible."

During my breakfast at the Range, I met Bobby from Holman Island (it's how he introduced himself), who was sitting at the table beside me reading my column (about fishing on Slave Lake) in the *Yellowknifer*. I was filled with no small sense of satisfaction, having reached an audience I never would have through any of the major papers, none of whom were distributed in the North anyway. Bobby—he wore the obligatory baseball hat and could have been anywhere from forty to seventy years old—told me that he'd learned to play hockey in a Fort Smith residential school— "The only decent part"—becoming so good that he was offered a tryout with the Maple Leafs, but declined because of responsibilities to his father. "I was a good centre," he said, "and I worked well with my wingers. But my career ended after I fell into the boards and was paralyzed for six months. I lay in the hospital and drew on the strength of my ancestors. I knew they'd look after me, and, eventually, I got better. Now I study the caribou, and tell white people that it's not only about their science," he said. After breakfast, I told him, "It's an honour to meet you," because it was. He slapped me in the shoulder and said, "All right! Hang in there, buddy!" winking as he left the diner.

There were two women sitting at a table along the far wall below a whiteboard with coloured plastic letters from a child's playset spelling out a few longstanding menu features: HAMBURGER CHICKEN NOODLE SOUP FRIES. Their names were Eve and Lucy, and they'd come down from Cambridge Bay for a cousin's wedding. Lucy was a big woman whose beatific face was pinched with great folds of flesh. "They call me Mama Grizzly," she said, extending a hand the size of a dinner plate. Eve was smaller—a toy bear—with dark hair bundled on her head and Coke-bottle glasses. We had coffee together and they told me who was getting married (Sally and Rick), how the couple had met (at a town social), and what they did (Sally worked for the government and Rick was a shift worker in the mines). They asked me who I was, where I came from ("Toronto, eh?"), and what kind of music I liked.

"All music," I told them.

"All music?" they said together.

"Well, maybe not all music. Maybe not . . ." I said, remembering my time in Simpson, "maybe not Toto."

"Who?"

"Exactly," I said.

They laughed as if they'd been tickled.

Returning to the *Yellowknifer* after my time away, I found that the place was the same as it ever was. The reporters barely looked up to welcome me back—still no jeujing—and only Karen could manage a "So how was it?" This led me to perform a centre-of-the-newsroom soliloquy about my adventures vomiting in a float plane, graphically describing what it was

I'd expunged until Karen threw her hands over her ears and Mike waved an arm, "Okay, okay . . ."

I grabbed a copy of the *News/North* weekly and headed to my desk. The company's newsprint aggregate of stories from across the North had become my favourite read for its comprehensive and important stories—"Residential School Survivors in NWT Have Claims Pending"; "Gwich'in PhD Candidate Talks Racism"; "Abandoned Fuel Pipelines in Fort Res to Be Assessed"; "Man Gets Two Years for Bloody Hammer Attack"—as well as far-ranging columns from people like Roy Erasmus Sr., who wrote a post-addiction wellness column called "When the Heart Says No," and a firebrand dispatch by Cece (pronounced "Cease") McCauley. McCauley was the first female Dene chief in Inuvik and leader of the Women Warriors of the Sahtu, whose motto was "We're tired of waiting for men." The ninety-something writer—McCauley kept her age private—was, in many ways, the Don Cherry of northern journalism. Her hand never left the trigger and her opinions were unfiltered and inflammatory, upsetting many readers. One of the Métis writer's latest pieces was about her experiences in residential schools, which she called "the greatest years of my life," and she achieved a national profile after assailing Jean Chrétien in curlers. McCauley—an honorary chief—was married to a man who used to carry volumes of Shakespeare with him to the trapline, and, in her eighty-eighth year, she once barricaded her grand-daughter and a sleepover friend from a hungry black bear who'd invaded her kitchen, "rummaging through the fridge and eating pickles," according to a CBC story.

Cece had once been photographed for *Maclean's* magazine holding up a single uranium rock as a way of bringing to light the legacy of endemic cancer deaths in the Sahtu, the result of unmonitored mining at Port Radium. She wrote in plainspeak with ellipses and exclamation marks, and her work both validated *News/North* as an equal-time soapbox while sinking it into an occasional carnival of opinion. Still, I looked forward to her column whenever it appeared.

The latest issue of *News/North* had the usual complement of stories about people from the communities who'd travelled abroad: a class of kids on a school trip to Wrigley Field in Chicago, another to Victoria ("The young students got a taste of life outside the NWT!"), and yet another to Inuvik, where they studied tundra biology. If the *Yellowknifer* liked to think its content rode above that of its Territorial satellites, this was only barely true. When I returned to the office, I found writers working on stories about a couple who kept goats in their yard; a holidaying local who was bitten by a centipede in Hawaii—"We'll write about it because he's getting hits on *social media*," said John, horking out those last two words; a yoga festival for which John had taken unpublishable photos ("They were better suited for another kind of paper, if you know what I mean," said Karen); a judicial hearing concerning a fellow who'd exposed himself on the Frame Lake trail ("It was a hung jury," said Mike, drawing a polite smattering of applause); and a story about whether or not the Loch Ness monster might have boarded a trans-continental flight, changed at Edmonton, then Calgary, then Edmonton again before coming North to allegedly retire to the murky waters of the lake.

Ewan was assigned to cover him or her or it, or whatever one is supposed to call a mythic water lizard. After heading out to source the story—the sighting had been reported by a young Dene man who swore he saw an enormous reptile in the lake, "a big smiling face with teeth," he said—he returned claiming he had evidence of the beast before producing a staged photo of a green dollar-store dinosaur wading in a pool of standing parking lot water.

"Jesus Christ," said Mike, rubbing his face with the weariness of a man consigned to run exiled sea monster stories. Walter viewed the photo and then said, shitting no one: "Photos like these are, actually, always just in the shadows a little." The writers turned to see if he was serious (he was). "Gimme a second," he said, walking over to his station before spitting out Ewan's image with the toy reptile darkened, as if it were sitting for witness protection.

"Guys, guys," said Mike. "You wanna know the real story?"

We turned to Mike because Mike always had the real story.

"Old Slavey," he said.

"Old who?" we asked.

"Old Slavey," he repeated.

"I think I met her in a bar one night," said John.

"Old Slavey was its name. Jesus, we invented it," said Mike. "There was a guy here, a writer. He was sitting around looking for a story and he just wrote it, about a beast who lived in Slave Lake, a dinosaur, a Loch Ness thing. I don't think he was sober at the time."

"You mean Old Slavey isn't real?" I asked, feigning disappointment.

"He's as real as you want it to be, buddy," said John.

"I'm just telling you what happened. It was, like, our biggest story ever. It still is, for fuck's sake," said Mike.

"What do you want me to do with this?" asked Ewan, holding up the photo.

"Give it to me, I'll darken it some more," said Walter. "No one will buy it if you can see his little teeth."

"It looks like a lobster," said Karen, late to the game.

"Lobsters scream when they die. It's what I'm told," said John.

"No, they don't," said Julius. "It's not scientifically proven."

"They do. They scream when they die," repeated John.

"They don't scream," said Shawn. "They quietly suffer." The young writer turned to me:

"Like all of us."

I followed John and Glenn Werkman, a lifer reporter from Alberta, outside for a smoke. I first encountered Glenn at one of the *News/North* softball games—the *Yellowknifer* had a sad-sack team called the Brewsroom for whom I occasionally whacked a bat at grapefruit-sized balls—having joined the paper deeper into the summer. He was an older salacious Buddha with a beard, glasses, and suspenders who growled when he spoke, bridging stories about sex or drinking (or drinking and sex) with phrases like "the whole shiteroo," a term that I was determined to use for myself (which, I suppose, I just did). If Yellowknife was a little lost in time, Glenn came to us direct from 1973: part Bobby Riggs, part Paul "The Bear" Rupert. I honestly couldn't imagine him working for any other paper in 2016.

While chewing on a dart, Glenn asked if I'd visited the offices of the *Deh Cho Drum*—a *News / North* satellite paper—during my time in Fort Simpson. I told him that I had, but the offices were dark.

"They were probably hiding," he said. "Like Anton, the poor bastard."

Anton had been dispatched to Inuvik, but things had gone badly for him in the Far North. Because he ran the Inuvik paper alone—most of the *News / North* editors were their own bosses, at least in principle (they still had to answer to Yellowknife)—the only people with whom he interacted were story subjects, and the isolation had him drinking as a way of getting from day to day. Anton had hoped to deal with the collapse of his marriage down south by moving here, but the detachment only worsened his misery. After a few issues at the *Inuvik Drum*, he stopped answering phones in the office. He couldn't be reached on email and he didn't answer texts. When a former employee went to check in on him, he was curled up in the dark under his desk.

"I should try that," said John. "Think anyone would notice?"

"Not until you started smelling," said Glenn.

John and I stayed outside and he told me about something that had happened while I'd been away: a small chemical spill on 50th Avenue, which he'd cycled over to cover. He told me that, when he got there, police seemed particularly bothered by his presence. They shouted at him "Stay back!" in barking-dog voices, "even though there was nothing going on."

"There were a few guys in hazmat suits," he said, "but that's about it. Buddy, they didn't want me coming anywhere near them or the spill. They have a real attitude, and it's getting worse. The RCMP think they're some kind of special breed, but they're not, at least not anymore. And this idea of being 'royal' and 'mounted,' they've gotta get rid of that. Lissen, I covered the crime beat for twelve years for CityTV in Toronto and believe me, a cop is a cop is a cop," he said, meting out the words.

If the situation between John and the police—between the paper and the police, too—was already fraught, there weren't many signs it was getting better. John was right when he pointed to mutual distrust, saying "Cops have a resentment for journalists that's getting right up there with people's distrust of lawyers. I understand hating the paparazzi, but I'm trying to do stories that will help this place in the long run." I also wondered if his being from Toronto had anything to do with their attitude toward the writer, although this was tougher to square considering that Yellowknife was the only place in Canada where, whenever I mentioned I was from there, people reacted the opposite way everyone else in Canada does. There was very little attitude or resentment, partly because everyone who wasn't Dene came from somewhere else, and partly because Toronto might as well have been Istanbul, another place on the far side of the tundra.

John may not have recognized it at the time, but an incident during a recent campfire party at Fred Henne Park hinted at the kind of trouble that would hound him for the rest of his time in Yellowknife. There, he was confronted by an angry and drunk off-duty RCMP officer named Jim LaValle (not his real name), who stumbled over to give John a piece of his mind. "We were standing around the fire—me, Glenn, and Sarah—and I was saying something about the RCMP," he said. "We were talking about the Moncton shootings [where a local citizen had besieged police with a firearm]; how the cops had been sent into a situation where the guy had an automatic weapon, and how the RCMP brass wasn't charged under the *Criminal Code*, but, rather, through Workers' Compensation. I was telling the story and I probably said, 'Those bozos . . .' I wasn't flattering the RCMP, but I was defending the officers who'd been killed, who never should have been put in that position in the first place. What happened next was, LaValle came over from the next campsite and started yelling: 'Listen you piece of shit!' I looked over. Three times, he fell face-first on the rocks, but he still came over, trespassing into our site. He was shouting, 'I'm Jim LaValle!' He was laying into me and it was getting ugly, but he was pretty drunk so nothing came of it. Honestly, we talked it out and he was hugging me by the end, but it got me thinking that the RCMP were taking me very seriously, and that word had spread to keep an eye on me or something. It was all very strange, and a little scary. I tell ya, buddy, some nights I'm looking over both of my shoulders."

18

YELLING AND SCREAMING

I t was on the Canada Day weekend that the North finally caught up to John McFadden. I'd spent Saturday playing floor hockey at Cody Punter's invitation with a group of young and fit RCMP officers, figuring it would be good to get in the company of the police beyond the glare of the newspaper. But there was another reason: I needed to do something other than drink and listen to John tell stories. I required some distance from him, partly because I thought it would give me some perspective on all that was going on, and partly because, when talking to Glenn about the RCMP's media liaison and Elenore Sturko's personal antipathy toward John, he asked me, looking over his glasses: "How do you know John didn't say a lot of awful things to her?"

"Because he said he didn't," I told him.

"Right."

"What do you mean, 'right'?"

"I mean, it's John's story; it's his words. I'm not saying he's lying, I'm just saying, we don't know. Okay, we believe him. But do we believe him because he's our friend, or do we believe him because they're true?"

The notion that it was all a misdirection—that John had provoked the force and insulted Elenore's sexuality—made me question my instincts about him, and an encounter at the courthouse with Ms. Sturko—a petite woman with close-cropped hair and a ruddered calm to her voice—didn't make things any clearer. After I introduced myself, she said, "I know who you are. When I toured with a few friends playing music, we read your [first] book aloud to each other to pass the time during long drives. Thank you for that."

There are few things that a villain can do to make themselves seem less villainous, but admitting that they've read aloud one of your books to their guitar-winging friends while touring Canada is probably one of those things. Even better—or worse—her words didn't feel engineered by the RCMP or drawn up after a gathering of spin technicians to make her seem more credible in my eyes. She meant it, and I could tell. During our conversation in the quiet foyer of the courthouse, we talked about rock and roll and touring Canada and it was all very pleasant. Elenore had joined the force after leaving a media job with the CBC, hoping to bring stability to her and her partner, Melissa's, life, with whom she had three children. She could have been a character in one of my songs, for fuck's sake.

After exchanging a few more stories—"Did you ever have the wild rice at that place near Blind River?" and "How often did you gig at Amigos in Saskatoon?"—I confessed: "I'm a friend of John McFadden's."

"I know," she said, looking straight at me.

"I like John," I said. "I don't think he'd ever do anything to . . ."

"Okay," she said, pushing out a breath of air.

"He's not a homophobe," I said.

"It's not that," she told me.

"It's not?"

"No. Well, he said some very inappropriate things. Hurtful things."

"Things about your sexuality?"

"We were on a ride together and he was asking me about my wife and kids and it was all very personal," she said.

"But you were on a ride together. Isn't that what people talk about? Their families."

"I'm a police officer. We were on a ride. It's not the place to talk about my personal life."

"Okay, but that hardly seems like the type of thing that . . ."

"And then he called me for a bridal issue that the newspaper was doing; asking me all of these questions about my life . . ."

"John said that he thought it would be interesting: someone from the LGBT community in a bridal issue . . ."

"That's not what I got from it."

"He was slighting you, you think?"

"No, he was just . . ."

"Pushy?"

"Pushy, mean, confrontational . . ."

"For a story in a bridal issue?"

"It didn't matter what the issue was."

The officer stopped, as if to comport herself.

"I'm trying to understand what happened," I said. "I'm trying to understand why things have become so bad between the two of you. They weren't always this bad."

The officer put a hand to her brow. She began to mist over, becoming affected by our conversation. Cops aren't supposed to cry in the foyers of city courthouses, but it's what she was at the edge of doing. She waved her hand and told me, "You don't know; you don't." Another officer came and took her away.

I wondered if Elenore Sturko and Glenn Werkman were right: maybe I didn't know. Maybe I just assumed that I knew. I weighed a few other things that I'd learned about John: he'd had four DUIs in Ontario, and been charged three times; he'd been banned from a bar in Peterborough (although the ban was short-lived); and he'd had an assault charge, later dropped, from a woman, a girlfriend, who'd given him an STD ("I threw her wallet at her feet, and she called it 'assault,'" he told me, shaking his head). A former Toronto co-worker of his wrote to tell me how John would come into the City building late at night with girls he'd picked up in a bar, promising them a tour of the studio. "One night, he brought in two *skanks*," he wrote, "and they were hammered, obnoxious. The *Breakfast*

Television producer came in to give him shit and they got into a fistfight in front of the girls. [It was right around then] that John got fired from City."

I'd never seen John too far out of his mind—at least not yet—but Lydia Bardak's thoughts were "I love John, but he has a serious problem." Someone else who asked not to be named said, "He's an alcoholic with a hearing problem. He's not going to get better unless he helps himself."

In a 2016 incident, Lydia Bardak sought to get John barred from the Folk on the Rocks music festival—she succeeded—after claiming the reporter upset her mother while appearing drunk during an interview. John denied this happened—he played me the tape in which he seemed cogent and unslurring—but Bardak wrote a nasty letter to *Yellowknifer* management as well as to the music festival complaining about him. John obtained a copy of it and carried it with him wherever he went, producing it, crumpled, out of his pants pocket whenever anyone asked him about the circumstances of their argument. I asked Lydia why she'd copied John's employers in the complaint, and she said, "John has a drinking problem and John has to straighten up or else . . ." I asked what the "or else" part was, but she gave me a sideways glance that suggested I was playing dumb, which I wasn't. When I told John what she'd said, he called her a series of names best not printed here, then sighed a deep sigh, exasperated after getting it from the city's patron saint of the homeless, no less.

Still, because John was a vulnerable man whose demons lived in his breast pocket and because he'd befriended me in the crazy North, I resisted scratching too hard at him. Most people who talked about him in the above terms also walked a line, and, besides, alcoholism had a sliding scale in the North, where drinking was a Territorial sport, especially in a town with more bars per capita than anywhere outside of St. John's. Not only that, but if John had an unflattering and secret nocturnal existence, many others in Yellowknife had other lives buried within them. If John was capable of the occasional deception, he wasn't alone, but since he'd emerged as a popular figure at the centre of a gathering storm, something had to give. The town would eventually hold him up to the light.

I finished playing the game with Cody, a two-hour marathon in the heat of the rec centre with two dozen police officers and other security personnel in sweat shorts and T-shirts. Even though I was a writer from Toronto and a friend of their sworn antagonist, they treated me fine. No one shot at my head or tried running me over in the crease. In the dressing room, they thanked me for coming out and everyone scattered. The game nearly killed me but I was glad I'd gone. Cody drove me back to the Narwal, where I had dinner before strolling around Old Town feeling like a seven-thousand-year-old man: back stooped, arms hanging at my side, legs screaming. I ambled back to the cabin and thought about how I wanted to celebrate the Canada Day holiday. There were text messages from John. I ignored them.

I passed out on the pleather, destroyed by the game. I woke up, took a sleeping pill, and slept for fourteen hours. In the morning, I checked my phone: more messages from John.

Dozens more.

The story went like this. On Saturday night, John and Sarah were drinking at the Black Knight. It was a normal evening where a normal crowd had gathered around the brass rails, swinging kitchen saloon doors, and table-stands, nursing pints of beer and listening to the bar's subscribed satellite transmissions of 90s American rock. The mayor was there. He found John at around 10:30 p.m., enjoying a smoke outside. An event was going on up the street at the Elks Club, so people were gathered there, too, hunched over smoking in the parking lot. Every now and then, a homeless man or woman wandered past the pub, regular rounds looking for change or dead ends left in a large silver keg that served as an ashtray outside the club. The summertime drew everyone into the street under the pink glow of northern skies, or into the bars, where they celebrated the fact that it wasn't minus 45 with blinding ice and snow. "In

July, you have to look hard to find someone who hasn't had three beers in them by midnight," said Glenn, on a night when he had at least three beers in him.

While he was outside, John saw two cruisers carrying four police officers pull up to a white cargo van across the street with its windows painted black and bearing stolen Alberta licence plates. He immediately went to get his camera from Sarah's car. The police looked for and found the driver of the van—a "grossly inebriated" man with a long goatee named Rocky. Afterwards, the police, in John's words, "started tearing the van apart. They were just going at this thing." It's why he got his camera, wondering what was inside the vehicle. There could have been bricks of heroin, bags of coke, a weapons cache. The lights of the police cruisers whirled. People in the Elks parking lot shouted and pointed, wondering what was happening. They butted out their smokes. They came a little closer.

John stepped into the road. "You're fucking John McFadden!" said one of the officers (the cops deny they were ever verbally aggressive), moving toward him. John moved, too. The journalist said that the officers ordered him not to get any closer. John barked that it was his right, as a reporter, and the public's right, to know what was going on with the search of the van (afterwards, police hinted that the crowd outside the Elks were triggered by John's words and actions, "stirring them up," according to Constable Bill Maxwell [not his real name]). John said: "I appreciate the thought, but it's not me who draws crowds; it's cruisers with their lights flashing." The police maintained that John was "yelling and screaming," but it's also possible he was simply being loud. Anyone who knew John knew the voice. When you heard it coming, you either turned around or charged forward, depending on what kind of night you were looking to have.

John insisted that he had only "two pints and a Caesar" at the Black Knight, and that Sarah bought him drinks. "Everybody knows I've blown all my money by Saturday," he said, proving an awkward point. Sarah stressed that John wasn't drunk, a notion supported by the fact that he was able to manage his steps as well as operate his camera—he shot for three and a half minutes—although, after bringing this up with Glenn, he said: "You know John McFadden; I know John McFadden; everyone knows John McFadden. If you put John McFadden at the Black Knight for three hours, what's he going to look like? Let's be real here. He's not gonna be no fucking priest."

John took pictures of the cops doing whatever they were doing. If, in the beginning, the police didn't know who John was, they did after a time, because it's what one of the officers—Constable DeMarco—told his partners. They warned the writer to stay on the sidewalk, and he complied, but after police moved away from the scene—it's uncertain where they went, although John believed that they dispersed in an effort to entrap him—he came to the open side-panel door of the van, and, allegedly keeping to the sidewalk, thrust out his camera and shot the (mostly empty) insides of the vehicle, a photograph that produced nothing in the way of insight or evidence or proof of what was going on, leading one to question why the cops had attacked the contents of the van with such fervour. When the police returned, they descended on the reporter, telling him he was under arrest for obstruction. John forced out a laugh, a little bemused, a little bewildered. The police cuffed him using plastic tags. They pushed his head into his chest and his body into the cruiser. They shoved him in the back seat. Two officers climbed into the car. They drove.

"When I was in the back of the police car, I thought, 'This will be great. Here's my story for Wednesday. People will support me and I'll be really hard on the police,'" said John. "I told the officers, 'Guys, you've been smoking some bad weed. You've gotta get some good weed to smoke.'

"[One of the cops] was as rude to me as anyone has ever been in Yellowknife," said John, which seemed to matter as much to him—the rudeness—as the way in which he was allegedly treated. "My hands turned purple from the cuffs. They were killing me. When I got to the jail, they shoved me through an open doorway. I turned back to face them and they put my head against the wall, hard, smashing it in" (the police later said they feared being spat on by McFadden, something that happens when dealing with the detained). "My glasses broke. There was blood, and I still don't know where it came from." The police walked John into the cell, where he made like he was going to strangle himself with his shirt until they let him call someone. "I was angry as fuck," he said. "It suddenly dawned on me what was happening."

A few hours passed and John phoned his lawyer, then another, then another. No one answered, so he phoned his MLA, Robert Hawkins, who secured his release. John went to Sarah's, who helped him clean up. It was late. He was shaken and scared. He headed home on foot but stopped at McDonald's to get something to eat. There, he discovered two men sitting near the bins behind the restaurant, sharing a bottle. John sat down. He drank with them and told his story.

PONY DOES A TRICK

The next day, John talked and I listened.

"I wasn't drunk," he insisted. "I had two pints and a Caesar over three hours. I wasn't pounding. If I'd been staggering drunk, I would have walked away. They said I was 'lightly slurring.' What the fuck is 'lightly slurring'? There was no warning. They never once said, 'Don't come any closer or you'll be arrested.' We debated on the street about whether I was obstructing them and I insisted that I was not. I was on a public sidewalk. They backed off, so I took a step closer. The van had some shit in it. Turns out it was a plumber's van and buddy who owned it says they were looking for drugs. I think that's one of the reasons I was arrested: they thought they'd find something on me. The cops admitted that they thought that we were buddies and that we were in cahoots. But I'd never met the guy."

John knew that something was coming—he'd said as much to me over the previous few weeks—but he still seemed shocked that it happened the way it did: in full view of his local on a Saturday night, although maybe that was the point. "They have issues with me and they know who I am. I think they were waiting for me to take one step closer and arrest me and that's what they did. They said I was obnoxious and loud, but the charter of rights isn't only for people who are pleasant. Two of the cops said I was inside the van, but if I see police going through a van, I'm not going to put my fingerprints inside it. What am I, an idiot? Wait, don't answer that."

Finally, laughter.

"The whole thing didn't last five minutes. I remember them saying: 'Don't yell at us.' I'm loud at the best of times, but I never shouted, not once. I know not to swear at cops, but my back went up when the guy asked, 'What the fuck do you want?' It was a debate, only debates don't usually end up with a reporter thrown in jail. Three hours, I was in custody. You know what I think? I think they charged me to get me off the police beat. I think they want me gone."

Over the next few days at the newspaper, John was in and out of Bruce's office, "wound tighter than a two-dollar watch," he said. He looked even more sleepless than usual, his face drained of its natural animation. He came to work wearing a laundry-pile Hawaiian shirt and shorts and sandals, as if waiting for a cruise ship that would never come. The paper closed ranks to decide what to do. With the story all over town—CBC, the Moose, and *Edge YK* all covered it soup to nuts—the *Yellowknifer* decided to show neither support nor indictment of the writer. They played the middle, as Bruce suggested they would. They ran a photo that, even though it was a colour pic, looked like a mugshot. John wasn't quoted—nobody expected him to be—but Bruce wasn't either (the story said that he'd refused comment, which I thought was the most meta-*Yellowknifer* moment of all time). John felt spurned, partly because in his eyes the paper hadn't stood up for one of their writers—one of their allegedly *assaulted* writers—and partly because, after other reporters read the story, no one had come over to ask how he was doing or if he needed any help, worried, perhaps, about how such a gesture might play out with their bosses. Bruce removed John from the crime beat and laid it in Shawn's hands. If Shawn was already overwhelmed, the extra work nearly wrenched the life out of him. Everybody was drained, and now this. It didn't help that the junior reporter now occupied the beat of the person sitting next to him in the newsroom, who rubbed his forehead wondering how things could possibly get any worse. It was, at best, a divisive reassignment, and because Mike and Ellen had taken their holidays at what would turn out to be the worst possible time, it fell to Bruce to recalibrate office tensions, something he was challenged to do, spending most of his time removed from the news force. John didn't write much—"The situation is too toxic right now," said Bruce—and instead he slumped in his chair, taking defeated smoke breaks, where he told me, "I'm about this far away from quitting and leaving this fucking place," showing a distance between his thumb and forefinger. His nights were spent at the Black Knight looking around the room and pointing suspiciously at the RCMP personnel in the bar: "That guy, that guy, that woman, that guy . . ." I didn't think he had to worry about being watched—it's not as if he became more clandestine, either, when it came to drinking or smoking weed—but after heading to the washroom, I looked into the bottom of a urinal to find John's business card lying on the blue mat soaked with piss. I moved to another urinal.

There were still stories to write, papers to make. The following day, I sat at my computer terminal listening to John struggle with his breath—his asthma had worsened with the anxieties that came with a potential two-year maximum sentence in the North Slave Correctional Centre—while writing bumpf about the 150th anniversary of the Twin Otter, working the keyboard with single tired taps instead of the flurry by which he attacked his rig. We'd gone to the airport for the event—maple sugar squares and a constituency of airplane nerds in red commemorative hats—winding past the Yellowknife golf course, where, in the late 1940s, a DC-3 crash-landed on the first tee and was, according to Mordecai Richler, "immediately converted into the golf course's first amenity (a clubhouse), filling that office until 1952, when an American order recalled every DC-3 in good enough condition to fly," hauling it away and sending it into battle during the Korean War.

John was so distraught that he asked me to drive the company car, even though, because of insurance issues, I wasn't supposed to. Since there was no drive-check program in Yellowknife—"It's impossible to get arrested for impaired driving here," he told me, sounding like someone who'd tested and re-tested the theory——I took the wheel and we headed to the hangar through the rain, which was another thing: in a semi-desert climate with annual precipitation, including snow, of just under thirty centimetres, the weather suddenly turned. After John's arrest, the skies emptied for the first time all summer: nearly two days of dark clouds sitting overhead like players in a rugby scrum, pushing back and forth into each other, but never away.

Mark Heyck, the mayor, was at the hangar. He couldn't believe what John was telling him: how he'd been thrown in jail for taking pictures. John repeated his mantra, "Two beers and a Caesar!"——I thought it was a good name for a party rock band——and he asked the mayor: "You saw me. Was I impaired? Was I intoxicated? Was I being belligerent?" The mayor answered that he hadn't been.

"Thank you, sir. Thank you," said John, pacing the ground and assembling the first few pieces of his defence.

John felt persecuted and his sense of self-worth was fragile. In the North, it was hard enough to be alone as well as persecuted and alone. Also, because he'd come and gone from so many media outlets, you wouldn't have blamed him for wondering whether it was happening all over again——bad shit coming down and finding him because of the way he carried himself and the way he lived. Even at the best of times, he was an alarm bell waiting to go off. In one two-week span, he was given a black eye by Julius after a money dispute, the first of three fistfights he'd have with his roommate; was told he had to clear out of his cabin and find a place to live by his landlady, who sneered at him and said "I don't like you" after John made an offhand compliment about her legs; and set the Yellowknifer building's security systems off when coming in to get his camera during a late-night house-fire call. Wherever he went, all anyone wanted to talk about was what he'd allegedly done, what the cops had allegedly done, and what he thought might happen. On top of his foghorn voice and machine-gun laugh——there were times when John and I would be talking on a residential street, only to have neighbours come out and tell us to quiet down—the reporter had a target on his back. For some people, John's arrest was a case of a fuck-up finally fucking up, and a lot of people steered clear of his presence, worrying how they would be perceived. "He's a heat-seeking missile," said Glenn, "and not in a good way."

A few days into the mess, I received a gift from muckrakers' heaven, which I imagine being a place where everyone drinks for free and fedoras hang from tree knots and writers are encouraged to wear the same blazer they bought in 1981, or something like that. Before the gift was delivered, I tried keeping things light around the office, but it wasn't easy. If I'd established myself as a kind of journalistic charlatan—a book writer trying to wrestle himself into a set of clothes that everyone else wore freely—people had stopped feeling particularly comforted by the newsroom pony because of what was going on with John, but then the pony did something exceptional, at least for a pony.

One afternoon, I was scrolling Twitter during a perfunctory "Yellowknife" search—an instance of print journalism deciding that if you can't beat digital journalism, you might as well use it—when I came across a freshly posted item from CBC news, reporting that the city's KFC outlet was closing after fifty years. The words were out of my mouth as soon as I read them: "They're closing the KFC!" Everybody turned in the chairs: a collective squeaking of wheels. If I hadn't, technically, broken the story, I'd at least broken it in the *Yellowknifer* newsroom, making me feel, for a moment, very important, but also useful in having swung the hot lights away from my friend.

Suddenly, all anyone could talk about was KFC. Editors and reporters volleyed questions at me: "When is it closing?" "What's going on there?" "Is there really no more chicken?" Affecting a veteran cool that I'd done very little to earn, I spun in my chair and crossed my arms behind my head while fielding their inquiries, making up most of my answers before confessing that I had no further insight into the matter. Still, it felt good to be part of the news-making team, a sensation that accelerated once Ellen came over from her station to ask me one of the most affecting questions I'd answer that summer:

"Can you get me a quote?"

"Yes, yes, I can," I said.

"Go, buddy, go," said John, goosed, for a moment, to life.

Walking away, Ellen said, "There's a little bit of newsroom excitement for you, eh, Dave?"

She was right.

The pony was happy.

I asked Shawn for the number of the store's owner—this presented me with my first problem in the possible construction of a story: was KFC a "store," a "restaurant," an "outlet," or a "chickenshack"? Or was it all of the above?—but before calling, I positioned myself the way John did at his desk: notebook flipped open and a pencil in my teeth waiting to fire a hard question at whomever answered. The phone rang once, twice, a third time. I imagined a group of people huddled in a room discussing what to say and how would they spin this and *what if he knows don't give anything away for christsakes don't let him know that you know.*

Someone picked up.

It was a woman, one of the KFC employees.

"Hello there, this is Dave Bidini from the *Yellowknifer*," I said, a ripple of excitement moving through my words.

"Oh," she said.

"Hi, yes," I said, pausing to remember John's approach. "How are you doing today?" delivering my query with, I hoped, the sensitivity and sympathy of someone concerned with her well-being.

"Okay, fine," she said.

"Can I ask you your name?"

"Winona," she said.

"Ah," I said. "Hello Winona. We've heard that the KFC plans to close down on August 26. Is that true?"

"Sorry, what?" she said.

"Closing down. The store is closing."

"Um, hold on," she said, holding the phone to her chest. She was quiet for a while—I thought I heard the muffle of voices on the other end—and the longer she remained disengaged, the more I felt like a bit of jerk, understanding that jerkdom is one of the qualities needed to be a halfway decent reporter. I couldn't stop thinking: what if Winona didn't know about the store's closing? What if she was hearing this for the first time? What if losing her job meant her family suffering and what if her family suffering led to all those things associated with hard times after the end of an income? What about her kids? What about their future? Winona seemed like a nice person. And there I was, working on my scoop. In this moment, one thing I did not feel like was hardboiled. Now it was me who was pressing the phone to their chest, worrying about what came next. I thought breaking into tears would ruin whatever reputation I'd fabricated, so I sucked back the emotion. Winona returned to the line.

"Oh, okay, yes, but you have to talk to the boss. He'll be in later," she said, sounding almost sunny, which made me wonder if the discussion had gone like this:

—Is it McFadden?

—No.

—Is it that Shawn kid?

—Don't think so. Sounds too old.

—Is it the Japanese one?

—Who?

—Never mind. It's not Bryant, is it?

—No, he's away, I think.

—Okay, must be that new guy. Tell him to call back, which he won't. We're fine.

I told Winona I would call back, which I would not. I told Ellen what I had, or didn't have.

"Did they confirm the closing?"

"They did, sort of. They didn't unconfirm it."

"Okay. Write it up," she ordered.

I started scribbling—if I wasn't hard-boiled, maybe I was at least deep-fried, with onions and peppers—and after a while, I had the story. I filed and then Ellen asked about a photo. She suggested waiting until they removed the giant chicken bucket, which the store planned to do later in the week.

When the day of the de-bucketing came, John and I stood on the road and watched as a truck winched the candy-striped bucket from its pole, lowering it onto a flatbed with a city worker peeking over the lip like a kid on a teacup ride. We stood in silence, sparing a moment to wonder what it all meant. Was the bucket coming down a metaphor for John's troubles? Was he the bucket or the dude trapped in the bucket? Did the end of the chicken shack represent the end of old Yellowknife? What would happen to the bucket? What would happen to Winona? Would the communities ever get their chicken again? Would someone buy the bucket and put it on a stick in their backyard? Neither of us had answers. A few more workers tied the bucket down and then the truck drove it away, leaving a hole in the middle of the sky.

"I've got your headline," said John, shading his eyes from the sun.

"PICKING UP A BUCKET OF CHICKEN."

"Hey, it's pretty good," I said.

We stood there for a moment looking at where the bucket used to be.

"Buddy, I tell you, it's all I've fucking got," he said.

JAYSUS MOY LAG

The dust began to settle post-arrest. News arrived that the paper planned to pay for John's lawyer and cover whatever legal costs he incurred. "So, that's nice," he told me, wringing his hands. "It'll probably run them six or seven grand, so it's not cheap," he said. When I approached the publisher, Mike Scott, and mentioned the costs, he remonstrated: "Of course we're paying. He's our writer and our employee." Bruce Valpy was more blunt: "You can't go around throwing writers in jail for doing their job. We have to defend that any way we can." The search began to find a lawyer for John and the paper's motor ran a little steadier, allowing me time to take my next midsummer trip around the Territories, this time closer to the Arctic Circle, or "next level North," which is how Randi put it after hearing of my plans to go deeper into the Northwest Territories.

I wanted to go to Tuktoyaktuk because, all my life, it felt like an impossible place I would never have a chance to visit; like Pluto or Patagonia or Keith Richards' rec room. It was a name, or word, I'd heard spoken in films about the North that teachers had screened in public school classes, and its name stuck like a popcorn kernel in the cavity of my imagination, every hard "k'" embedded there, one driven in deeper by the one that followed. If I knew very little about the Northwest Territories—if we, as Southerners, knew very little—we knew even less about the settlement on the far reaches of the northern shoreline at the hem of the Arctic Ocean. And yet here I was, two plane rides and a boat trip away. This was the North, too. Once you made it *up here*, you were never far from the unreachable.

I reached the top of north via Inuvik, hoping that a series of float plane rides would go better than the last. I was encouraged to find that my immediate vessel—a First Air AIR-42—seemed like any other short-haul carrier, the seat-pouch card with emergency warnings in Dene and Inuktitut notwithstanding. I had the good luck of sitting next to a half-Irish, half-Dene man named Harold Peely, a mining shift worker bound for a two-week run in Norman Wells, the Sahtu's hub of the natural gas industry. Harold grew up in Cambridge Bay and was the acclaimed throat-singer Tanya Tagaq's boyfriend when they were fourteen years old. I liked Harold immediately. He was small-featured and whippy, bouncing in his seat when he spoke, and wore a leather jacket with an embroidered Harley's logo on the back—automobile, racing stripe, dancers with huge torpedoes—that a friend of his had made before dying in prison. He raced snowmobiles, had fought Jordin Tootoo in a northern summer league hockey game, and once partied in Nunavut with the California folk-pop-hippie group, Dr. Hook, of all bands. Harold was also a guide who hunted caribou and bear, but, in the summer, he slugged it out in the mines, something he'd done since he was sixteen years old.

Like Susan Chaffee, Harold immediately made a point of telling me how many people he'd beaten up, all of it with a smile like a burning wick. In a gesture of transparency, he also told me how many people had beaten him up, most recently his wife. "She knocked me out with one punch! Right here, where I'm most vulnerable," he said, pointing to his temple. I was about to suggest to him that I didn't think he was the only one who was vulnerable there, but he said, "I know what you're gonna say. But most people get hit here," he said, tapping his cheek. "You can hit me here a hundred times and I won't go down. But I was teaching my wife to box, and *bam!*, she tagged me in the temple. I was flat out!"

he shouted, surging back in his chair. "My wife and I fight all the time," he confessed. "She's pretty tough. Still, ten years of marriage. That's pretty good, eh? Our daughter's two and our son's adopted. We took him in because, a while ago, my wife was assaulted pretty bad. She can't have kids anymore."

Harold spoke of tragedy like it was just another plot point. No matter how hilarious or mischievous his stories, something terrible always happened in the narrative: his brother was an addict, his parents were alcoholics, and, years ago, he'd lost a son to fatal illness. Pathos wandered through his life like a mourning violinist past a chirruping crowd, but if Harold acknowledged the sadness and the pain, he didn't dwell on it. If it were me telling one of his stories—say, about confronting a local drug dealer ("From B.C. A real punk") who'd sold methamphetamines to my teenage son, and I told the dealer that I was going to bury him in a hole in the middle of the ocean where he wouldn't be found again ("We could do this. Easy," he said, in case I doubted him)—I might have paused to gauge whether it was appropriate to share a story about the darkest struggles of life. But Harold treated death and sadness with the same weight afforded the wonder of life, not forgetting to be hilarious, which he also was.

I was only overnight in Inuvik, home to the most northern stoplight in Canada as well as the utilidor, a massive and insulated above-ground water tubing system that caterpillars through town. I boarded another plane bound for Deline—the land of the northern prophets—travelling in a Twin Otter with beige single-row seats, beige seat belts, and beige-framed windows patterned against beige walls. As we nosed through the clouds, a northern plaid was revealed—lakeblues, landgreens, and redroads—sitting between tungsten mountains (the Mackenzie range) dotted with forests like a five o'clock shadow. Although I am not the most devoted window-gazer—once, I remember slumbering while flying over Rome, only to awaken at the sight of the Eternal City fired in sunlight below me, and feeling like a doofus for nearly missing it—my forehead was pressed

against the warm flat of the window watching as the landscape trans-
formed into a set of enormous moth's wings: great circles of red, grey,
green, auburn, and brown, scabbed at the edges like a melanoma. The
ground looked soupy and damp—stomping Yetis would have been swallowed whole by the mud, I thought—which, I learned, was the result
of permafrost warmed by the sun, melting the colours into great sets of
watery eyes. There was a retarded summer beauty about the land—
exactly the kind of North I'd hoped to discover: neither monochromatic
nor endlessly barren—and you could see the terrestrial fight being waged
between the seasons, one emerging while another refused to pass.

Before getting to Deline ("Del-een-ay"), located in the Sahtu (North
Slavey) region of the Territories, we pit-stopped the Twin Otter at the
Tulita (formerly Fort Norman) airport—it wasn't so much an airport as
a courtesy parking lot with planes instead of cars—before climbing on
twenty minutes later. The plane tipped, if slightly, as our pilot came
aboard. He was heavy-set and sixty-something, wearing a white, short-
sleeved aviator's shirt with gold epaulets. He was fadingly handsome with
crimped blond 40s film-star hair and blond forearms—like Simpson Air's
Ted Grant, you could see the trace of an airman's style in his composition—and he settled on one knee in a crouch at the front of the cabin
while rubbing a gammy leg, which made him wince at the touch. The pilot
sighed a long, tired sigh, wrung his hands together, sucked in a breath as
a way of winnowing his gut, and announced, in a deep Australian brogue:
"Allo folks. I'd be Roger. And I'd be your pilot for today." Behind him in
the co-pilot's seat, a younger, thinner man with dark features was doing
all of the, well, *piloty* things: clicking switches, writing in logs, and pulling
down levers as the plane began to quietly purr. Roger adjusted his crouch
to continue speaking and said, "Jesus, my leg," which, in his Queenslander's
tenor, came out sounding like "Jaysus moy lag." He turned to address his
co-pilot. "Stanis, I may need ya, mate. You done? You all right?"

Stanis, a Bosnian who was putting in his hours co-piloting across the
North, said he was all right. Which made one them.

"Jaysus moy lag," repeated Roger, rubbing and wincing.

"Okay," he said, trying to forget about his lag. "The first thing I have to say is that I've been at this game a long time, but this business of flying in the North is, well, new to me," which, in terms of things you'd like to hear your pilot say is probably right up there with "Just so you know, I could have an appendicitis attack at any moment" or "Has anyone seen my blindfold?" Roger smiled politely—truth be told, it was more of a squint than a smile—and pointed ahead: "But don't worry, friends. We'll get ya there."

Whenever I travel by air, the less I know about my pilot, the better. While crossing that divide between aircraft and gate, I'm often terrified that I'll see him or her with an Aleister Crowley book open on their lap, dowsing a locket over the pages while snorting heroin off their co-pilot's jacket sleeve. I'd rather not see them at all, choosing instead to imagine it's Han Solo sitting in the cockpit and the movie is going to end up fine. One of the last things I want to hear is a confession by the person in whose hands I have entrusted my life that "flying in the North is, well, new to me," or "we'll get you there," because, after all, Roger's promise didn't cancel out crash landing in a forest clearing; hunting small prey for food before settling on grubs or plants that may or may not cause terrible hallucinations; choosing a leader who has covered himself in bear shit as a way of declaring superiority; fragging said leader after megalomania takes hold; cooking and eating Roger because, let's face it, he was old and had a gammy leg; and discovering, finally, that a quiet, unassuming member of our plane-crashed party has, in fact, devised a brilliant plan to reach town. Because, technically, that defines "gettin' there," too.

Roger remained in his crouch—he'd been down long enough that he probably needed help standing up—and told us about the plane, although there wasn't much to tell, the aircraft being the size of a long cigarillo with very little options in terms of flight, landing, or escape. I noticed a woman across from me tearing at her arm rest and another guy huffing and snorting in what I assumed was a state of mild distress triggered by our pilot's confession. Roger forged on in the spirited manner of his people, splashing against whatever sense of foreboding had seeped into the cabin. He told us, "Now there are many ways to leave your lover, but there's only one way to leave the aircraft," thumbing behind himself at the exit near the front of the plane.

Roger twisted around to show us what safety equipment we had to pull down and where—it was a painful pantomime, and I saw him mouth the word "bollocks" as he turned away—but as he did, I corrected him:

"Fifty ways."

Roger said, "I'm sorry?"

"Fifty. There are fifty ways to leave your lover."

"And you've actually, like, exacted this science?" he asked, the word "exacted" sounding like a plate skimming across a concrete floor.

"Not me. Paul Simon."

The guy behind me laughed.

Huh hu huh hu huh

"'Fifty Ways to Leave Your Lover' is a song by Paul Simon," I said. "He did the research, not me."

"Well, it seems as if this Mr. Simon has had his ups and downs, eh, mate?" said Roger, for a moment blithely forgetting that he was about to propel ten strangers into the cloudless air in an old vessel over terrain with which he was admittedly unfamiliar.

"All right then, fifty," he said, clapping his hands and nodding.

Roger continued with whatever else was required of his speech—flight duration, altitude, no smoking—as the plane purred louder. When he was done, he turned to climb slowly, achingly into the cockpit just as a squawking voice came over the radio. Stanis answered and said something to Roger. Stanis went to the door and cranked it open, at which point a small fellow with feline eyes, a crooked baseball cap, a jean jacket too big for his frame, and a deck of Players smokes winched in his breast pocket joined me, the Aussie, the Bosnian, and the rest of the passengers. He was greeted in North Slavey and, suddenly, the cabin sang with life, rewarding me with the traveller's joy of hearing new sounds from a different tongue voiced in a faraway place.

Roger sighed and winced some more before breaking the news to us: "I'm sorry, folks, but Canadian flight regulations demand that I go over the security commands once again because of the new passenger who has just joined us."

"But it's only Tony," said a voice from the back of the plane.

Huh hu huh hu huh

Roger rubbed his leg and looked up.

"Now, Tony," he said, "there might be fifty ways to leave your lover . . ."

21

THE HEART OF A LAKE

We made it to Deline. At the gift-shop-sized airport, I was met by the proprietor of the Grey Goose Lodge, Suzanne Hall, who vanned me down the road to my accommodation. The first thing I saw after coming into the town was a graveyard at the top of the village. Many graveyards possess a mournful beauty, but this one was adorned with colour-splashed wooden baby cribs stilted to the earth above each plot. The cribs reflected the Sahtu Dene's belief that man returns to child-hood after death, a near-Hindu concept enforced in a manipulation of the body, the spine being cracked to lay a person to rest in the foetal position, curled to fit in a circular grave. Charlie Neyelle, one of the few crinkle-faced and kind-mannered elders remaining in the village after the scourge of Port Radium, told me that "in the old days, people believed that when a person dies, they curl up like they're in their mother's womb, which is why they're buried this way. People tie a rope under the person's knees and around their neck and pull it until they hear a crack in the back. When the Europeans came, they used coffins, so we built cribs to show where our people were. We also believe that after a person is gone, their souls wander around, and sometimes they need help, especially if they've lived a certain kind of life. This way, they come back to their family line, and find themselves." After expressing my astonishment—it was the only graveyard where I was reminded of life rather than death—Suzanne told me, "For our first date, one of my boyfriends took me down there. He said that he wanted to introduce me to all of his relatives."

Deline (population 550) was surrounded by what you and I might call wilderness, although there was no word in the Dene language for such a thing. The town rested tight to the southwestern shore of Great Bear Lake, the biggest in Canada, and eighth biggest in the world (behind Lake Baikal in Russia and just ahead of Lake Malawi). It was the natural focus of the area—unlike in Yellowknife, the water was visible from everywhere in town—to say nothing of being the largest remaining unpolluted lake of its size in the western hemisphere and the site of the first northern Canadian UNESCO biosphere, shimmering blue in the vast light of the day.

Great Bear Lake was at the centre of the Sahtu Dene's origin story, which concerned the misadventures of an angler named Touye, who, one day, found himself fishing at his favourite spot along the shore. The entire community relied on the angler's catch for food—he set four hooks for these purposes—but, with his line in the water, a trout swam past and stole one of the hooks, meaning he wouldn't catch his usual complement, threatening the community's provisions. "Back then, you couldn't just run to the store and buy a replacement if something broke or was stolen," said Morris Neyelle, a former Sahtu leader, who spoke with his top bridge removed to reveal two white-toothed fence posts. "The man had to get his hook back!" he told me, his eyes lighting up while telling the legend.

The angler used his dream powers to become a medicine man. From there, he turned into a loche, the largest fish in the Sahtu, and chased after the trout. He descended to the centre of the lake, where he saw a light, and through the light emerged the presence of a giant beating heart—a *tudze* in Slavey—surrounded and protected by every manner of aquatic species, some of them monstrously large. The angler-turned-medicine-man-turned-loche understood that the beating heart was the life source that sustained the lake and the greater world. "The Dene people view water as a living thing," said Morris, threading together the latticework of his fingers. "Like a human being, if it drinks poison, it will die. The health of Great Bear Lake is a key to survival," he told me. It was a theme integral to life in the Sahtu.

The graveyard's beauty was sustained through the village itself, its dirt roads and painted homes possessing a care and detail beyond what I'd seen elsewhere in the North. When I told Suzanne this, she said that there were clean-up initiatives every spring after the thaw, dozens of families stooping to pick up whatever garbage had been hidden during the winter. My impression of the town's glow might have been owing to my time spent in Yellowknife's worn baseball mitt, but I was also thinking about how Diane, the Parks Canada guide, had described Sahtu spirituality, a church in which four prophets were worshipped, the foremost being a famous seer named Louis Ayah ("Eye-ya"). She also described hybrid Catholic/Dene church services that combined traditional drumming with scripture readings, a rare harmony born out of a collision that, historically, had resulted in the suppression of Indigenous life. Morris, who, in the early 1990s, helped rename the village from its former Fort Franklin, explained, "It works great. When the drumming starts, the priest goes out for a smoke." The same dichotomy between the Sahtuot'ine and the non-Indigenous world was found in a story told by writer/teacher Miggs Wynne Morris who wrote about a Deline wedding she attended where, at the end of mass, the crowd broke into a "familiar, nasal" Slavey hymn before the newlyweds eventually turned and walked down the aisle to Dionne Warwick's "That's What Friends Are For."

Because I was only swinging through the Sahtu—one and a half days—and because there was so much story here for such a small place, I had to climb on the carousel and hang tight, a discovery-by-speed routine that hadn't been necessary over my long days in Yellowknife. I leaned on Suzanne to direct me to the key figures in town, starting with a march after midday to the council chambers—only a few minutes down the road from the Grey Goose in a relatively new building—where local politicians, along with hunters, had convened to talk about caribou, or, rather, their disappearing ranks. I was startled when Suzanne led me past the reception area through a set of doors directly into the chambers, where the role of the federal government's involvement in the issue was being discussed among men in sweaters and suit blazers, as well as dudes in hunting caps and camouflage vests.

Deline chief Leonard Kenny was at the centre of most discussions. He greeted me during the session's adjournment before guiding me into his office for a chat about his vision for Deline.

Leonard was a stout man with a retreating hairline and a wide face that hid nothing. He had smooth skin over high, pointed cheekbones, a feature that I'd noticed among many of the passengers on my plane, as well as the few citizens I'd come across in Deline. He landed in his office chair with the entire weight of his body, allowing himself a reprieve from the demands of his job, which saw him attending meetings like the one out of which he'd just emerged; planning a forthcoming session of Dene Nation chiefs; organizing a lake-preservation "Waterheart" conference in which David Suzuki was the featured speaker; and working to secure reparations for the Port Radium tragedy. Pointing back through his door to the council chambers, he told me, "When it comes to issues like the caribou, we're building our own conservation plan, something that will come out of discussions with the community. The caribou numbers are down, but we don't think they're threatened. The government, on the other hand, wants to pass a law where even the Indigenous community would need tags when hunting, even though we're Treaty Indians. My people don't like it," he said, laying his hand flat on the table.

"We've always maintained that we are stewards for land, water, and animals, something that goes back to the elders, to the story of the beginnings of the Sahtu [the *tudze* legend]. In our tradition, we only take what's needed, but at the same time, the Yellowknives, for instance, have taken a lot of caribou, maybe too many. When Dene Nation arrives here we'll figure out a way to approach it consensually. Rather than simply object to the government's strategy for the caribou, we'll present a plan explaining how we want to do it. That's how we figure out issues. We work together with everyone. It's how it's done," he said, holding it out his arms.

Along with local facilitator, activist, and politician Danny Gaudet—the driving force behind so many projects in town, and someone who was so busy that there was simply no time sit down with him during my short stay—Kenny had helped Deline become the first town of its size to adopt Indigenous self-government, an effort thirty years in the making, and a remarkable achievement among Dene groups throughout the Northwest Territories, and around Canada.

"My summer's booked solid and I have no holidays," he told me, looking out from his desk through a half-shuttered window into the daylight. "There's having to organize the rollout of our government, but another big thing is Port Radium. People are studying readings—they've been monitoring the region for a while—and there are twenty-four recommendations coming out of the company having mined here without proper protection. We never ended up settling on a financial agreement. I don't know if you know what happened in the 30s and 40s . . ." he said, before taking the time to guide me through the story.

Leonard said that in 1930 near Cameron Bay (later Port Radium) on Great Slave Lake, two men, Gilbert and Charles LaBine, discovered radioactive pitchblende, radium, and uranium ore. Mining Canada immediately classified the payload as "insidious and deadly" and declared that "the hazards involved in the handling of high-grade radioactive materials make necessary the adoption of certain precautions," suggesting regular examinations of workers, none of which were carried out. Instead, the mine opened in haste, employing the Sahtu Dene to dig for the rock—it was the first-ever paid employment for the Sahtuot'ine—as well as sherpa it in ninety-pound bags on their backs to boats travelling south along the Mackenzie to Fort McMurray, eventually landing in Port Hope, Ontario. Locals called it "the money rock," and since the work was rugged and the carry heavy, the men occasionally lay on the bags to sleep. After delivering the ore, they took apart the sackcloth and gave it to their wives, who used it to make tents. The towns around Great Bear Lake became wracked with epidemic cancer deaths to the point that Deline was known as the "Village of Widows," having lost an entire generation to the disease. "Every one of my uncles and grandfathers worked over at Port Radium," Morris later told me, looking me straight in the eye. "And now, they're all gone."

In 1941, the Canadian government quietly purchased the mine. The U.S. government ordered sixty tonnes of uranium, which they used in the Manhattan Project, eventually producing the atomic weapons that devastated Hiroshima and Nagasaki. The attacks by the U.S. military on Japan affirmed one of the Dene spiritual leader Louis Ayah's prophecies about an expensive and powerful "glass" rock and "men with white faces climbing into a big hole in the ground." Ayah also envisioned a "flying bird; and a big cigar-shaped stick dropped on a land far away" where another hole was made and where everything burned for days. According to author Richard Van Camp's book *A Man Called Raven*, Ayah foretold the devastation of a people—the Japanese—whom, he said, "looked a lot like us," yet lived in a distant place. These prophecies spread, and one story had the Canadian government coming to Ayah in wartime and asking him to stop Adolph Hitler's heart. Ayah said he couldn't bring himself to harm another human being, but guaranteed that Nazi boots would never reach the shores of North America.

The Prophet Ayah's visions began when he was a child. He knew every word in the bible without ever having picked it up. He had other apparent powers, too: knowing who was coming to visit him on a pilgrimage before they arrived, and sensing whenever a "brewpot" (homemade alcohol) was being made in town. One of his visions had "strange animals coming to town . . . three of them," and, on April 2, 2008, a trio of polar bears arrived on the shores of Great Bear Lake, having made their way, remarkably, from the Beaufort Sea, some four hundred kilometres away. It was the first time anyone in Deline had seen a polar bear, and they were shot to protect people from harm. The beasts were mounted in the lobby of the Grey

Goose, both to honour the animals' memories and to remind people of their elder's prophecies.

One of the guardians of Ayah's visions was a man named George Blondin, an archivist and former chief of the Deline First Nation, who passed away in 2008 at the age of eighty-seven. Blondin was a remarkable person who lived a remarkable life. Born in 1923 on the Barren Lands, he was judged to have the early powers of a medicine man and taken out of residential school in Grade 3 to live among his grandparents, who, according to legend, were capable of supernatural conjuring. His paternal grandfather, Paul Blondin, was said to possess eagle medicine with the power to leave his body and fly, while his maternal grandfather, a man named Karkai, used yelling medicine to stop a grizzly bear in its tracks in order to save a young girl.

Eventually, sicknesses carried by white settlers eviscerated the Sahtu Dene, and, by the early 1940s, only George and his father escaped the ravages of a flu epidemic, not the last time they would cheat death. His father grew sick with pneumonia and was taken to a hospital in nearby Norman Wells, where, according to Blondin, his dad's lungs sounded like "porridge boiling." George was convinced that he would end up alone in the world, but when he returned the next morning, his dad was putting on his mukluks, telling his son: "We gotta go visit our traplines." The previous night, he'd dreamed of remarrying and having more children, his hair turning white in old age. A few years later, this would all come to pass. George would have a stepmother and eight half-brothers and sisters.

Even though George's dad had wanted him to become a medicine man and a healer, he exhibited no special powers. One elder foretold that he'd leave his mark as a great storyteller, but it wasn't enough for George's dad, who, in one final attempt to prove or disprove his instinct, sent his son to a medicine man in nearby Cameron Bay. The man confirmed that Blondin was left wanting in this regard. He told the father: "Your son is a storyteller. That's how he should remain."

George and his dad ended up working at Port Radium. After the site was exhausted, Blondin moved to Yellowknife and got a job at Giant Mine, the first Indigenous person hired because of his experience hauling "money rock." He worked for fifteen years, then went back to the land to record stories from hundreds of elders. He wrote his first book at a camp on McGill Bay using notepads and candles. Stephen Kakfwi remembered that "George could walk into a community and engage elders and community leaders and musicians [at once]." He was the single-most influential teacher of his generation.

In 1988, he joined a group from Deline who travelled to Japan, where they offered the *hibakusha*—the survivors of the nuclear attacks—an apology. The group saw this as a first step in healing the damages of the past as well as the beginning of a new positive legacy, manifested in the dream of self-government, which, in 2015, the town voted 84 per cent to approve.

"The prophecies helped guide us toward independence," said Kenny. "Ayah foretold that, after the [inevitable] death of the oceans, people would come and shake our hands. He saw the rest of the world running out of food, while fish remained abundant in our lake. He saw people coming by the thousands with camps popping up everywhere, and part of having self-government in place is about us being ready for the world when they arrive," he said, expressing a political selflessness that was almost startling to hear. Charlie Neyelle's beliefs were similar to Kenny's. "Everywhere, there will be anger and depression," he told me in a voice as old as the sawing of a tree branch in the wind. "People will come here to find the answer. The town will be waiting."

Deline used to be called Fort Franklin. The explorer was here for two years during his travels around the North, but many locals couldn't say his name without looking as if they were sucking on a lemon. While Yellowknife had its Franklin Avenue hill and other places across the Western Arctic promoted themselves in proximity to the Northwest Passage, Deline was racing in the other direction, cutting nearly all connections to a person who, for a handful of years, was a major symbol in Prime Minister Stephen Harper's efforts to illuminate the legacies of the North.

"Let's face it," said Morris, "Franklin was a bad dude. The elders heard stories from their grandmothers, about how women were kidnapped by gunpoint and made to serve the crew. The locals brought the Europeans caribou and herring, but they were treated badly, living in fear for two whole years. Finally, people got together and snuck out during the night. When they came back five years later, there was no one left; Franklin and his crew had killed them. In Émile Petitot's journals of 1870—he was an early missionary here—he talks about Franklin's killings. He said that he witnessed thirty-two murders while he was here. When he went back to France, they told him that he couldn't say these things about Franklin, which is why it took so long for the diaries to come out. People think that Franklin went down at sea, but I think the Inuit killed him. He was a bad dude and people had just had enough."

After Franklin came the terrible diseases, and after that came the residential schools. There was often an overlap in the hardship. Morris remembered, "My dad went to residential school in Fort Providence in 1924 and he was there for two years. In 1957, my mum was taken to hospital because of TB and she didn't return for five years. The nuns kept her even though she'd recovered well enough. People were dying all around her and she was given food that was rancid, black food that they said she had to eat unless she wanted to die of starvation. When the planes came to take people away, families ran into the bush and hid because other relatives had left to disappear forever. This all happened. But I'm a forgiving person. It's our turn now. It's a chance to do something different."

Considering what Deline had suffered through, their resilience, hope, and resolve—and kindness—were astonishing. If Indigenous communities across Canada had been profiled in the Southern media by the tragedies of Attawapiskat, the gangs of Winnipeg's North End, suicides in

Nunavut, the deaths of countless women, and the unsolved murders of teenagers in Thunder Bay, here was Deline: a beacon of light and possibility. And it was happening in a region that the rest of Canada had largely ignored: the Northwest Territories.

Later in the day, and with the tangerine sun still high and ripe in the sky, I stopped at the edge of the Grey Goose lawn to draw my sunglasses from my valise. Bending over, I sensed something swoop above me. When I stood up, I saw two large ravens settling on a fence post along the side of the road. I looked at them, they looked at me. After putting on my sunglasses, I could have sworn that they laughed.

I was more aware of the ravens in Deline than anywhere else. Although I'd encountered the birds in Yellowknife and Simpson, they were a more voluble presence in the Sahtu, squawking to each other like a group of old men gnawing on cigars, sounding nearly human. One afternoon, a bird landed near where I was standing and made whistling sounds like a person running their fingers over the holes of a flute, while, later that evening, I came out from my hotel room to find a group of them—more than three and they're known as a "conspiracy"—gurgling like emptying drains. You couldn't look into the sky without a feathered black thing darting across your eye line.

The raven—*datsǫ́* in Dene—was seen as a smart, clever, and prescient bird, even though the rest of the world has a different view, painting it as an inauspicious creature, its presence dubious and foreboding. I wondered what Edgar Allan Poe was thinking while writing his famous poem in which he described the raven as "ghastly, grim and ancient," although it was worse in parts of Sweden, where these birds are considered the ghosts of murdered people. I thought there was a flickering intelligence behind the bird's stare, and since their brain is among the largest of any bird species—the concept of displacement (communicating objects or events that are distant in space or time from the communication) is also singular to them in the animal kingdom—to meet their eye was to tunnel into what I perceived were the mechanics of avian thought. There was a sense of play in the glance that returned to you, a social frisson, even. Some Dene have described ravens—who are devoted to family and who mate for life—as "dogs with wings," and it's how I felt whenever I was close to them. There was very little skittishness or concern in the presence of humans. They seemed to encourage the company.

In his book *The Barren Lands*, Warburton Pike talks about an expedition in which a raven flew overhead, turned on its own back, and set a direction that the explorers followed, eventually leading to a food source in the woods. Lawrence Nayally, whom I'd met at CKLB, also conveyed this behaviour to me, citing a legend about looking into the sky for the bird should you ever find yourself lost or in need of food. Some people in Yellowknife talked about the ravens being a social nuisance, but almost everyone cited their cleverness and persistence. Glenn told me, "One night, I was parked outside the Black Knight, having left some cat food in the back of the truck. I went out for a smoke and I saw about thirty ravens tearing it apart. They were in there helping themselves, so I got in the truck and I drove away. The birds took off, but, going down the highway, two of them followed me, flying right behind the flatbed. It was an amazing thing. When I got to the dumpster to get rid of the stuff, I found the rest waiting there, standing around the edges of the receptacle. I watched them finish the stuff as I drove the truck away."

Because there was a mysticism about Deline, I couldn't help but project a mysticism on the birds, too. As lords of the sky, they seemed to guard the dominion of the village, and during my last few hours in Deline, I had the strange, yet not unsettling, sense that they were watching me as I walked through town to the cabin where Ayah had died, "right there in the corner of the room," Charlie told me. The cabin was unlocked twenty-four hours a day and welcomed all visitors. It hadn't ever been vandalized by bored or disaffected teenagers hemmed in by winter for three-quarters of the year. "You can go there anytime," Morris said. "Just sit and think. It's okay."

Once inside, I saw that the cabin wasn't the kind of velvet-roped shrine that forced you to be careful about where you left your boots. In some ways, it was very plain. At the back of the room was a set of white cabinets above a counter with two or three coffee urns and six rolls of unwrapped paper towels, under which a stack of fold-up chairs were propped. The far wall with exposed logs was bare save for four modestly sized photographs of the prophets—Ayah, Andre Andre, Naedzo, and Joseph Bayha—and a few tables holding vases with plastic flowers over simple brown carpeting. The front of the room had a light green hand-made shelving unit with dozens of framed photographs of people in the community who'd passed away. On the middle shelf was an enormous laminated photo of Louis Ayah: broad fur hat; deep, sunken eyes; a pro-nounced brow; stoic nose; and a tufted chin where I imagined a great beard had once been. Underneath was a table covered with a white linen sheet holding porcelain figures of Jesus and Mary, some prayer candles, and a set of goblets patterned about a large bible opened to Genesis 2:24: *That is why a man leaves his father and mother and is united to his wife, and they become one flesh.* It looked like an altar, if absent the kind of don't-touch sanctity that I remembered from mass in the early days of being dragged to church as a kid. Near the altar was a chicken-necked microphone stand with a pair of small speakers keeled at its side. There'd been some kind of performance here. It probably wasn't John Prine, but my mind raced for a moment to the fantasy.

The wall nearest to the door had a couch beneath a set of windows. It was the kind of couch that looked easy to crash on, friendly and sagging as it swallowed your frame. With the wind knuckle-tapping against the windows, I thought of great deep summertime cottage naps or sleeping on the chesterfield in old Reaction Studios on Stafford Street in Toronto, where the Rheostatics made our second album, filling my subconscious with the sounds of a mix being born. I took my writing book and laid it open it across a low table in front of the couch. I searched for my pen in the depths of my travel bag. I unleafed a new page and looked around the cabin.

I fell asleep.

The exhaustion of the summer—the research and work; the travel; the colour, sound, and life that had flown at me from every direction—guided me down. For what was probably only twenty minutes, I sank into the darkness of a most unknowing slumber, the couch holding me like a warm palm. It was a great black sleep and I would have slept through the rest of the day and into the night had I not, suddenly, burst out of it. The skreeing. The gabbing. The squawking.

Ravens.

When I pulled myself up from the couch—I took a minute to find my arms—I looked out the window to see three birds in a cacophonous state: beaks snapping, wings flaying, feet hopping about. I saw them, they saw me. Had they followed me here? What did they want? Why had they waited until I was sleeping to start talking?

In many ways, Deline was an impossible place, yet I'd seen it with my own two eyes. I'd listened to elders, spiritual leaders, working people, and civic representatives talk about finding strength from within, and knowing love as a result of that strength. Words like "forgiveness" and "awareness" and "unity" weren't thrown about as platitudes heavy as manhole covers, but, rather, used in common parlance. I remember Charlie—the closest Deline had to an avowed modern spiritual leader—leaning in close to me and telling me in a rough whisper: "There are all kinds of religions, but, in the end, your body is the church's house." He waited to see if I'd processed what he was saying, then he poked his belt with his finger. "It comes from right here," he said. "In the belly button." Then he laughed and instructed, "Write that down," making sure I remembered the joke.

I gathered up my things, looking for one final time at the gallery of prophets on the wall. I reached around to find something in my bag to toast them—an Altoid or waiting-room candy would have sufficed, but I couldn't find anything—before realizing that this kind of ceremony wasn't a thing here. I left the cabin and went outside, finding the ravens in their spot on the window ledge. I asked them, "What the fuck, guys?" before understanding what was going on. They were the manifestation of three close friends—two men and a woman—each of them lost in the last few years, two by cancer, one in a car crash on a drive from Calgary to Regina. The birds even looked like them: the eyes, the manner, the joy, mischief, and light. They'd found me in this far northern place of magic and I'd found them. They turned to each other and nodded. This happened. I saw it.

They flew away.

22

GET OUT THE COOKIES

I left Deline and returned to Inuvik. The next morning, I was booked to travel up the Deh Cho (*Kuukpak* in Inuvialuktun and *Nagwichoonjik* in Gwich'in) to Tuktoyaktuk. I'd been on the fat middle of the river in Fort Simpson, but Inuvik was settled along its northern neck just before the Delta, which flooded yearly, creating new channels and a different aerial doodle, its arms moving about like a centipede doing the rhumba. The Delta was, according to the *Canadian Encyclopedia*, "a vast fan of low-lying alluvial islands covered with black spruce," with three main passageways to the ocean. It was also largely unmappable, owing to its amorphous nature. You had to know it in order to be on it, and as I gathered my things in the hotel room and waited for my ride to the river's boat launch, I hoped that whoever was taking me out would know it.

I was collected at dawn by a gregarious, frazzle-haired middle-aged woman named Barb, who was celebrating her birthday and who'd just come from rear-ending her neighbour's car (Barb worked for Tundra Tours, who did summer river guides of the Delta). She told me both of these things after I climbed into the van, then asked: "Do you think it's bad luck to hit someone's car before going out on the river?"

"I think it's bad luck for the person whose car you hit."

"Oh yeah, that too," she said, chewing a nail.

We drove at dawn to the muddy banks of the river, which curled along the edge of town like a snake guarding its prey. A few of the other passengers were waiting—five of us were travelling to Tuk, but I was the only one staying there—along with our captain and guide, a young man named Kylik Taylor, who'd returned to the North after training as a mixed martial arts (MMA) fighter in southern Ontario. He'd come back to Inuvik to re-engage with his Gwich'in roots, learning traditional ways from his dad's family, who, he said, "lived in Inuvik when there was no town, just land and a few trees."

Kylik was far less sea-bitten than I'd hoped for. He was neither salty-bearded nor peg-legged and his shoulder looked like it hadn't ever, not once, been shat on by a parrot. Instead, he was very fit with a wisp of brown hair, lean build, and handsome young features, seeming suspiciously telegenic for someone who'd spent time being wind-whipped on a daily basis. Because it didn't look as if Kylik had ever been bitten by a whale or chased by a polar bear—in fact, he looked a little like an Arctic version of the alt-pop lord Beck—I worried that navigating the moving shapes of the river would be beyond him, a suspicion that only worsened after he tapped the steering wheel and told us that the boat—a twenty-four-foot Hewescraft called *Indigo*—was taking its maiden voyage. After watching Barb—who was going on the trip with a few friends to celebrate her birthday—fawn over the young guide whenever he spoke or explained what to do in case we capsized, I decided not to judge him on his northern handsomeness.

It was a calm morning on the river, cloudy and soft. The motor purred as we met the waves heading north, chugging past the low, ghostly Richardson Mountains and through weedy channels. Kylik told us to look out for a snowy owl he'd seen a few days earlier, and Barb announced, "Oh, seeing a snowy owl: that's good luck." We swivelled our heads and looked out both sides of the boat—there was cowling to protect us from getting wet and help us stay warm, but we unsnapped it for the journey—and, after a moment, Kylik shot out his arm and pointed: "There." We all swivelled in the same direction and saw the enormous bird—plump, charcoal and white—its great swooping wings cruising the air. Barb and her friends *skreed* in delight. I might have *skreed* a little, too.

We purred on, passing old fuel barges anchored along the shore. The barges were still used because of the distance, and cost, of transporting goods by truck. The river was huge at certain points, then smaller as the weeds rose around us. It was a fascinating trip because of the ever-changing scale of the place and the way in which the boat had to swerve whenever the route winnowed through circuitous passageways. After about half an hour, Barb, whose day was turning out to be awesome, announced, "Time to get out the cookies!" tearing open a bag of Dad's and passing them around. Together, we produced our respective foodstuffs. I'd over-compensated after my experience nearly starving in Nahanni, packing every ridiculous thing I could find in the snack racks of Inuvik's only— and yet, twenty-four-hour—variety store, hugging to my chest a package of mini-Skor bars, some weird tasting BBQ-flavoured popcorn, a bag of small carrots, five Kit Kat bars, and a six pack of Five Alives. We ate and chatted and *ooohed* as the mountains sunk into the land, giving way to the occasional bald hill overlooking the river. Kylik, who proved more seaworthy than I'd suspected, told stories about his life on the water, an oration that was still new to him, although I appreciated him making the effort. Even though he didn't *dargh!* a single time, Barb prompted him to tell the story of how he almost drowned a few months before. She did this by saying, "Hey, Ky. Tell Dave about the time you almost drowned."

One fall day, our captain—his full name was Kylik Kisoun Taylor— found himself on Big Lake in his kayak (*Kylik was in his kayak*; say that five times fast). A freak wave sent his craft over, popping the skirt and sinking the boat. Because he was wearing a life jacket with a SPOT locator device and cellphone, he felt secure at the outset, but it wasn't long before the cold water got the better of him. His hands started to swell and he had trouble moving his legs. "I got to the point where I was freaking out," he said. "I thought I better just call the RCMP because I didn't know how much longer I could swim. I tried to call but I was drowning, I was sinking." Finally, Kylik touched the bottom of the lake, so he bounced up and down and made the call. But his mouth filled with water as he relayed his position, and, in his words, "I was starting to lose my mind. I was starting to lose function. I couldn't think straight and was double-guessing myself: 'Am I actually in Big Lake?'" A local man ended up hearing his call on the scanner and went to rescue him. Kylik was okay, but the event left its mark. I wasn't sure whether being with a captain who'd cheated death on the water was lucky or not, but I supposed I would find out.

We made a few stops before our arrival in Tuk. We docked at a place called Reindeer Station, a hamlet that had been created because of a (failed) attempt by the federal government to reroute the migratory pattern of Santa's caribou, bringing in Scandinavian Sami herders to care for the animals. The only things left in the riverside village were a few abandoned shacks and what looked like a welcome centre with a haggard REINDEER STATION banner still strung across the front porch. This is to say nothing of the bugs, which, as soon as we appeared, stormed us in great swirling crowds, their needle barbs sharpened for the occasion. I pulled my hoodie tight to my face, but knew this would fall short after seeing Kylik pop on a mosquito net while tromping through the tall grass. Kylik spoke for a moment about the history of the place before aborting his speech, realizing that "there once was something here and now there is not," didn't amount to the greatest narrative, especially with people waving their hands about like acid casualties. We folded our arms over our heads and ran to the floating dock.

We cruised for another twenty minutes—more food, more stories— and, at one point, the boat followed a bald eagle as it arrowed down one of the channels. "Seeing an eagle: that's good luck!" said Barb. This led us to one of the bird's nesting grounds on a hill, where we docked the boat and climbed the sandy slope overlooking a narrow band in the river, which, Kylik said, was a swimming ground for caribou. Clouds of yellow swallows greeted us as we came over the hill—"Oh, seeing yellow birds is good luck, too!" said Barb—and, at one point, I looked down to find a huge eagle feather at my feet. "Oh my God," said Barb. "An eagle feather . . ."

"Lemme guess," I said. "Good luck?"

"Oh, really, really good luck."

I picked up the feather and handed it to Barb.

"Happy birthday."

"Getting an eagle feather on your birthday. That's the best luck of all," she said, holding the feather to her chest.

"Let's head out before it gets too late," said Kylik, looking at his watch. "Everybody ready to hit the ocean?" We cheered that we were. Our captain headed down the hill and we followed, filling *Indigo* for the last leg of our trip and bound for the edge of the continent.

Because of the relative closeness of the Delta shores and the intimacy in which the river narrowed—it was almost like a northern everglade—I was jarred once we found ourselves expelled into open waters at the top of the Deh Cho. The river disappeared and we were taken by the vastness of the sea. The brown-green silt was replaced by the ocean's cold blue-grey and, if the river had offered a strong enough current, here the waves swelled and the mist rose and the boat fought to stay on course. I checked my stomach, fearing the worst, but I was okay. Barb packed away the cookies and the rest of us stood snapping the cowling into place. The wind howled and it grew very cold. We pulled up our hoodies and tightened our scarves. Soon, fog appeared and we were swallowed into the mouth of the ocean.

It happened in an instant. It wasn't like city fog, the kind that announces itself in rolls of wet smoke. Rather, it was like a descending dark veil, taking away everything around us. I could see only what was in front of me: my companions, a few empty gas tanks, and the boat's cowling flapping as the wind raged harder. We were now driving forward into one translucent thing, a single tiny vessel alone in the Arctic Ocean. We shivered in our jackets and fleece.

We hung on as the storm——at least I think it was a storm; I couldn't be sure if it was like this all the time——pushed at the waves, conjuring them to grow even higher. We had reached a northern place where I felt truly lost, a place where, if we'd disappeared, nobody would have known where or when it had happened. I imagined the boat going over and someone finding our Dad's cookies in the wreckage. He or she would pick up the sad soaking bag and tell another member of their search and rescue team what they'd found.

"Well, at least they had cookies."

The rain kept coming. Kylik worked the wipers hard. I trained my eyes on him and saw that he wasn't squinting or peering or probing ahead with his eyes, or even chewing a lip or scratching a chin wondering where we were headed or how. Instead, he bore a hole through the intensity of the fog, shoulders and jaw squared, legs and arms taut. Because he was strong and young and had the form of a former MMA fighter, he was able to steel himself against the nature of the ride, and, for the first time, I was grateful that he wasn't old or grey bearded and had never had scurvy. He checked the GPS and I saw him nod to himself. The boat rocked through the waves. No one said anything. No one had to.

Suddenly, there was a tear in the veil. Kylik pointed ahead: "See!" We lifted our heads and spotted a crooked finger of land. This was Tuktoyaktuk, a sliver of shacks reaching into the sea. I'd never felt so far away from my country while continuing to be in my country. I was distant from everyone——my family, my friends, my city——and Canada stood at my back. Beyond the grey waves, showers of mist, and a thinning wall of fog, we approached the village at the edge of the land. The waves settled and the sun knocked against the sky. I felt a tap on my shoulder. Barb was holding out the cookies but I stared ahead, sobbing in the rain.

23

TIME AMONG THE HOSERS

The boat landed at Tuk and I wiped away the tears. We moored at the foot of the isthmus beside a fishing boat filled with guns, gas cans, and life jackets. Sitting in the stern were two large, cement-faced men with dark beards wearing toques and Sudbury dinner jackets, cast by whatever spirit conjures this kind of broadly Canadian welcome. Not that the men were especially welcoming—this may have made them more Canadian still—and, for a moment, I wondered if they could see the print of tears and red of my face before realizing that I didn't care. If you're concerned about pride or appearance while on the ragged hem of the Arctic Ocean, you probably aren't here in the first place, although these men looked tough enough to suggest that sentimentality or a tender examination of self was low on their list of feelings, somewhere below hunter's remorse, or growing melancholy at having to jackhammer a grave out of the permafrost, which is how they did it here. In the past, I've waxed on about how we're all wound into the scrappy and resilient identity by which our country is defined, but the presence of these two sea-bitten Northerners made me feel as if I were a giant ambulatory latte—foam mascot torso, bow tie, tights—holding a moleskin in which lurked the beginnings of a terrible novel about a yoga instructor who falls for a macrobiotic Pilates blogger. Not even my greasy Jays cap—okay, it wasn't exactly greasy; maybe soiled; okay, maybe not soiled—affected the way I must have appeared to them. The wind-carved lines of their faces and broad rucksack shoulders pointed to my precious southerness and how, if self-preservation for them was about slaying enough wild meat to carry their family through the winter's darkness, for me it was about making sure my car was filled with high-test unleaded gasoline, because, you know, regular unleaded gasoline, well, that'll be the downfall of us all.

"Not too cold out there today. Pretty foggy, though," I said to them, pretending to know something about anything.

"How'd ja come in?"

"With Kylik."

"Oh, Kylik."

"Yeah, Kylik."

And we ended there. I stepped along the creaking dock to the land—it was wreathed in a low mist, making it seem even more like a watery dream—and hauled my bags along the side of a dark muddy road, waiting for someone to pick me up and bring me to my lodging. It was around 12 degrees Celsius—late-fall Ontario temperatures—but the salty bite of the Arctic wind made it seem as if the sky might erupt with snow. The rest of Kylik's group—they were only staying for a moment before heading back—climbed the road to visit the Northern Store beyond the wharf, Tuk's one-stop supply for dry goods, electronics, vacuum cleaners, tires, and everything else under the sun.

After a small moment in which I felt adrift, and slightly abandoned, in a new place (when travelling, this experience is partly euphoric, partly terrifying, and partly lonely), a red truck with Jackson Pollock mud splattered across its flanks pulled up and bleated its horn, even though I was the only person around. The driver was a young woman in sunglasses and hunting jacket: Rebecca Pokiak, the daughter of James Pokiak, whom people called the "polar bear hunter." Rebecca rolled down her window.

"Are you the guy I'm supposed to take into town?" she asked, with an impressive and pronounced uptick.

"I'm Dave," I said, waving.

"Oh," she said, looking into her lap. "I think that's the name," she said, flipping through some papers.

"You're from Inuvik?" she asked.

"Well, not *from* Inuvik. But I came from Inuvik," I said.

"You come from Inuvik?"

"No, I come from Toronto."

"Toronto? I'm not sure."

"I am," I said.

"You're what?" she said, in a perplexed uptick.

"I'm from Toronto."

"And what's your name?" she said.

This went on for a while. I realized that I didn't know any more than Rebecca, having been brought to the top of the world without any instruction beyond that.

"You wanna get in?" she asked, leaning over and opening the door of her idling truck.

I said that I did, and so I climbed up, the running boards and height of the vehicle making me feel like a small child scaling the top bunk. Along with her pronounced uptick, Rebecca had the most Canadian of all inflections—her "lows" sounded like "loe" and you would have phonetically written her "hellos" with three l's and four o's. It was like hanging out with the McKenzie brothers' sister: "Okay noe, I think there's suppoe-sed to be anoether felloe later too and that's why I'm confused, eh." After a moment, she decided that I was, in fact, the right person before telling me that the timing of my visit was awkward: Rebecca's mum, Maureen, the facilitator of the trip, was abroad working, and my responsibility had been left to her daughter. Rebecca pointed to the door and said, "Okay, so Eileen will be here soon. She'll get you. Then I'll see you later, okay?" I climbed down from the truck.

"Who's Eileen?" I shouted as the vehicle pulled away.

Rebecca sounded the horn, which I took as a kind of answer, although which kind, I wasn't sure.

24

≡

SWALLOWED BY
A BIGGER THING

Moments after Rebecca left, a van pulled up driven by a dark-haired, fortyish Inuvialuit woman in red fleece and sealskin gloves: Eileen Jacobson. She called me into the truck, looked straight ahead, and said: "We're going to the airport. Gotta pick up a group, then we go on tour. So, welcome to Tuk. Okay?"

Eileen worked in league with the Pokiaks as tour operators, hosting anywhere from three hundred to a thousand (mostly day) visitors a year. She also drove a taxi and had once run a big-game caribou hunting business with her husband, Billy, until caribou harvesting restrictions forced a change. She had a way like an arrow moving forward, her thoughts always trained on the next thing. At the beginning of our ride, she reached over and tapped one of my lapel buttons—a Blondie *Parallel Lines* pin I'd bought at a record store in Toronto—and said, "These. Like little girls wear." I stared self-consciously down at the button long enough that I almost missed my first view of town: wide, dirt-packed roads that undulated across the flung-noodle peninsula where elevated rows of small homes and shacks were Popsickle-sticked to the ground, their crooked railings draped with drying animal pelts—caribou, muskox, and polar bear—and roofs crowned with antlers, bones, and various grey skeletal matter. Every manner of snow machine, toy bike, barrel, the occasional stove, set of tools, and more pelts were scattered about in front and back lots. Because of the proximity to the roaring northern ocean, some of the homes had boarded-up windows, "partly because kids won't break windows; partly because of the weather; and partly because families move out and live in the bush in the winter," said Eileen, who spent much of the year on the land in Lac Rendezvous, east of the Anderson River. Tuk wasn't a dirty place, but it was impossible for it to be well-kept with winter booting its rib cage eight months out of the year. Some stretches of it appeared the way Toronto does after a spring thaw: fists of cigarette butts, piles of cans, juice boxes and other garbage tossed as if caught in one of those "Ah, no one will see it under the snow" lapses. Last year, record winds of 127 kilometres per hour had nearly blown two structures down, one of which—a large blue shed where the CAT used to clear the dump was housed—was bashed in at a 45-degree angle. When I asked about the town dump, Eileen nodded her head. "We call this our Walmart," she said, although whether she was being funny or not, I wasn't sure.

Since there were no trees to frame the ocean—or frame anything—Tuk had a sense of openness and space, and because the buildings were squat and the population small—just over eight hundred in 2017—you could see the whole of the town wherever you were standing, peering into it like a child at a diorama. The air was redolent with the salty perfume of the sea mixed with bug dope, tobacco, diesel, and drip coffee, pots of which were brewed most hours of the day, partly because Tuk was a dry town, and partly because coffee is a perpetual warming agent. There was another smell I couldn't quite identify. It was smoky, but not quite forest-fire smoky; more like a summer BBQ grill after being used, even though I saw no BBQs and there were no restaurants in town.

Tuk was surrounded in all directions by the sea. It flooded every view, and sometimes just flooded, the edges of the shore soaked in great pools that would have produced impressive marshland were anything allowed to grow (flooding was the reason Tuk didn't sustain a larger, more active airport). Sandhill cranes stood like little white toothpicks along the edges of the water, which shimmered a little when the sun was out, but was slate grey when it was not, darkened further by the silt expunged from the Mackenzie River.

Unlike the Maritimes with its high-cliffed Atlantic grandeur, or north-western British Columbia, with its verdant Pacificana, Tuk's geography possessed its own drama in that its size and proximity against the vastness of the ocean made it seem as if it might be swallowed at any minute (this year, they'd lost eight feet of beachfront during a three-day storm). With the peninsula stretching out like the long sleeve of a sweater holed by moths, you wondered whether another gap would be enough to irrevoca-bly weaken the land mass, a condition accelerated by sea levels that were increased because of melting ice floes and severe global warming. Local government had enforced some areas as no-build zones and there had been plans discussed about moving the settlement farther inland.

Eileen pointed out that "at one point, it was thought that the place would just erode and erode until nothing was left, being so close to the sea and all. But, as you can see, this hasn't happened. Yet." Knowing this, it was hard not to see Tuk as yet another disappearing thing swallowed by a bigger thing whose condition had changed because of what we'd done to it.

It wasn't until we were on the other side of town close to the James Gruben Airport—this took no more than five minutes—that I realized I had yet to see any people. When I voiced this to Eileen, she said, "Everyone's at home, dabbing." At first I thought she was referring to some kind of awful drug use that had consumed the place, but she said, "Bingo night. Everyone plays." I asked her where the hall was, but she told me: "No, at home." I must have looked confused, because she continued: "The TV shows the bingo and everyone stays in and plays. They dab," she said, pre-tending to stamp a pad on her lap. I asked if it was a local station that aired this show, but she said, "No. CBC. It is very popular. We also get the satellite TV; all things. I watch the Blue Jays, even in the bush." I pointed to my baseball hat hoping to re-establish the credibility I'd lost with my girlish band pins, but she continued: "Bautista. Encarnacion. I miss the other one, Johnny Mac." She said they'd won that afternoon, and we kept talking baseball while winding through town. A few months after coming home from the Northwest Territories, I was a guest on the Blue Jays' radio broadcast, and told Eileen's story, only to receive an email from a few people who knew her and Billy from their time researching the Eskimo curlew, which had vanished after numbering in the millions (Billy claimed to have been the last person to see one, in the mid-1980s). One fellow, Joachim Obst, wrote to say that "years before Eileen (and her husband, Billy) ever had a satellite phone or big screen at their remote camp, they listened to the bush radio station (SBX 11) and got the news about the Blue Jays from hunters and trappers talking on the waves." Another friend, Bob Bromley, noted how "SBX would help pass news, weather, aircraft charters, and loving messages from family members. It was listened to by everyone, especially residents in communities who wanted to hear news from the land, and between communities."

Eileen and I arrived at the airport to wait for the tourists: twelve of them coming by Twin Otter from Inuvik to spend a few hours in Tuk. The terminal was small, dark, and empty. Eileen went over to a plywood wall and turned on the lights. The baggage ramp was nothing more than a naked set of steel rollers with a pile of old *Inuvik Drum* newspapers stacked at the end, and when the phone rang at the lone, unmanned check-in counter, Eileen went over and answered it: "No, no, not here yet." The ribs of an old kayak hung against one wall and a set of yellowing black and white photos of Inuvialuit elders hung on another. There were a few rows of blue bucket plastic chairs, and Eileen and I each sat in one, looking out at the runway on the other side of the window to see if anything had landed (nothing had; planes were often delayed because of the unpredictable weather and low ceiling). I asked her about the complications of dragging a satellite television into the bush and she said, "No problem. My son hooked it up. Internet, too!" While completely debunking my idea of roughing it—in fact, making the idea of roughing it seem far more palatable—I wondered about Eileen's routine in the bush, and she told me, "We spend about eight months there: hunting, trapping. We shoot snow geese, tundra swans, ducks. We hunt muskoxen, caribou, wolverines, foxes. No problem. I've been doing this for long time, since I was a girl." It seemed like good times: slaying beasts, then watching a twi-nighter from Fenway Park. I told her this, but Eileen harrumphed. "No, we shoot geese during baseball season, but the rest is wintertime. Which is hockey season," she said, explaining to the doofus from Toronto that hockey was played in the winter.

The tourists finally arrived—a dozen tablet-waving sixty-somethings from the United States and Canada—and together we headed for a closer view of the town, which was our first lesson: "Tuk is not a town, village, or city. It is considered a hamlet," said Eileen. I liked the idea of that, and, looking around, it made sense. Tuk was hamletesque in that it was nestled—not *tucked*, because that would just be a terrible pun—on a bar of windswept land. Pointing at the water through the window of the van, Eileen said, "We call this both the Arctic Ocean and the Beaufort Sea," treating the note less with pride than with the fatigue of a tour operator having to explain it.

As well as having a clear eye line to the water and beaches with wind-rows of driftwood scattered about—the product of the Mackenzie's spring breakup—Tuk possessed other satisfying natural features. One of these was nature's enormous carbuncle, the pingo (*ibyuk* in Inuvialuktun), which sat like a set of large grassy soufflés around the peninsula and proved no end of fun to say. Pingos are created when lakes attempt to drain through the permafrost and are, instead, pushed up from the earth, having over-grown their old beds. Even more distinctly, some pingos had divots at their peak, as if a great-booted giant had stamped on the hill, only to get his foot stuck before pulling it out. These hills sat in the distance like mossy, decommissioned UFOs (one of the guidebooks called them "brown ice volcanoes," which proved too scatological for me) and were a further reminder that the profile of the North as a single thing—white, empty, uniform—has been drawn by those who never spent time here. The modesty and quiet of Tuk made the presence of the enormous pingos seem even more profound, leading one to imagine them coming unscrewed from the dirt and spinning away before landing among their own kind in an ancestral hillside or mountain range.

Another thing that made Tuk beyond the average seaside hamlet or ocean cove was a second alien presence: the Distant Early Warning station, or DEW line. Long empty of engineers—it has since been replaced by automation and the Northern Warning System radar—the station had been built by NORAD during the Cold War to warn North Americans of Russian planes coming over the top to invade. When Metallica played here in 1994 as part of a Molsons' beer promotional operation for a long-forgotten ice beer, drummer Lars Ulrich said that the best thing about the DEW line was that "Russia will bomb here first instead of New York or LA," which was one way of looking at it. Construction started on the large metallic apparatus in 1955 without any local consultation. In 1957, the operation brought teams of European and American scientists to Tuk, and that's how come Eileen ended up with two sets of German cousins. The DEW station was an odd and wonderful thing to find in Tuk, not only because it made one want to air-synth Geddy Lee's keyboard lines in the Rush song of the same name, but because it was the last thing you'd expect to find in a place so distant and wild.

The DEW line consisted of three towers—one tall and two squat—each with canvased white geodesic domes at the top. It sat on a modest promontory over the settlement. Trying to be polite, Eileen said that she thought they looked like giant soccer balls on sticks, but what they really looked like were what my wife would have called, observing delicacy in the presence of children, "man parts," right there on a hill overlooking the city. Since there wasn't a ton of things to do in town—there were, basically, two stores (the Northern Store as well as the independently owned, and new, Stanton's Inuk grocery store) and no shops, hotels, or cafés—I drew no endless source of joy turning from looking at the pingos on one side of the cove to the DEW line on the other. Many travellers come north to gaze upon forests, mountains, rivers, and lakes, but we rarely spend time taking in the grandiose relics of Cold War paranoia, its swollen balls laid against the permafrost and its massive rod pointing to the sky.

Eileen drove her van and spoke to us on a headset. The summer had been moderately warm, so far, although Eileen groused about a few weekends past where temperatures had climbed to 21 degrees Celsius: "Too hot," she said, pretending to cool down with a wave. Despite the relatively fine weather, I noticed people in town walking around hoodied, with their hands in their pouches, and it wasn't until I climbed outside the van during a stop at Eileen's house that I realized they weren't affecting a northern gangsta look, but instead protecting themselves from mosquitoes as big as bobby pins that seemed determined to suck all the blood out of anything that moved. We scurried into her nice home and she announced to the group that we were going to put our feet in the Arctic Ocean. "Only our feet?" I said, guessing that a hint of male genitalia wouldn't be too shocking in a town where a giant cock and balls lorded over it. Eileen sighed and said: "Well, we used to let people skinny dip. But we did it in front of the old folks' home and they had to stop. Too much excitement."

Before ending the tour, we came across a pond where kids were riding snow machines—"snowmobiles" to you and me—through the shallows. They roared from the banks one after another, skidding and bouncing through the muck and whooping as if they were part of a strange helmeted rodeo, exactly the kind of thing you'd find in a make-your-own-fun town, and a place where a lot of people couldn't wait for winter to begin so that they could ride snowmobiles. "We call this 'skipping,'" said Eileen, as one machine came to rest in front of us, revealing a young man driving, and another person behind him: a boy who couldn't have been more than five. Their faces were streaked with black gunk as they looked at us—goose-white tourists sitting in the van brandishing cameras—with a kind of hard-earned look that said: "You realize you'll never do anything as fun as this, right?" The older kid popped a smoke in his mouth and passed the infant a bag of Doritos. They sat on the machine eating and smoking as Eileen tugged at the wheel, turning the van away.

We returned the elderly tourists to the airport, and then Eileen brought me to my accommodations: the Tuktu B&B on Mangilaluk Road. There were caribou antlers above the door frame and, inside, three windows pointing to the sea. When we walked into the small main-floor kitchen, we both shivered: the last people to stay there had left the windows open. But it was okay. Rebecca arrived a few moments later with her two kids: Edward, who wore a Blackhawks cap and a Superhero hoodie, and Isabel, her younger daughter. The place was outfitted with three bedrooms upstairs, a tall electric heater that we discovered in a closet, a large satellite TV and Wi-Fi. After seeing the big screen, I experienced one of those guilty travellers' moments where I felt compelled to click nostalgically through the remote looking for something to remind me of home. I decided that a quick look wouldn't compromise my sense of awayness, so I flicked on the set and came upon channel 725 and a commercial for CBC's broadcast of the Pan Am Games. Feeling guilty, I turned the set off and rushed to the window, where I saw a single fishing boat purring across the water, its captain holding a rifle. I called to Rebecca, who was coaxing Isabel into her dirt-caked truck, and asked her why the fellow in the boat was carrying a gun. "Oe," she said, bundling the little girl under her arm. "First, you harpoon the whale. And then you shoot it through the head."

THE VULCAN APPETIZER

The creation myth of the Inuvialuit (or "Siglit," as they were known by Europeans in the nineteenth century) is a Noah story that predates Christianity. It starts with a hunter living on a pingo overlooking Tuk before it was Tuk. He had a wife and a son and they shared their home with an orphan girl. One day, the hunter headed out on the land to check his traps, only to find a sealskin bag filled with water. The bag grew bigger and bigger, and when he told his neighbours about it, they laughed and mocked him. He decided to build a raft and a cabin in case the bag burst, which it did, water pouring out of it for months on end. The land was flooded and the man's neighbours died miserably and, soon, even the pingo was set adrift on the water. The family floated on the raft until, one day, the boy—who was the spirit of a raven (or, simply, "Raven,")—paddled until he discovered a small island: the top of the lost pingo. He harpooned the pingo and pulled it out of the water like a bathtub plug. The waters drained, the family hauled the pingo back to its original home, and the land was suddenly rich with lakes and rivers and fish. The boy married the orphan girl and they had many children. These children end up becoming the Inuvialuit.

Eileen Jacobson's lineage was Kittegaryumiut Inuit, although she told me that "the last of the true Inuvialuit died years ago," with everyone having assimilated with someone else. Inuit—the most widespread

Indigenous people on Earth—had originally gathered in great numbers in the Western Arctic (as opposed to the East) because of the bounty of the region, with longer sustained warmth and ice-free seas, providing better fishing and a greater food supply (to say nothing of copious amounts of driftwood allowing access to wood in a place bereft of timber). There were, and are, twenty different species of fish—char, burbot, inconnu (the "she fish"), lake trout, cisco, and whitefish among them—in ocean and lake waters as well as every manner of northern game, from polar bears to wolves to caribou. It's hard to imagine a place with such marauding winters being favourable to dwellers, but, relative to the rest of the North, the West was less challenging by degrees, and, in this environment, Inuvialuit culture and society burst to life.

The early Inuvialuit lived in sod houses, a model of which had been assembled near the point. They called this construct an *igluyuaryuk*, and entire families resided in it, guarded comfortably from the hellish winds and cold winter (the explorer Vilhjalmur Stefansson, who lived in the Western Arctic, suggested that wintertime temperatures inside were between 24 and 29 degrees Celsius, the building ventilated by a small hole in the roof). Inuvialuit families believed that children were the reincarnation of lost relatives, and in some instances, kids were named after grandparents, leading to a bewilderment among early-visiting Europeans after hearing toddlers being called "mother" or "father" by their parents. In the excellent book, *Across Time and Tundra* (written by Ishmael Alunik, Eddie D. Kolausok, and David Morrison), the authors talk about how kids were rarely, if ever, struck "because it could damage their souls . . . and there was strong prohibition against scolding." They also suggest that "it was better to risk letting a child play with a sharp knife . . . rather than damage his soul—and offend his namesake—by [chastising them]." This attitude would have proven handy after that time I was caught by the cops smoking hash in Dave Crosby's parents' Pacer while on our way to the Albion Mall. Still, not having to kill enormous beasts for food was a trade-off I was willing to accept.

Like most other buildings in Tuk, the model sod house had been compromised by the weather. Its protective pickets were bent like a set of wrecked teeth and its walls leaned together like bodies in a football huddle. Instead of symbolizing the indefatigable spirit and invention of the North, the condition of the building mirrored the fact that part of living here was about allowing yourself to be knocked about by the elements, surviving winter, rather than conquering it. That the sod house sat on the point greeting new arrivals to town was, I thought, no accident.

Inuvialuit culture had had a fine hold over most of the greater Arctic until recent times, when, suddenly, the East rose while the West stayed the same or weakened, its people having moved from hunting and gathering and trading into a wage-based economy with the advent of the DEW line and other construction projects. This brought expected complications: traditions lost to the modern world; behaviour affected by diet, money, and vice; and an unstable economic climate. These days, when people think of the ribbon of land across the top of Canada, they mostly think of Nunavut, the Eastern Arctic's foothold, even though it suffers from the same changing nature. The East gained independence and a national profile with a televised birth-of-a-nation ceremony; grew more accessible through daily flights from Ottawa; and was defined by the stories of popular folk heroes like Jordin and Hunter Tootoo. Before visiting the Northwest Territories, I'd been flown twice to Iqaluit on tourist trips with the purposes of writing about the place, and I knew more musicians who'd played there than anywhere in the Northwest Territories. Since the federal government hadn't flooded the West with jobs the way it had in the new territory, the region remained neglected, and rather than the pages of its history flying open, the story of the Inuvialuit had been nearly waxed shut. Such was the extent of written material about the place that, in the Toronto Reference Library, there was one book about the Western Arctic for every five books about Nunavut. The region was to the rest of the greater Arctic what the Northwest Territories was to the Yukon, which was what Yellowknife was to Whitehorse.

I thought about this while settling on the landing outside the Tuktu. My meditation was broken, however, once a truck appeared rumbling across the muddy road until its grille kissed the tip of my boots. Rebecca leaned out the window: "How ya doon?" I told her that I was fine. Isabel and Edward were with her, and so was her husband, Robin, a quiet young man in a Blackhawks hat who spoke after a second's thought in a measured hoser drawl like a 33 RPM record with a nickel on the tone arm. The truck was strewn about with various pieces of all-weather ensemble and a deck of open-topped smokes on the dash. We rumbled across a pothole-bitten road to a spot along the shore where Rebecca and Robin needed to check their fishing nets, which they'd put into the water the night before. If the shoreline near my lodging was wide and empty, this one, on the opposite side of the peninsula, fell in scuppered cliffs to the sea. It was different in another way: there were people here.

(At this point, I think I should pause to ask if you like Raffi. I should also ask if you *are* Raffi, and if you are: Hello, Raffi! Since you wrote the popular and sensitive song "Baby Beluga"——which, let's face it, has been haunting parents for the last forty years or so; I mean, it's a good song, but no melody repeated twenty-seven times over an infant's mewling can sustain itself; okay maybe "God Only Knows" by the Beach Boys, but that's about it——I feel compelled to tell you that next few chapters may be difficult for you to read because they're about the evisceration of beluga whales for the purposes of survival in inhospitable climates. The whales get speared and shot, and I'm sure they feel pain and may even scream out. That they're known colloquially as "sea canaries" probably doesn't help. Still, it's the way it is, and if it bothers you——not just you, Raffi, but your fans, your *Raffi-a-lites*——you might want to skip ahead a few chapters to where I describe what it was like to dance in my bare feet on the sloped sand of Frame Lake in the aftermath of the Folk on the Rocks music festival at four in the morning and the only thing that got eviscerated was my consciousness. Why don't I meet you guys over there in a little bit?)

If other hamlets had town squares or cafés or diners where locals gathered, Tuk had whaling camps on the edges of the sea. Here, families came to strip, clean, cut, wash, boil, cook, and dry beluga meat from whales they'd harpooned and shot the day before (mostly males; the Inuvialuit left alone pregnant mothers or mothers swimming with their black-skinned calves). I scuffled down the banks and came upon a wooden rack hanging with a quilt of beluga meat—milky white hunks with pink insides—and, beyond that, a large, sunglassed woman brandishing an *ulu*—the traditional half-mooned blade—used to slice enormous strips that she slung over her shoulder like a wrestling belt before pitching it to wash in the surf (traditionally, Inuvialuit women did all the cleaning, dressing, and cooking of game, a fact that was confirmed after I noticed most of the men plunked on their asses listening to CBC North on the radio). At her wooden table was a large hillock of meat—a deep bloody purple—which she used to make *mipku* (a kind of beluga jerky) in one of the hamlet's makeshift smokehouses. The smokehouses accounted for the BBQ scent I'd sniffed on arrival. There were dozens of them around Tuk—small, nailed-together structures with pipes hanging over flame-burning stoves built with beach driftwood—and locals tended to them like Russians to their dachas or the English to their gardens. Once I identified them, it was all I could smell; smoked whale meat being the abundant, delicious aroma of the hamlet, and the one that returned to me whenever I remembered my time here.

Rebecca introduced me to the nearest family. My presence was met with a kind of choral shrug that suggested that whatever I was doing wasn't half as interesting as what they were doing (they were right). After a moment, the clan's matriarch—a pipe cleaner of a woman, sunglassed in a kerchief, slacks, and yellow Crocs—took me in her cool hand and walked me to a drop sheet where a square of warm muktuk had been pulled from a black pot burbling over a small fire. "Ever had it warm?" she asked in an old person's croak that sounded like a cabin door being opened. I told her I hadn't, and so she kneeled down—the kneeling took a while—reached for the nearest long knife blade, and sawed at the meat, cubing it for me to sample. "Now," she told me, her face growing severe, "eat it all of it." Everybody laughed because it's what people do when they get to make fun of whale-eating writers from Toronto who wear little girl band pins on their denim jackets. But the joke was on them. I noticed a cap-encrusted bottle of HP sauce lying on the sheet, and so I splurtched it across the translucent white meat, making the warm, just-oceaned muktuk taste and look like a strange kind of Vulcan appetizer. I devoured it all.

The Inuvialuit use almost all of the whale. They kept its round white melon skull as a ball and used its stomach as a bag, "to carry around knuckleberries [a.k.a. salmonberries] and things," Eileen told me. Muktuk was an exceptional source of vitamin C, important to northern dwellers who spent parts of the year in near darkness, and since the animals yielded so much meat, it helped sustain families across long winters. When they were done taking apart the carcass, families slipped the unused meat into the water, feeding the rest of the sea life to keep the circle turning.

We marched farther down the shore until we came to Rebecca and Robin's fishing line. They climbed up on their truck's flatbed, embraced two blood-caked tubs in their arms, and hopped down, carrying them to the edge of the waves. "Now, we're gonna show you how we net the fish," said Rebecca, a smoke plugged in her upper lip as she bent to pull in the line. Together, she and Robin tugged the line out of the water—parts of it had been mended using sinew harvested from belugas—and, suddenly, sparking silver and gold fish appeared entangled in the mesh, one white-fish after another, about twenty in total, with the occasional inconnu. Robin grabbed one around the belly and said, "Hmmm, a little soft," its lack of density owing to the time spent in the water, a little longer than was ideal (about eighteen hours). The next one, though, was fat and taut, and Rebecca pitched it into the tub. After doing this a few times, she called Edward over and told him to find a rock. He did and she pointed to the crest of the fish's skull. Edward brought the rock over his head and then cracked it down on the fish. He didn't do it in the kind of zealous—or ominous—way one would have imagined a young Charles Manson doing it, but, rather, he was careful and officious, getting it done in a manner that, I sensed, made Mum and Dad proud.

Once the entire catch was tubbed, we drove to the Pokiaks' smokehouse, which stood in front of a large open sled-dog pen. I wanted to look at my phone for the time, but resisted. It was almost more fun not knowing or caring. Besides, it could have been morning, afternoon, or evening, partly because of the everlasting daylight and partly because I was detached from any kind of schedule. The measurement of time passing seemed frivolous in a settlement that had been undiscovered for so long that no one knew how old it was, although some estimated the first people arriving about twenty thousand years ago. What Robin and Rebecca were about to do—ritualistically clean their catch beside a traditional smokehouse within view of the water from which the fish had only just been pulled— was an ancient task, and if I'd been to wild Africa, eternal China, and old Europe before, here I sensed a whole other meter of age based on land, sea, and sky, as opposed to the things men had built around it.

After putting two fish on a table below some tarp used to blunt the wind, Robin turned to me and said, "Now we're gonna show you how we cut the fish." Rebecca said she was tired, so she took the kids to buy Pepsis while I sat and took notes: how, despite a forest of insects beehiving around him, Robin worked away at the catch, eloquently gouging out a hunk at the bottom to remove the eggs, then cutting underneath the tail. Next, he ran the edge of the blade along the spine, butterflying the meat in two pink halves and making cuts with space between each chunk so that they would dry in perfect fingers that, after being smoked, you could hold and crack in half, leaving the skin as wallpaper on the plate.

Rebecca and her daughter were leaving at the end of August for school in Whitehorse. They'd all gone down the year before, but Robin found the city and experience wanting, making him the truest Territorian of the bunch. "Too far from the land," he told me while cutting and butterflying. "Lots to do, but not what I want to do," he said. This year, Edward would stay with him at home so he could continue to go out on caribou, muskox, wolf, and fox hunts, to say nothing of a pursuit of the scavenging and villainous wolverine, in a way the most terrifying and nefarious of all northern beasts. "They're sneaky and intelligent," said Robin. "What they do is climb into trees and, when the caribou pass under, they jump him and tear it apart from above."

"They're like the heel that everybody hates who waits until the other wrestler has his back turned before they attack," I said.

Robin smiled for the first time—his moustache fanning out like two dark wings across his face—and if I'd thought a reference to Ric Flair would have broken the ice, I would have played it earlier.

"So," said Robin. "You're from Toronto?"

"I am, yeah. Ever been?"

"Yeah, once. I was there."

"What were you doing there?"

"I was performing," he said, his eyes trained on the fish.

"Performing what?"

"Fiddle," he said.

"What kind of show was it?" I asked.

"It was called Strings across the Skies. It was a contest for fiddlers, and we won, a bunch of us, from Tuk. I was eighteen. We played at Roy Thomson Hall."

"Really?" I asked, although I shouldn't have.

"Yes, really," he said, laughing, and letting me off the hook.

"What was that like?"

"It was fun, man. I was eighteen, and the drinking age was nineteen. But still we got some drinks in us."

"I've never played Roy Thomson Hall," I told him.

"I also played on the Orkney Islands."

"Man, I've never played there either," I said, although whether-I'd-played-there-or-not was not the way I meant to judge his adventures.

"We were supposed to go to New Zealand, too. Never happened."

"Man, that's too bad," I said, forgetting to mention that I also hadn't played there.

"Well. I dunno. Something happened. We didn't go."

"Yeah," I said.

"Yeah," he replied.

In Tuk it was easy to think of people as remote and disconnected and floating near the top of the Earth, and while that was geographically true, travel is everybody's business, and so is art, and that's how come the spare-worded Robin got to play shows on a set of small islands off the Scottish coast, and other places, too. Before coming here, I felt grateful being able to live in a busy city full of life and energy while occasionally jetting to the wilds of the North, but it was purely southern, classist, economic-bracket bias that allowed me to think that it couldn't happen the other way: men and women who live in the North getting on a plane for a taste of the other world, living on the land and in nature before dropping in on malls, restaurants, Blue Jays games, streetcars, MDMA, and record shops. As Robin hung the last of his fish, I tried to decide which was better, but thought better of it. From down the road, small Isabel darted toward us, the wings of her bright yellow jacket waving as she moved. "Daddy please!" she shouted coming forward before finally settling at Robin's side, where he flicked the knife into one of the fish, gouged out a nest of eggs drooling in fat and blood, and held them like a tangle of grapes above the young girl, who opened her smiling yap and swallowed the moist whole of the bounty.

26

THE END OF AWAY

The following morning, I rode with the polar bear hunter. I imagined—and hoped for—a bearded northern Zeus arriving on a sled pulled by stags wearing a vest made of oxen wool and an antlered head dress, but James Pokiak drove a Ford F350 and wore a hat from Disneyland. He was also smaller and more compact than I might have thought, with friendly eyes and a thin moustache, sitting low behind the wheel as if the hulking truck were driving him.

Because we had only part of a day together, I immediately turned on my tape recorder and asked the polar bear hunter, who'd just turned sixty-one, if he might start by regaling me with a few harrowing tales of stalking the great northern beast, of which two-thirds of the world's population lived in Canada. "Well," he said, looking over as if, perhaps, measuring my ability to stomach what he was about to say, "polar bears are, you know, pretty shy." It was the equivalent of Darth Vader tittering through his face shield: "Jedis? I dunno. I think they're kind of cute." Maybe sensing my disappointment, James continued: "Well, there was danger a few of the times, sure. But, you know, nothing we couldn't get out of."

"You make it sound like anyone could do it, even me," I told him, waiting to see if he might pull the car over to hold his side while laughing.

"It's true that I had to take down a few bears at the tent after they'd gotten close to our camp," he said, "and it was pretty scary. But the adrenalin rush pushes you, and you do what you have to do. Still, polar bears are not as aggressive as grizzlies and they're usually pretty timid," he continued, the softness of his voice making the beasts—and the idea of taking them— seem as benign as picking up a hamster from the carpet.

James Pokiak's view of the polar bear was shared by others who'd lived among them. Nineteenth-century naturalist Robert Brown once wrote that "the impressions which we have imbibed regarding the polar bear's ferocity are due more to old notions of what it ought to be rather than what it is," and the fact that, according to *Arctic Dreams* author Barry Lopez, "the same bear that [can] knock a beluga whale senseless with a blow . . . can also pry tiny thalia from a kelp strand with a single claw," belied one's impression of the *Ursus maritimus* as simply a marauding beast. If Inuvialuit culture viewed the hulking bear—average weight six hundred pounds—as a solitary and wan figure adrift in a kind of lonely, white reverie, Western mythology painted the picture of a much more terrifying and murderous creature. In his book, Lopez recounts a journey into a bear den by one of explorer Gerrit de Veer's men, who found the place "fearful to behold," with, according to Lopez, "hoar-frosted hairs dangling from its ceiling and ice-covered, claw-scraped walls."

Among early European visitors, stories were passed around of fresh graves torn open by bears and a nocturnal stalking by the animals across ice camps, where bodies were devoured. This resulted in a period in which explorers shot any bear on sight, no matter how far from the ship. Lopez wrote that, "in November, 1876, Sir Allen Young [killed] a young female from the deck of his steamship. He lassoed one of her cubs as a gift for the Prince of Wales. The female was butchered and the cub wrapped in her skin in the hopes of appeasing him. Three or four days later the cub succeeded in tearing free of the ringbolts. He was then placed in a small cage, where he remained for the duration of the voyage. The cub roared for hours on end . . . and was tormented by the ship's dog, who stole his food and bit his paws. By the time the ship reached England, the cub lay prostrate in his cage, convulsing and panting. He died almost a week later."

Polar bears have been ascribed the same characteristics as other bears—brown, black, grizzly—but they're remarkably distinct in personality and nature: long-nosed (and -necked) instead of flat-faced; narrow-shouldered instead of broad-framed; and territorial for only as long as they stay on an ice floe (in the beginning, they weren't even classified as the same species). Such is their duplicitous and singular nature that conferences and symposia have been held to study the great mammal, most recently as they relate to climate change and the protectionist agenda of governments. James knew these events first-hand, having travelled the world—Switzerland, Germany, Hungary—to speak at them, but his political and environmental focus had morphed because of recent American sanctions preventing the import of pelts from Canada and elsewhere.

"You shoot a bear up north," he told me, "and there's no point unless a tourist can bring it home as a trophy. This is a real problem and we're trying to get our government to address the issue, because it used to be a good way of employment before. Now, there's less and less. People aren't coming the way they used to and they're going to other places to shoot for sport. When the Americans listed the polar bear as endangered, there was an over-harvest elsewhere, and so people thought we were up here slaughtering them. But we'd never do that. We need the polar bear. They are important to people in the North."

In the opinion of Daphne Maxwell and Clementine Berger, two environmentalists I'd met while at the Grey Goose in Deline, "Misinformation has been the result of the northern media talking to itself and the southern media ignoring the northern media. What gets lost is the fact that the people who are harvesting bears are being demonized even though no one pays more attention to the bears than them. They're caring for the animals, in a way." This reminded me of something James said: "As hunters and anglers, we have to be environ-mentalists. We have to respect wildlife, and in Tuk we co-manage all of the species—we have co-management boards, too—so if anyone knows what's up, we do."

Clementine suggested that "when it comes to endangered species, the things that drive decisions come from politicians wanting to leave a legacy. What makes the issue of the polar bear more complex is that they live off-shore and, because they do, multiple countries manage the species, so you get public figures trying to make their mark above the others. There are things happening beyond the polar bear other than being simply affected by climate change. Populations are increasing because of more cracks in the ice, which means more seals, which means more bears in communities causing problems. It's difficult messaging to an audience in the south that isn't even close to ground zero. All they hear is 'Climate change is bad, save the polar bears.' Unless you understand the link between bears and Indigenous people, you can't start to make an argument. Some governments, it seems, would rather trust the word of scientists than learn traditional knowledge."

If details on the bears' survival had been wrongly documented, recent media reports from Norway didn't help, including sensational stories about how polar bears were turning to dolphins as a food source, the result of the aquatic sea mammal swimming in warmer waters. This news only heightened the U.S.A.'s call for a worldwide ban on harvesting.

"Because the U.S.A. listed the polar bear as endangered, trophy hunting in the North was almost shut down," said Daphne. "The Americans claimed that our tags for export were too easy to produce, but while Canada actually manages the hunt, the Russians couldn't care less. There's more poaching in Russia and in a place like Norway, where there are no Indigenous people who overlap where the harvest is. Our job," she said, "is to get people off the idea that making polar bears endangered will work toward helping climate change. People think they're saving the planet by protecting the polar bear. But it's just not true." This echoed something else that James Pokiak said: "The threat to the polar bear comes from climate change, not from hunters."

The decline of, and threat to, the polar bear trade was ill-timed considering that something was about to happen that would finally open up the hamlet to visitors, many of them prospective hunters: the first permanent all-weather road into Tuk and a de facto completion of the Trans-Canada Highway in 2017. People in town mentioned "the road" more times than at a Cormac McCarthy book club. It was a remarkable development in a region—the North—that had seen many recent and unprecedented developments after centuries of relative stasis: renewed oil exploration, the birth of Nunavut, the push for Arctic sovereignty, the effort to discover whatever remained of the Franklin expedition, and a general rise in the nation's consciousness about the land mass that stretched above them. The all-weather road—120 kilometres long and costing roughly three hundred million dollars (mostly federal)—would allow a generation to do that which their ancestors never could: escape.

The road was also positioned by some as welcome relief from the absurd costs of air and boat travel—a round trip cost four hundred dollars for an eight-minute flight from Inuvik—as well as the risk of navigating a thirty-five-kilometre winter ice road, which took two hours to drive and where a speeding ticket was eight hundred dollars, to say nothing of how much more perilous it had become with global warming messing with its seasonal durability. The new road linked Tuk to Inuvik—some feared the former end of the Dempster Highway would become nothing but a glorified gas stop for people heading to the Arctic Ocean—but it would also sew Tuk into the rest of Canada and the world. Year-round ground transportation meant a constant flow of supplies to town and access to a demographic of tourists who didn't have to save for a lifetime to afford the airfare required to get there.

The construction of the road happened exclusively in the winter, allowing trucks to carry forty-ton loads across the ice. Special geotextiles were developed to protect the permafrost with an eye to how the land might change—or, rather, melt—with rising temperatures, a condition exacerbated by warm run-off in the early summer. According to a piece written by Chris Windeyer for the *Edge YK*, "At one of the sites, crews [plan to] install plastic culverts instead of metal ones. [It] may not sound like exciting science, but the idea is to reduce the amount of heat that gets into the roadbed [using the same kind of] corrugated metal used in traditional culverts. At another site, scientists from the University of Manitoba will build an embankment with layers of gravel and geotextiles. The whole thing will be laced with sensors to study how much the surrounding soil moves."

A report prepared by the N.W.T. government for the region suggested that the road would increase tourism spending by $2.7 million a year, an extravagant number considering that it cost no more than $70 a month for the unemployed and the elderly to rent their subsidized homes, and the average personal income was just over $35,000 a year. Merv Gruben, the former mayor of the hamlet and one of the main champions of the road, told the *Globe and Mail*, "We need the hotels, we need the RV parks, we need the garages. We have to expand our schools and our health centres. Tuk's never going to be the same again. A lot of people will be moving here." Merv reinforced his point over the phone, telling me, emphatically: "The road will let people see parts of their land they've never seen before. Just after we started putting it in, I took some elders for a drive out there and they wept, having set eyes on places they'd never been able to see before."

In the polar bear hunter's eyes, the road would make it easier to get into the community, "but it will be easier to get out, too," he said. "It works both ways, you know."

I asked him if he was worried that people would be inclined to leave Tuk forever, but James said, "No. Even if people leave, they will always come back. Right now, we're stuck and it's too expensive for most people to fly. With the road put in, a family of five or six can travel a lot easier. Besides, there are lots of young people sitting around doing nothing for themselves, and there's a whole world out there. When the road opens, it will give them motivation, but it will also show them how lucky we are to jump on a snow machine. They'll also appreciate what it's like to be here. That's my hope, anyway."

"So you're not worried that they'll go to the cities and want to stay?" I asked.

The polar bear hunter laughed gently.

"Why would you want to do that? It's so much harder to find places to hunt and fish down there."

When James spoke about the road—its impact after years of isolation— he gathered his thoughts as if arranging a set of puzzle pieces. "The road will bring a whole new set of opportunities," he reasoned. "But I'm concerned with how close it is to the Husky Lakes [a.k.a. Eskimo Lakes]. There's good fishing there and I'm worried about how it might affect the quality of the water. A long time ago an oil company wanted to come in here and build a road and we said no. But times have changed. People seem more willing to try it."

Doug Matthews, an energy writer long involved in northern issues who was living in Tuk with the purposes of readying the town for the opening of the road, said: "The highway will present a large psychological challenge and the hamlet has to be prepared for it. Right now, for instance, our office closes at 2 p.m. on Fridays, but with the opening of the road, people will be able to come into town any time they want. We're putting together funding for programs that will help prepare people for this. We're talking to elders, priests, students, alerting them to the enormous changes that are about to come." I asked Doug if there was a fear that it would be a little like inviting people into your house only to become aware of all its shortcomings. "Yes," he said. "People have been living here naturally, isolated from everything else, and, suddenly, there will be strangers coming to look, lots and lots of them. The trick is to make people feel less self-conscious or worried about the appearance of the place, yet at the same time be careful that it doesn't look too weathered or ragged. I mean, we've got all of these old fuel tanks every-where. Nobody ever thought anything of them before, but, frankly, it's a good reason to paint the fucking things."

Doug shared in the romantic notion that the road would, finally, connect all three oceans—Pacific, Atlantic, and Arctic—and he felt great symbolism in the fact that it would harmonize with Canada's sesquicentennial. "It's the equivalent of a modern-day Last Spike," he said. "It's the final tie between the people up here and the rest of the country. I think that's reason enough to celebrate it and give it focus, as opposed to simply dwelling on how the town will change. It's also sym-bolic that the road, itself, is being built by two Inuvialuit companies—E. Gruben's Transport and Northwind Industries—and the planning is all being done locally. This is a northern effort. It's not as if people are being airlifted in and outsiders are telling everyone what to do. There's an entrepreneurial crowd here, always has been. The skills that made the Inuvialuit self-sustaining traders and hunters can be applied, and the fact that the community has been around as long as it has bodes well for whatever changes the road presents."

The other change—or potential change—that loomed on the hori-zon was greater oil and gas exploration. Locals had seen this movie before, based on a dalliance between heavy industry and the almost chimeric—some would say cursed—prospect of bountiful natural resources. Imperial Oil was the first to discover oil in 1970 in the waters of Tuk Harbour, kickstarting the Beaufort Sea exploration programs of the 1970s and 1980s, with Dome Petroleum, Gulf Canada Resources, and Esso Resources all operating from the harbour and its shore-based facilities. The town benefited, if modestly, from municipal infrastruc-ture, a few new roads, improved waste management sites, and an extended airstrip, but collapsing world oil prices in the mid-1980s and the cancellation of the National Energy Program stopped any further work in the region. Companies pulled out, leaving the casks of old equipment and off-shore stems that you could see from the shoreline, and, in the end, all the promises—no matter how divisive or conflicted within the community—were just that. Author Kenneth Coates called it "a northern vision gone sour," although the windscreen was always too muddy to know what lay at the end of the road.

Still, interest renewed in the area in the mid-2000s, and over the past ten years, billions of dollars of exploration parcels have been awarded to BP, Esso, MGM Energy, and Conoco, among others. One of the conspiracy theories I'd heard floated, both in Inuvik and here, was that the new road was part of the oil companies' demands, as well as certain international interests looking to acquire future water rights. It wasn't hard to see that an all-weather road would increase corporate accessibility while decreasing the cost required to be here, and the same applied to a deep-water port, which some said was required to facilitate tanker traffic, and even cruise ships, one of which appeared every summer, its passengers ferried into Tuk by motorboat. Merv Gruben said that "with the opening of the Northwest Passage, and there being no port between St. John's and Dutch Harbour, the road could prove vital to getting goods down from the North and to the west. If the port is expanded, we can provide service to whatever is happening off-shore. We could be a supply point for fuel and oil."

When I asked how he felt about this, the hunter's face grew hard, showing me what, perhaps, the bears had seen before their moment of truth. He said: "Shell, Chevron, BP: they all attempted to drill before, but they failed environmental impact screenings, and nothing shows me they won't again." To him, industrial development wasn't the inevitability that others thought it would be. "What if what happened in the Gulf—the oil spill—happened here?" he asked, shaking his head. "There's no answer to the blowback, and the majority of our livelihood and food source would be destroyed. The fish, seals, and whales—they would disappear. The tailing ponds in Fort Mac are so big you can see them from space, and they've already found toxins here in the Mackenzie River. You get a simple rainstorm and the run-off is increased. I'd be completely happy if nobody drilled in Tuk Harbour."

I read him parts of a *Globe and Mail* story in which an Inuvialuit man, William Dillon Jr., commented on the 1970s legacy of oil companies by saying, "They train us, and then they disappear. They come back again with another idea, creating work, and then they start to train us again. That tapers off. The money runs out and then they disappear again: boom and bust, boom and bust, every year."

James nodded and said: "The drilling would create jobs, okay, but new wealth would affect things like crime, drugs, and alcohol [currently, Tuk is a dry town], and because we're a small place, it would change fast. It would hurt our hamlet. We don't need it."

While the future of Tuk—and the greater North—hung in the balance, recent numbers cast shadows over everything: twelve billion barrels of oil buried across the Territories, Nunavut, and Yukon; seven million hectares of land under permit or lease in the same area; a seven-thousand-kilometre decrease in distance that a ship would save by taking the Northwest Passage for a trip from Tokyo to London; and the highest per-capita unemployment rate in Canada: 12.3 in Nunavut, 7.6 in the Northwest Territories, and 6.9 in Yukon. While it's true that issues concerning Northern Gateway and Mackenzie Valley pipelines as well as the sinking price of oil had slowed the thunderous footsteps of change, I sensed that people in Tuk knew that something was coming. The only question was when, and for how long.

27

PLAYING COUNTRY MUSIC WITH RICKY KIKOAK IN A TRAILER IN TUKTOYAKTUK

I t was the next day—Sunday—that Tuk started to jump a little. Like everyone else in town, I arose past noon and was ready to meet the day. A fellow named Gary, who was Rebecca's cousin, lived beside the Tuktu in a wind-battered home with a hammered-together staircase leading to a bare weather-clawed front door, and I found him outside in his Atlanta Falcons sweatshirt smoking every ten minutes. We had a few exchanges from each other's front stairs, before deciding that we couldn't completely understand what the other was saying. Still, we forged through as most strangers would, covering—and yet, not covering—the weather, sports, Toronto, fishing, whaling, the conditions of the roads, and more weather. It was fine. I asked Gary whether there were any shops in town. "Shwops?" he replied, as if I were speaking a strange dialect. I pantomimed the act of shopping—pretending to walk around while carrying two heavy Christmas bags at my side—before realizing that I looked like I was riding in a wheelchair.

"Shwops?"

After leaving Gary, I visited the locally owned Stanton's grocery store (the Northern Store was owned by a company in Winnipeg), which, in its own way, was like coming through the looking glass. Away from home, the most mundane features of life can be informed with a sense of curiosity and intrigue—"Wow, I've never seen this brand of creamer before!"—and you're struck with a certain melancholy while communing with goods you would have shouldered past in your local store: "Aww, this Kraft Dinner came a long way to get here, too."

Stanton's was a compact supermarket with teenagers working at a long lunch counter with a cash register at the end. The counter had a truck stop cappuccino maker and a square contraption that, in excited pink and teal script, promised "Onions Ring And Fries! Hot! Now!" I probably was staring too long at this magical box, because one of the kids—a boy in a Pittsburgh Penguins cap—asked, "You want onion rings and fries, sir?" Dreaming of the snack's hot, greasy burn, I told him that I did, at which point he put his hands flat on the counter and sucked in a long breath before telling me, in a severe tone that he should keep in reserve should he have to break the news to a customer that their family pet has been accidentally harpooned in the parking lot, "Um, sorry, but the machine, you see, is, well, broken." I told him that it was okay, even though it wasn't.

I spent the rest of my visit wandering the aisle writing down food prices in my notebook. I must have looked like some kind of confection detective, although no one seemed to object. The food was outrageously expensive, partly because, with no ice road, Tuk was at the mercy of food being airlifted into the hamlet, to say nothing of having to rely, and subsist, on non-perishable goods, a fact that, in the mind of Merv Gruben, would change with the all-weather road, "giving everyone more choice and probably improving diet and health, too," he told me.

At Stanton's, a jar of Cheez Whiz cost $11 and a quart of milk was $9, which partly explained all the creamers. Ritz crackers were $7; McCain's Superfries, $7; a tub of Breyers' ice cream, $12; a Dr. Oetker's pizza, $9; and five sad German sausages could be had for $17. Plums were $9 a pound and lemons were $8. A bag of onions cost $8, cherries were $15 a pound, and the Stanton sold a Trivial Pursuit game that cost $47. The only upside was that there was plenty of everything—crowded shelves and lots of stock—provided you could afford it. On my way out of the store, I stood in front of a wall taped with announcements and billfolds: Sam Pingo's Fishing Camp; Workshop on Dealing with Change, Or: Loss Is an Inevitable Part of Life; Don't Pluck Geese around Private or Public Houses (Do It Upland!!!); If You See a Wild Dog Do Not Give It Food (Loose Dogs Will Be Shot on Site!!);Tuktoyaktuk Hunters and Trappers Taking Names for Shotgun Shells; and Study of Beluga Whale Habitat Meeting Cancelled Will Reschedule. Another announcement—attributed to a person named Heavenly Elias—was titled Residential School Survivors and Intergenerational Survivors Meeting with the subject line:To See How You Are Doing.

There were a few posters promoting upcoming events. One of them had a colour photograph of a jumpsuit Elvis on it—a promising sign, I thought—although, on closer inspection, it was revealed to be a singer named Ernest Monias, headliner for Tuk's fourth annual fall music festival, to be staged in the mud and gravel divot at the centre of town, where a small plywood stage sat beside a set of green bleachers. Ernest, a Cree performer born in Cross Lake, Manitoba, and known to audiences as "Elvis of the North," had played the previous three festivals. Whenever I brought his name up, locals stepped back as if I'd just bonked them with the flat of a tennis racket. One elderly woman, whom I encountered on a later visit to Stanton's, swooned: "Oh, he just plays and plays and plays and the crowd screams and screams and screams," she laughed, which, considering the relatively quiet nature of the Tukanese, seemed unlikely. She also warned me, tsking as she spoke, "If you have daughters, watch out. Ernest and his band will go on a tear, and they don't set the best example for young kids around here." I told the woman in my finest Elvis drawl, "Thank you, thank you very much," then moved on with the satisfaction that, if I discovered nothing else in the North, at least I'd found the Pelvis, shaking it for the Inuvialuit lo these confounding years.

I walked out of the store and carried on through the hamlet, passing the local radio station, which was housed in a log cabin. CFCT had gone on air in 1972 after an endowment by Toronto's CHUM radio's Allan Waters, who also supplied the broadcast technology. Before CFCT, there was no radio in Tuk other than the occasional signal from Inuvik and Radio Moscow coming across the pole. Pioneered with the help of a local French missionary named Father Lemeur, CFCT began with an all-volunteer, open-door policy. Anyone could come in and program whatever they liked. Announcers had one-way conversations with family members in the bush; elders told Inuvialuit folk tales that lasted deep into the night; deejays played records shipped north from Yellowknife (Doug Matthews remembers hearing "Bat Out of Hell" for the first time on CFCT); and local RCMP constabularies hosted a show that aired in the middle of the night called "Pigs in Space." The programming was different every day.

CFCT was run by John Steen, a member of the Legislative Assembly, the mayor of Tuk, and, in Matthews's words, "a serial businessman and original owner of the Hotel Tuk Inn." The volunteer policy ended around 1981 in one of those radio moments you wished you'd heard but never will. According to Matthews, a woman named Mary Dean (not her real name)—John Steen's long-time girlfriend—"got juiced one night around one in the morning and began calling out John over the airwaves because he hadn't paid her wages for working in the hotel. The Mounties came down to the station to remove her and the whole thing was broadcast to the entire town. Needless to say, John killed the volunteer idea after that."

In the mid-80s, the radio station fell on hard times, lacking the funds to sustain itself. Steen announced to the community that he'd finally found his saviour: Russian state radio, who'd written the station a letter offering free programming such as "Moscow Mailbag" and "Soviet Press Review" at no cost, to keep the station alive. News of a possible Soviet broadcast presence in Canada made the wire service—it might have been fabricated and planted by Steen; no one is sure—forcing the hand of local government, who forced the hand of the North's corporate neighbours: a consortium of Canadian oil companies who eventually donated money to the station. Today, CFCT's broadcasting is infrequent, and even though I asked around town if I might tour the place, maybe play a little Meatloaf, no one was certain who had the key or whether any broadcasting was scheduled for the station. CFCT's decline was explained by Matthews, sighing, "With TV bingo, no one needs the radio anymore," which made me think that "dabbing" might have been a bit of a scourge after all.

I left the log cabin station and made my way to the end—or, as locals insisted, the beginning—of the Trans Canada Trail, passing the seniors' home, small hospital, and wind-savaged graveyard, all of which were sandwiched beside one another. The trail was one of those manufactured destinations that was supposed to make you feel like you were standing in a place heavy with symbolism—it was marked by a tall and pointy steel red and green maple leaf sitting atop a round plinth with a weathered bronze plaque in the front—but, in Tuk, all you had to do was walk to the shore and face the ocean to feel the weight of the place and its distance from everything else. I half-heartedly clicked a photo of the sad leaf and was amazed less by the government-cited end of Canada and more by the fact that the plinth had stayed rooted in its spot, exposed as it was to the howling wind and the sea. A few kids passed me on BMX bikes—they said, "Hello," and I said, "Hello" back—and I went in search of the now-derelict Tuk Hotel Inn, which opened in 1977 and hosted the alien invasion of the Molson Ice Party concert in 1994: Metallica, Veruca Salt, Moist, and Hole airlifted north as part of an extravagant brewery promotion. Perhaps owing to the middling nature of the groups' collective legacies, or maybe because a handful of rock groups appearing under a tent to a few hundred contest-winning beer louts in the Far North meant little, in historic terms, compared to how oil companies or European explorers had affected Tuk, there wasn't much local narrative about the event other than what went down at the Hotel Tuk Inn, which was now nothing but a faded, pink-porched building where bored kids had broken whatever remained inside. Before closing in 2014, room 104 at the inn had a yellow sign taped to the door identifying it as the Courtney Love suite, named after the singer of Hole and widow of the legend, Nirvana's Kurt Cobain. Tourists were encouraged to sleep where Courtney Love had slept—although, to be fair, Ms. Love slept in lots of other places, too—and, according to former owner Paul Voudrach, who ran the inn along with his wife Norma and their ten children: "They were the noisiest bunch of people I'd ever met." I figured the Tukanese would have been left with a deep impression of the musical airlift—after all, you could scribble the list of southern bands who'd played in Tuk on the length of your pinky, and one of them was Anne Murray, who isn't even a band (Blue Rodeo was here in 1999)—but the only thing anyone ever told me about the show was that a few elders arrived at the gig, listened to "one of the bands," then excused themselves, politely. After considering the matter, I decided that it's probably what most of us would have done were we surrounded by a pack of drunken *Kablooniks* awkwardly moshing to "Enter Sandman" and drinking crappy beer for free. In the end, the Molson Polar Ice Party beer promotion was probably just that.

After looking at the old building for as long as it takes a tourist to decide that there isn't much to see—and, really, no one will notice or judge you if you just wave your hand dismissively and chalk up the outing to a failed search for something that ends up being nothing—I turned to retrace my steps across the peninsula before noticing my neighbour, Gary, standing on the crooked staircase of what I thought was Rebecca's porch and smoking (this appeared to be Gary's métier: standing on porches and hauling butts). Since Rebecca told me to drop by if I was ever around—she'd pointed out her place while driving to the whaling camp—I walked over to Gary and asked him, as clearly as I could, whether his cousin was in.

"Rebecca?" he said.

"Yeah, Rebecca. Is she in?"

"No," he said.

"Oh."

"Yeah."

"Okay."

"Rebecca doesn't live here!"

I told him that I was pretty sure that Rebecca lived there before realizing that she did not. I realized this because, as soon as Gary spoke, a group of thinly moustached, Levi-ed, baseball-capped Inuvialuit men appeared from behind the house holding coffee mugs. Over Gary's shoulder, a huddle of women came out of the house and stood on the staircase behind him, dragging on smokes and looking at me through heavy-lidded eyes.

"So, Rebecca's not here?" I asked Gary.

One of the baseball-capped fellows approached me and said, "No, Rebecca's place is there," pointing back down the road. He was missing the nails on his fingers and his hands were soot black. He had campfire eyes and brown teeth and he spoke the way Gary did—Inuvialuit-accented English—although he seemed to better understand what I was saying, and vice versa. Over Gary's shoulder, the women retreated into a dark alcove at the top of the stairs, curiously peeking out every now and then to see if I was still there. The other men came forward, hands pressed into pockets, the ocean raging behind them. After a moment, I noticed what was hanging off the side of the house: an enormous muskoxen pelt drying in the sun: dark-brown with bronze-black edges. The man who'd addressed me was named Terry, and seeing me look at the animal skin, he asked the best question I could have hoped for after finding myself among strangers in a new place:

"So, what do you think, buddy?"

The skin was big enough to roll an entire family inside. Though I'd seen belugas eviscerated at the whaling camps, I felt something stronger in the presence of the pelt, knowing that it had once covered a great snorting beast rumbling across the tundra, and that it was these men who'd skinned it and hung it like a flag in their yard, although they weren't showboating. In fact, that they weren't riding around town on the flatbed of a moving truck holding the oxen's skull above them like a tournament trophy made what they'd done seem even more formidable.

"Go on, go on, touch it if you want," he said, waving me forward.

There was a creaking sound and I noticed the women looking out from their alcove, watching the white guy with the little girl buttons press his delicate hand against the oxen skin in front of the men whose entire arms had only just been inside the beast, pulling out pink guts and knifing apart the rest.

"How's it feel?" asked Terry.

"Feels good," I told him.

One of the women—she had a voice like a nail scratching concrete—said something in Inuvialuktun and her friends laughed. It was the kind of laugh that suggested that the joke probably had something to do with how the out-of-his-depth-dork-from-the-big-city looked next to the master hunters, which is to say, they were probably joking about my penis size.

"Mind your own business," said one of the men to the women. He was smaller, grey bearded, and a little like an Inuvialuit Yoda. I gestured to the women.

"You know them?" I asked him.

He laughed.

"Yeah, we're all family, you know," he said. "For better or worse."

"I know how that works," I said, very nearly crossing off my list "Making a Mother-in-Law Joke with Inuit Hunter" as something I could tell my friends.

Terry asked: "Hey, you want some coffee?"

I answered him, immediately regretting the unmanly indecisiveness of my words, in which I explained how, "Well, you see, after six o'clock, I can't really drink coffee because, well, it kind of keeps me up and, well, it makes my stomach feel a little . . ." before stopping and telling him that, yes, I would.

"Hey, what time is it anyway?" I asked.

One of the younger men, a dark-eyebrowed fellow with a buzz cut and sloped face in a grey hoodie whose name was James, said, "One second, I'll tell you." Part of me expected him to look up and read the sun's arc—more cultural prejudice—but instead, he reached behind him and pulled out an iPad.

"Nine o'clock," he told me.

I was startled by both the hour—during my time in the North, getting used to perpetual daytime was the most challenging feature—and the easy presence of technology in such an elemental land. James had picked up the tablet on a recent trip to Inuvik and he'd loaded all kinds of songs. After learning that I was a musician, he played tracks by Dr. Dre and Pitbull and other rap artists whose names were lost on me, the music riding above the waves that surged against the breakwater behind Terry's home (a set of large boulders had been put there to stop the thinning wedge of the land, which, before the shoreline eroded, was the site of a curling rink). The music produced another global symphony—east L.A. beats, rushes of ocean water, a piano figure looped, an electric guitar slashed across the fat of the body—that played to a story shared in low tones by Terry, the man who looked like Yoda, James, and a few others, including a young woman in a red hoodie whose name was Monica, about making a hand drum using the stomach of a caribou.

They stood in a semicircle and performed the pantomime: holding up the fallen beast on its toes before sinking in the knife blade, carving the artery just below the neck, slicing down and clipping an upper intestine, then moving around behind the animal to shear away the wall of the stomach so that it came away whole. At least that's how I think it went, though I can't be sure. This is partly because listening to the hunters speak in the late sunlight on the edge of the Beaufort Sea about how to carefully stretch an animal skin over the wood of a drum while "In Da Club" by 50 Cent played on James's iPad made me feel as if I were stoned. And partly because, a few minutes later, I was.

One of the men disappeared behind the house. Another followed, and then another after that. I asked Terry, "Hey, what's happening back there?" at which point he made a gesture using his thumb and forefinger: the universal sign for smoking weed. He kept his fingers to his mouth and nodded—I nodded back—before leading me to an old greasy workshop in a corrugated shipping container that the men had dredged up out of the sea. It was crammed with the bones of old snow machines and stacks of tool boxes, their drawers filled with dirty mounds of machine bits and black metal. There was a little desk lousy with stacks of paper and ashtrays spiked with an urchin of butts and ash. They passed two joints and we coughed deep rheumatic coughs while sucking in the harsh smoke, adding a texture—chest cavity drum rolls—to whatever was playing out of James's iPad. I started the conversation as if rolling a ball into the group's feet: "So, I thought Tuk was dry, eh?" After a shared glance, they giggled, which made me feel grateful that I'd been allowed to make a joke at the expense of the region's alcohol issues, which I wished I hadn't done as soon as I said it. This led to another hacking chorus, which led to two more joints being sparked. The next twenty minutes were lost to joy.

We emerged from the clubhouse—the container was painted orange, making my experience seem even more like something from "White Rabbit"—and, sensing that I was now putty in their hands, the old women emerged from their alcove to greet me, lined up in track pants along the bent staircase. The one with the crowbar nose spoke first.

"So where are you from?"

I told her and she said, "Toronto? Do me a favour, eh. Tell 'em we don't live in igloos, okay?"

"Okay. I'll tell 'em."

"And tell 'em we're not called Eskimos!" said another woman, whose face was like an old catcher's mitt: all soft folds and wrinkles pressed into each other.

"We don't ride polar bears to work!" said another.

"And we don't eat blubber. Well, okay, we eat a little blubber," said the crowbar.

And on it went. From out of the group of women—aunts, wives, sisters, and assorted matriarchs—a stoop-backed figure appeared wearing what I believed to be a housecoat (whether they all lived together in the house I couldn't be sure). She was carrying a plate and asked, kindly, "Do you want to try some breaded whitefish?" which, after "Would you like to time-travel back and see Led Zeppelin on their first North American tour?" is probably one of the greatest things a stoner can be asked. I took a piece. It tasted like an Arctic Fish McNugget: salty, tender, and delicious. I told the women this.

"Better than that white man's cod!" said one of them.

"Don't give him the recipe, he'll steal it!" said another.

"Lookit, he wants more!" said someone else.

The woman in the housecoat fed me the rest of the fish. At last, Tuk had opened up and invited me in. A truck was parked in the driveway and James sat on its fender scrolling through cute photos of his kids on his tablet. He showed them while I asked questions about his life. Returning the gesture, he asked if I was going to play any music while travelling through the North, and I mentioned that I planned on visiting the North Slave Correctional Centre in Yellowknife, where I hoped to do something for the inmates.

"The NSCC?" asked James, looking up at me.

"Yeah, you know it?" I asked.

"Yeah. I was in there. Eighteen months."

"What happened?" I asked

"I beat up my old lady," he said.

"Oh."

"I came home drunk and hit her. But I don't drink anymore. I don't do that sort of stuff anymore."

James seemed so gentle that I couldn't have imagined anything like this happening, but it happened a lot in the North; it happened a lot everywhere. James talked about the episode plainly and matter-of-factly— almost in passing—partly because domestic violence was more common-place here, and partly because he seemed to have come to terms with what he'd done. I asked James if he was with a different woman now and he said he was. The loneliness, the desolation, the poverty, the legacy of the residential schools, and the lack of education all contributed to a difficult life in the Far North, but the presence of alcohol—much sought after in a self-imposed temperate town where a contraband forty-ounce bottle of vodka cost two hundred dollars—didn't help. A few months after I left Tuk, three young adults were medivacked out of the hamlet because a local bootlegger had been cutting booze with antifreeze to increase profits. The kids' lives were saved, but doctors feared long-term brain issues. Until recent times, alcohol had been foreign to the Inuvialuit, and, in a lot of ways, the North was still a teenager when it came to booze and drugs, bingeing before any tolerance had been strengthened. Factored into the difficult economic and educational conditions, bad shit was going to happen, and people like James passed through darkness before coming out the other side. Doug Matthews said that the town had flirted with the idea of allowing social events to serve booze one night a week—possibly Friday—but no decision had been made. If, like the polar bear hunter suggested, the new road would lead to even more illegal alcohol, it was possible that things would get worse before they got better, although feeling the way I did—to say nothing of being stoned on smuggled weed—I had difficulty dwelling on the issue. I allowed myself a moment of traveller's bliss. James was better now and that's all that mattered.

As the hour approached midnight—and with the hue of the sky the same as it had been all day: mostly grey and only occasionally sunny, as if God were tapping on a faulty bathroom light—I turned my ear to the road and heard music: acoustic guitar and synthesized drums. I thought it was coming from James's iPad before realizing, in my sweet weed haze, that he'd actually moved from the fender of his truck to climb behind the steering wheel, at which point I decided that, as a rule, people in the Northwest Territories couldn't go twenty minutes without sitting in their rig. The sound persisted and I asked the group: "Does anyone else hear that?" The Arctic Yoda said: "Oh that's Ricky Kikoak. He's practising for the festival."

"But where's the sound coming from?" I asked.

"You okay?" asked Terry.

"Yeah, I think so," I said.

The Arctic Yoda pointed to a blue house across the muddy street.

"There. Ricky's in there."

Before coming to Tuk, I wondered if I'd get a chance to hear any local music: maybe a drum dance or throat-singer or some hymns voiced by Inuvialuit elders (I'd missed a singalong in the Kitti Hall community centre on my first day and was a month too early for the Elvis of the North). The sound that drifted across the street was that of a wobbly high lonesome voice set to the plinking of light electronica: a Neil Young 45 with a warp in it; Willie Nelson played on a Casio. It was strange and beguiling music, and, for a moment—for a *stoned* moment—I thought I might be having a Jerry Wexler/Ahmet Ertegun revelation—Wexler and Ertegun had, famously, crossed a Louisiana swamp in the middle of the night to sign Professor Longhair—discovering a new kind of music: an Arctic folk/disco hybrid created at the tip of the ocean. I excused myself from Terry's yard and crossed the street, standing under the window of the dwelling listening to the sound.

A woman's face appeared on the other side of the screen, her long dark hair swept over her eyes. It was Ricky's wife, Tina.

"Hey, you wanna come in?" she shouted.

"Okay!" I said, probably too excitedly.

I walked up the staircase and opened the door past a mountain of boots and shoes—all sizes—where I was consumed in cigarette smoke: Player's Navy Cuts made with a rolling machine that sat on a yellow linoleum table. "Come, come," said Tina, a smoke bobbing from her lip as she guided me to a couch in the kitchen and dining area. Ricky Kikoak—sixty-something with hound dog eyes, a few missing teeth, and long hair, wearing an undershirt and jeans—sat behind a small electronic drum rig—a V kit—holding a wide-bodied acoustic guitar in his lap.

"You sound great," I told Ricky.

"Well, I've been trying," he said, rubbing the back of his neck. "Trying to get ready for the festival. I have a band. Some guys. They're good, but we don't get together very often."

"You practise on the kit and guitar?" I asked.

"Yeah, well, sometimes," he said, tapping the shallow plastic of the bass drum while stroking a guitar chord with his right hand. "It's hard, you know."

"I play a little drums," I told him.

"Really?"

"Yeah," I said.

Ricky stood up, moved some clothes around, emptied an ashtray, buried some old chip bags into a kitchen garbage can, kicked some more shoes into a corner, and waved me toward the drum seat.

"Here, here," he said, handing me a pair of sticks.

I sat behind the cymbals, snare, and toms; plastic vestiges of 80s percussion that triggered electronic, and heavily processed, samples of real drums (one of the advantages of a V kit was having a volume knob to set the actual thump of the instrument; that and they were light, portable, and didn't take up as much room as a conventional kit. They also lasted forever and you could take them with you wherever you had to go). Ricky pulled his crane-necked mic stand across the room to a kitchen chair, where he sat down. Tina came over, gave him a smoke, then passed both of us mugs of coffee. Ricky had wired the mics—one for him, one for me—into a small PA with small speakers on either side of the room. Tina settled down at the kitchen table and started filming everything with her iPhone, even though we hadn't made a sound. At varying intervals, young Inuvialuit children appeared from an adjacent hallway. They were cousins of cousins of cousins, and two of them—twins—had been adopted by Tina and Ricky after their mother fell on hard times. There was also a young man who looked about twelve with a great bushel of dark hair on his head who came in every now and then to roll a cigarette, which he smoked while watching me play. At one point, the twins sneaked into the room and stared at me. Ricky laughed: "It's the first person they've ever met who's not from here." I extended a greeting to them. One of the girls ran away while the other held out her delicate hand, which I swallowed in the paleness of my palm.

Ricky opened a steno-binder scribbled with lines of verse and placed it on a music stand. Then he looked at me with a worrying glance: "I'm not sure what songs you want to do here." I told him to start and I would follow, and so he did, and after ninety minutes we'd played everything in his book: covers from John Prine to Ray Price to Merle Haggard to Buck Owens. I decided that, in its own stony way, playing country music with Ricky Kikoak in a trailer in Tuktoyaktuk was as good as going back in time to see Led Zeppelin (and probably a more onomatopoeic future lyric). At one point, he asked me, "Do you know Doug Sahm?" I expressed my love for the late Austin/Californian songwriter and spared a moment to wonder what the transient Tex-Mex singer would have thought knowing that one of his songs was being played so far from where it was born. At one point, Ricky told me he'd written his first song, called "Tuktoyaktuk," a paean to his home. Being a dedicated fan of paeans to home, I insisted we play it, and so we did. Even though the electro-drums went *plink* and *thwap* when they should have gone *boam* and *dud-duh*, it was fine. Ricky sang through his teeth in a bent Arctic twang and I scrapped a rhythm out on the kit. Tina filmed and the kids came and went. Outside, birds crept through the driftwood.

It was around two in the morning—the day glowed as if it were mid-afternoon—when we finally ended, sated, played out, weed-tired. I thanked the Kikoaks and the twins came to look at me one last time. It had already been the greatest day—maybe the greatest day of my summer up north—and when I crossed the street to say goodbye to Terry and James and the crowbar, I found a whole other crew of people in the yard. I pushed my hands into my pockets and turned back, a *Kabloonik* shuffling home.

Through the weed and music and company of all the people I'd met—people whom I doubted I might ever see again—I thought of what I'd tell John McFadden back in the newsroom, my mind emerging from its reverie to think about the trial, the newspaper, and Yellowknife. But just then, I heard a voice.

"Hey, mister! You wanna play?"

I looked down into the bleachered divot in the centre of town. There were about twenty kids—fifteen years old to maybe twenty-two, an equal number of boys and girls, a whole bunch of them named Junior—gathered around holding bats and gloves and standing over a jumble of bases and yellow balls.

"Hey, mister, c'mon down."

There are a few things that a sleepy-stoned fifty-two-year-old Canadian writer might want to find on the way back to their bed in the middle of a bright northern night. For some, it might be a handsome suitor waiting on the steps of their residence; for others, a bag of money discovered on the way home; and for others, still, an email announcing Steven Spielberg's plans to turn their book into an epic and expensive film. For me, however, finding a softball game about to begin under the Arctic sun at the edge of the ocean was it. I scampered down the hill to join them.

I was met in the dirt pit by a bright, smiling kid named Carl, who shook my hand and said, "Thanks for playing." That Carl wasn't so disaffected that he'd resisted asking someone four times his age to join the game endeared him and the group to me. They were nice kids. One of them, whose name was John, was a young goaltender and we talked about Carey Price before I asked him if he'd ever seen an NHL game.

"Never. But my dream is to one day go to Edmonton," he told me, looking into his blue leather glove.

On the hard flat dirt, I took my position in left field and stared at home plate, the old graveyard and its bent wooden crosses rearing over the diamond at the top of the hill. The game started and I shagged flies whenever I could, although I mostly chased after balls splashing around in muddy puddles of water at the back of the lot. I took my cuts, too, slicing a few balls into the ground while lining a couple at infielders, but some of my hits found holes over second and third. In the seventh inning, I homered—admittedly, the ball bounced off sets of shins and midriffs before arriving too late to the plate—and, in the ninth inning, I ran with all my spirit in my Australian boots and jean jacket with the girly pins to chase a ball stroked into the gap, reaching up with my glove and snaring it. I came out of my run like a Rockette, legs kicking while holding the ball in the darkness of my mitt. It was the third out and I ran off the field. One of the outfielders came over, tapped me on the back with his glove, and said, "Hey, nice balance, mister." The bottom of the ninth came and went—26–22 final—and the game ended. I thanked Carl. "No problem," he said, "that'll be, oh, twenty bucks." I told him that I couldn't possibly break my $250 bill, then turned to walk back up the hill with the kids still laughing at the joke. Carl shouted to me from home plate, "Hey, man, don't forget to tell 'em about Tuk." I promised that I would not.

28

THE NORTH SLAVE
PRISON BLUES

I returned to Yellowknife to discover that John's trial was scheduled for the fall. In the meantime, he wrote desultory pieces about quills and animals ("If I have to do one more caribou story, I'm going to grow antlers," he complained) and tried to hold whatever shit he had left together. He swung from the hope and possibility that he would be cleared—there was even gossip at one point that the Crown would drop the charges, but that was unfounded—to a sense that the cops were furthering their resolve to make an example of him. Mike and Bruce were equally nervous about how the trial would affect the *Yellowknifer* and their ability to freely cover the activities of a police force protecting its standing within the community as a group that didn't assault writers. If the paper lost its ability to freely examine what the cops were or weren't doing, no one knew what it would look like moving forward, a worry made even more pronounced considering what was happening in the greater newspaper world, the *Toronto Star* having laid off labour and environmental reporters and many North American publications challenged by the urge to chase clicks rather than let reporters sink into the matter of hard news.

If things weren't bad enough for John, his life became further complicated after tensions escalated between the writer and the Justice

Department, a situation for which I was partly—okay, mostly—to blame. It started innocently, during a visit to the prison—the North Slave Correctional Centre—where I was scheduled to play a thirty-minute set on acoustic guitar for a few dozen inmates. I'd wanted to put in some time because of what I'd taken from the community, and I knew a few people who had relatives or friends incarcerated in the prison. I sent a note to Sue Glowach, a Justice Department representative who helped facilitate this sort of event, and she fed me into an RCMP carousel where they ran background checks and cross-referenced my history to make sure I was fit for a visit.

Sue and I headed to the jail. We pulled up to the kind of dull, flat, square building that was so inconspicuous it was conspicuous, like a movie star in a baseball cap. The relatively new complex contrasted with the site of the former prison, near Tommy Forrest Field, positioned beside a trailer park and close enough to the edge of Main Street that, when songwriter Indio Saravanja was a boy, "you could stand and watch the inmates play baseball on the prison diamond," he remembered.

We were met at the front entrance by the convenor responsible for the inmates' social activities, a fellow named Stephen. Rather than uniformed with handcuffs hanging off his belt, he was dressed in civilian clothes—T-shirt, jeans, running shoes—with a fob looped around his neck. He *kachunked* us through the outer ring of the prison—a series of passageways leading to ante rooms leading to a small rec room/gymnasium with a few dozen chairs scattered about and some old Christmas decorations piled on a table—and, after settling there, he pointed through a window looking into the yard and told us, "See, you could escape from there. And there. And there. Oh, and from there, if you wanted," gesturing to a raised landing at the far end of a fenced enclosure. I wondered whether this was part of correctional centre routine—showing visitors how to escape were we, oh I don't know, taken hostage by prisoners—before deciding that Stephen was maybe just a little different.

"Has a jailbreak ever happened?" I asked him.

"Not during my time," he sighed, sounding disappointed. "There was a riot twenty-five years ago, but that was in the old facility."

"Okay, well hopefully one day someone will escape!" I told him, playing along.

"I hope I'm on holidays when that happens," he said.

"I hope I'm not in jail," I said.

And then everyone laughed.

It was all very weird.

"We'll probably have 2A and 13 and 17B and 6F and 3 and 7 coming," he said, listing the names of the pods—units of cells within the jail—who'd signed up for the concert. The rec room events—which included three-nights-a-week inmate jam sessions in a small room off to the side ("Lots of AC/DC and Metallica," said Stephen)—were arranged so that the men could meet people from other pods. "They're a pretty enthusiastic group," he said. "They love having visits."

"Who else has come?"

The convenor thought about it.

"You're the first one!"

A door cranked open and the inmates shuffled in. They were dressed in plain green T-shirts and sweatpants. Almost none of them looked at me, choosing, instead, to collect in little groups on fold-out chairs. A decorative wooden throne—"It's where Santa sits," said Stephen, before adding, "for the Christmas pageant"—was before the window, and, after a moment, an inmate with tubes in his nose wheeling an oxygen tank—a Dene man in his seventies—ambled across the room and took his seat there, staring out at the parking lot. I looked to Stephen for a clue about what to do next, and he made a goofy strumming motion while nodding his head, which, having had years of experience in professional entertainment, I took for the universal "Why don't you start playing now?" gesture. I cleared my throat and struck an A chord. The men scraped their seats across the tiled rec centre floor into crooked rows. They sat down and manspreaded and waited for me to say something that couldn't possibly render me as anything other than a white guy from suburban Toronto whose only reason for ever being in prison would have been if prison were a place where they put you for stealing the neighbour's Internet. I welcomed them and told them my name. There were no cheers or applause or signs of acknowledgement. I might as well have been in Regina.

"I just came back from Tuk," I said, starting the show as if it were the beginning of a stand-up comedy routine.

The silence lingered. The inmates' bored faces stared back at me until a fellow with a dark goatee and mischievous eyes piped up:

"Did ya get laid?"

Suddenly, laughter.

"Um, no," I said, giving him nothing to work with.

"Oh," said the goatee. "You want a number?"

During the first few songs, the inmates spoke with each other under their breath while I played. After one song, someone said, "Sounds like Johnny Cash," and then another said, "Sounds like Tom Petty," and then another, showing off for his friends, said, "Sounds like shit . . ."

"No, that's Nickleback," I said. "They're here next week."

I played on.

After one long song with many verses, an inmate told me, while digging his hands around in his waistband and scratching his nuts: "It's kinda ramblin'."

I choked back my courage and asked: "My songs or your balls?"

"Oh he said it!"

"Johnny's balls!"

"Dig 'em out, brother!"

And so it went. The most profound moment came during the performance of a Rheostatics song called "Legal Age Life at Variety Store," which includes the lyric "I am the king, I am, therefore, what kind of a fool am I?" While singing the line, I looked at old the wheezing fellow—the prison elder—sitting on the throne, his faraway gaze trained on the parking lot outside. The moment was heavy and I realized why "Folsom Prison Blues" was the kind of record that it was: in front of this crowd—whose lives were messed up no matter how many times a week they got to jam—it was very important not to suck. I dug in harder the rest of the way: biting off lyrics, thrashing at chords, hollering the lyrics. One inmate offered, "Now you're doing better!" I broke a guitar string and the show ended.

Sue drove me back to the newspaper. We talked about a lot of things, but our conversation inevitably turned to John, partly because it was impossible to talk to anyone in Yellowknife without his name coming up, and partly because Sue had dealt with John through her Justice Department's liaison with the press. "It doesn't look like it'll go well for him," she told me as we idled outside the paper. I asked what she meant—would it not go well for him in court? in life? in his career?—and she said, "Listen, I like John, a lot," which is what a lot of people said before they said something bad about John. It didn't go quite that way with Sue—she was a nice person, it seemed, who travelled around North America with her husband, Norm, a drummer, who'd come back from a recent studio session in El Paso, Texas, hosted by Terry Manning, the person who'd helped engineer the fourth Rheostatics album at Compass Point studios in Bahamas—but she openly questioned the veracity of John's story about what happened the time he was handcuffed and manhandled outside the courtroom from which he'd been excluded.

"I've seen the tape," she said. "John was interrupting the court proceedings by shouting, and the judge was getting angry, and you just can't do that. You cannot anger a judge or disrupt their courtroom," echoing something that Glenn had also suggested.

"But they'd given up his seat without telling him," I said, defending John. "It's his job to be there, and if he can't do his job, he can't work, and if he can't work, well, you know how this goes," I told her.

"Okay, but you know John," she said, which is another thing people in Yellowknife liked to say. "He immediately went to outrage: shouting and yelling. He could have said, 'Okay, let's figure this out. Let's figure out a way for me to be in there. Can I stand in there? Can I just sneak in the back?' John didn't do this. He didn't do any of this."

"That's easy to say," I suggested, "considering that neither you nor I was in that position. Besides, the security guard . . ."

"It wasn't a security guard, it was a sheriff," she said.

"Okay, the sheriff. He grabbed John."

"He didn't grab him. He moved him. I've seen the tape."

"But there were tears in his shirt and in his pants, at least according to John," I said, that last qualifier returning me to doubts about whether I wasn't seeing the forest through the trees, my impressions spun a certain way by John to reflect his innocence. I gulped back the notion and listened as Sue continued.

"Okay, let me say that again. Yes, he was grabbed, and the sheriff shouldn't have done that. But John immediately started freaking out and resisting when perhaps he should have stepped back."

"Stepping back without his footing?"

"Or, I don't know, something . . ." she said.

"But what about what happened next?" I asked her, remembering what John had told me: how an RCMP officer had come in, cuffed him, and led him down the ramp toward the courtroom exit, pushing him to the ground.

"I've seen the tape," she said. "He fell. He wasn't pushed to the ground."

"He wasn't pushed?"

"The carpet," she said. "He got caught in the carpet and he tripped. At least that's what I saw."

"Listen, I know that, in any confrontation, it takes two to dance," I conceded.

"And when you dance, sometimes you trip," she said, smugly.

"I just don't know how you tear your clothes and have a huge bloody wound on your knee by simply falling to the floor," I told her. "I don't get it. At all."

"Dave," she said, sipping her coffee and smiling. "I've seen the tape."

I thanked Sue for the visit to the jail and we parted ways. I wandered into the *Yellowknifer*, threw my stuff on my desk, and wrote down everything she'd said, freezing it on the page. John sat low in his chair at the end of the row of desks, tapping out whatever light news he'd been required to include on the day's run sheet. I sent him what I'd written. It would be the first he'd see of my work, any of it.

While sending him the Glowach transcription, I included other bits, too: some funny stuff, some conversations we had, and a few instances where people were critical of John, partly to demonstrate that my portrait of him wouldn't be a grease job, and partly to find out whether I had to worry about the repercussions of a main character who might suddenly read their words and want nothing of the book.

At first, we didn't speak of the writing. He didn't bring it up, so I assumed all was fine. John once told me, unequivocally, that he wasn't interested in reading books. "I get all my news and information from cable TV," he said with an almost unbecoming amount of pride. But a few days later, it all came at once: emails, text messages, and phone calls. John was freaking out, but it wasn't what I expected. Instead of reacting to what I'd sent him—it turned out that he had no concern about his portrait, warts and all—his outrage lay with Sue Glowach and what she'd said about him. He claimed that her words were libellous and irresponsible, and, possibly, enough to get his case thrown out. He was convinced that a Justice Department official talking openly—and negatively—about private information reflected an established bias within the halls of justice. He instructed his lawyer to take action.

Sue Glowach was livid. She emailed to express outrage that I'd passed on the details of our conversation. She assailed me for sharing an "off-the-record" conversation ("Off the record or not," said Glenn, "Sue fucking Glowach can't be going around telling people what she saw on that tape") but we never established that during our time together. She hinted that her reputation was spoiled and that, because of the email share, her job was in jeopardy. I felt like shit because I liked Sue. I was grateful that she helped get me into the North Slave Correctional Centre. John had taken my transcript and used it as leverage to subvert the accusations against him, which I understood because of his anxieties surrounding the trial, but I also thought that what he'd done was pretty shitty. Eventually, N.W.T. Justice contacted me to ask permission to use my writing in court, suggesting that I might be called to testify. After months of building John's narrative, I was now part of the narrative. It was an awful place to be.

I confronted him in the smoking area behind the newspaper, waiting for everyone else to leave before asking him a succession of "What-the-fucks?" He answered in as flat a tone as he could find, showing me, I think, that he could be this way if he tried, although it only made it worse because his manner seemed put on. "Okay, I expect you to be mad at me and that's fine," he said, holding up his hands. "But I had no choice here. My ass is on the line. Sue Glowach has no right going around telling people that I tripped on the carpet."

"But I sent that email to you. It wasn't intended for anyone else," I said.

"I appreciate that," he said, kicking at his feet.

"You betrayed me," I said, softening the verb a little.

"Well. You betrayed Sue, didn't you?" he asked, looking up.

"Fuck you, John," I said, still softly.

The reporter shook his head and made a sound that wasn't much of anything: no words, just noise expressed from the hollow of his throat. I wanted to tell John that he was a lousy friend—that what he'd done was a dick move, throwing me under a bus for his own purposes—but his choked silence stopped me. The reporter could have sunk a dozen different ways into new levels of serious concern, but after hearing him struggle to form a word, I thought two things: one, was John having stroke? And two, was he so twisted inside that he was robbed of his rumbling Peterbilt of a voice? It seemed more like the latter. I stopped and watched him smoke.

I could deal with whatever the Justice Department wanted or didn't want from me—my involvement, it turned out, wouldn't last beyond their initial letter—and since John lived in a cabin without heat or running water; had been blackballed, profiled, and arrested by the police; had all kinds of issues zebra-striping his life; and *still* didn't care what I wrote about him, it didn't seem right to lose my mind over what amounted to a desperate gesture. I didn't need to push him any closer to the edge. Besides, there was a pretty good chance he'd get there himself.

THE NORTHERN SHIRE

The situation around the *Yellowknifer* was fraught with tension. It was one episode after another. The relationship between Karen and John came undone, even though they'd been only casual friends during their time at the paper. It stemmed from an incident that happened behind the swimming pool near Frame Lake, which sounds like a plot twist possibly steeped in romance, but was not. Rather, John was wandering home early one morning—where he was wandering home from was never quite determined—when he looked down to find a knapsack containing a locked iPad, as well as packs of hotdogs and granola bars, which he ripped open and ate, never one to discern between found food or otherwise. After keeping the iPad for several days, and trying in his own technically challenged way to unlock it, he brought it to the bar and laid it on the table for people to see. Later, when John got up to leave, the iPad was missing. Coming into work the next morning, he discovered that Karen had taken it to the police.

"She stole it from me," he protested, his voice sounding even more like car wheels on a gravel road after so much anxiety and sleepless nights. "She stole it and took it to the RCMP, then said that I could go and pick it up in a week. I asked her why she did it and she looked at me as if thinking: 'Because you're a piece of shit and I'm not.' I've been thirty years in this business and I think I've earned a modicum of respect, but she talks to me and treats me like an out-of-journalism-school-piece-of-shit degenerate. I went to Mike Bryant and said: 'I need you to deal with this girl because I'm gonna make her fucking cry.'"

Mike talked to Karen, and he smoothed things between them, or at least tried to. Karen told me, "I took it from him so he wouldn't be charged with possession of stolen property. I was looking out for him."

When I mentioned this to John, he was outraged: "That would have been more of a stretch than what I'm being charged for. I don't have time for these kinds of people. Why the fuck didn't she tell me she was helping me locate the owner of the iPad, instead of stealing it from me and then trying to make me feel like a piece of shit? She should have told the RCMP that it was me who found it and that it should have become my property if the rightful owner didn't come forward." The truth of the matter was that John didn't own a computer. He needed one. His petulance over Karen taking it only reinforced a truth he was loath to admit: the only way he could get a laptop was if he found one in an alley.

John's antipathy reflected the divide between the generations of writers at the *Yellowknifer*. His take was "The hip thing today is how you can make yourself as marginal and distant as possible. That's what Karen does." The two writers were further separated in their respective career trajectories. If John was held captive in Yellowknife writing about meat wastage while awaiting his trial, Karen was on the verge of getting accepted into a prestigious journalism fellowship at Columbia University, and her *Toronto Life* piece would eventually be nominated for a National Magazine Award (she wouldn't win). This success translated into an interview at the *Globe*, where she was hired almost immediately. She left months before John's charges were heard.

John's conflict with *Yellowknifer* personnel didn't end with Karen. One morning, he and Julius got into a terrible fight on the doorstep of his cabin, the result of Julius trying to summon John out of bed to cover a fire in the neighbourhood. They wrestled for a while on the ground—John in his underwear, Julius in his street clothes—and the reporter ended up with a black eye. They didn't speak to each other for months, an impressive achievement considering that they lived in the same place and sat two desks removed from each other in the office. Crossing Julius off the list, John was left with but a handful of people he trusted and counted on as friends. There was Sarah and there were a few others. One of them— me—would eventually be leaving town.

John was drinking a lot. I knew this, partly, because I was drinking a lot, too, almost always in his presence. At least one writer said to me, "If this trial comes down to an issue of freedom of the press, do we want *him* speaking for *us?*" Another said, "You can't have him working for the paper in the day and then, at night, going out and acting like a hammerhead." Someone else: "The guy has a heart of gold, but, in the end, he's a fuck-up. He's been coming to this point [of arrest] ever since he arrived in Yellowknife." Everybody asked that I keep their names off their quotes. "No matter what he did, we all love John," said one writer. "We don't want him to get hurt after he finds out how people actually see him."

Karen told me: "There needs to be an intervention. There needs to be a lot of interventions. Yellowknife generally has a drinking problem. Nobody ever has any money, but a pint of beer is eight dollars wherever you go. When you're paying what I am paying—nine hundred dollars a month for shared accommodation with two other people—you can't afford to blow it on booze and cigarettes. I mean, watching John bum smokes because he has no money . . . it's all very sad and tiring."

John continued to live paycheque to paycheque. He grappled with a hard existence at a time of the year when, if you weren't rewarding yourself with warmth and light, you deprived yourself of the relief that summertime offered. With the burden of the trial weighing his steps, I asked him to join me on a tour of the houseboats, something I'd planned on doing before the summer ended. He told me that, not only had he never been on a houseboat in his three years in Yellowknife, but he'd hardly been on the water.

"It's a little out of my comfort zone," he said.

"You have no comfort zone," I told him.

He agreed that I had a point.

We were invited on the water by a denimed banjo player and bike mechanic, Ryan McCord, who'd once been sent a handwritten postcard from Stompin' Tom Connors that he had framed in his home. Ryan lived in The Woodyard in one of the old privy shacks—"shack" is not necessarily a disparaging term in the North—five minutes by bike from the city and thirty seconds from the soft-footed Great Slave Lake shoreline, where enormous weeds and rushes crowned the small squatters' community in overgrowth. For its reputation as a curious residential anomaly—it was so true to the original settlement that it made Old Town look like Century City—The Woodyard was still hidden because of its location, visible only once you were in it. It was part northern shire, part hillbilly shanty, and part Roald Dahl playground, founded in the early 1940s by two Norwegians, Hans Hansen and Einar Broten, the latter's tombstone reading: "A Man Who Drank 'Old Sam' and Didn't Give a Damn." Were The Woodyard in British Columbia or Nova Scotia, it would have been branded "an experiment in natural living," but because it was in Yellowknife, its slant-roofed dwellings and pipe-cleaner homes were just that. A large green-lettered sign warned visitors to ENTER AT OWN RISK, but because the sign was posted in a ditch at a 90-degree angle with fading letters and vines twirled at its edges, you passed through anyway. Besides, living in the North was already enough of a risk, and The Woodyard seemed verdant enough in the summer to soften however one fell.

We helped Ryan carry his canoe along a scrub path, passing a few ancient shacks—"That one used to be Slugger's; Peter lives here now; that's the dragon shack; see its dragon mural?" he announced in a low northern twang—before coming to a dock sawing with the waves at the edge of the lake. We stared out at Tony Foliot—rather, the Snowking's—houseboat, which reminded me of Popeye's cartoon tug, decorated with stars and flowers and painted yellow-blue with two Muskoka chairs platformed at the front. Over its shoulder, you could see a few more houseboats, and a few more beyond that. Their shapes and colours—aquamarine, red, purple, and Maritime blue—were pure northern pop art, particularly when set against Jolliffe Island's brooding hump of forest. Canada is often viewed through drab patterns and utility shades, but Yellowknife's lake-bound colours were the colours of joy and wonder. All of this in a northern capital city.

It was 9 p.m. The heavy sun ducked behind the city buildings—daylight hours were returning to normal with the waning of summer—but there was still a long golden glow across the calm face of the lake. Once we got on the water, John's harshness softened; his tensions unclenched. The cliché has the concrete-chewing city dweller feeling the complications of his life fall away while being suddenly close to nature, but you could sense John spooling out of that which entwined him. His legs stretched the length of the canoe and his hand tickled the lake as we cracked warm beers, passed joints to each other. From the water, Yellowknife was just another hunk of land.

Ryan paddled generously, going houseboat to houseboat. Each deck was coolered and filled with beer; music played on one stereo to the next; fishing rods were dropped in the water; dogs barked across the gut; and float planes buzzed overhead like giant dragonflies. There was one house-boat in the middle of the bay that showed up in endless tourist photo-graphs. It was painted Dutch orange and looked like a small Swiss cottage, anchored on a long tether that allowed it to swish imperceptibly in a wide arc, guaranteeing that whenever the residents, a young couple named Joel and Thea, awoke, their positioning, and view, would be different. The first permanent houseboats—owned by Gary Vaillancourt and John Alexander and built using two re-assembled Giant Mine bunkhouses supported by forty-five-gallon drums—appeared in 1982, and, currently, there were thirty-four on the bay, allowing for a lively water community, but with enough separation between homes that people felt unencroached. Canoes, rowboats, tugs, cruisers, jet skis, and rollicking fishing boats were tenants of the water, too, winding past the buildings like a hoser's Venice.

One fellow, a solar panellist from Alberta named Wade Carpenter, had built a floating dock from his boat to Jolliffe Island, using the land to compost, collect wood, or simply feel the earth under his feet. His cabin was like something out of *Dwell* magazine—wood-hewn and coolly stylish—but it also had the feel of 70s' outdoorsman Red Fisher in his dotage: a retirement home for Canadian icons. We stayed there longer than any of the other boats, sitting on his deck playing guitars and trying to remember Gordon Lightfoot songs before eventually paddling over to Matthew Grogono's sea-blue craft, where a salsa dance party was happening with a dozen visiting Cubans in straw hats and linen suits. Voices shot across the water. Barbecue smoke thickened the air.

Yellowknife Bay was alive.

John was embraced by the houseboaters. Most of them were aware of the circumstances of his arrest. One older, blue-jeaned fellow waved around a spliff the length of a Twizzler and told him (here was another thing about the bay: hippiedom without any hippies): "Man, we're fighting on the same side," an opinion stoked after issues surrounding the summer's houseboat fire, but established years earlier in 1996, when Grogono, the Snowking, and Gary Vaillancourt fought the city for trying to claim jurisdiction over the water (the government later abandoned its lawsuit against the residents, deciding that matching their resistance was beyond its energies). John took the houseboaters through everything that had happened, his tenor booming down the lake to people who might have liked to change stations, but could not. The houseboaters nodded in rhythm, having dealt with the city's shit for years. For them, the government, the cops, and the fire department were all the same: too straight to understand why they wanted to live the way they did, and too uptight to be unconventional in a place that defied convention.

Ryan let us paddle around like two guys from the city—we worked hard but got nowhere—and as the late evening dimmed, we headed to shore. I looked back to see John sitting high on the canoe bench like a beer-can king, unburdened and unchallenged by the case for the first time in what felt like ages, which was just as well. Soon, the aurora would begin, the days would wane, the air would cool to a snap, and evening darkness would rise to swallow the light. The trial would be everything.

After heading back up the hill from The Woodyard, John insisted we wrench whatever was left out of the night, demanding that we make last call at Harley's, Yellowknife's central strip bar. I begged off.

"I'm not a strip bar guy," I told him.

"Fuck that," he said. "You got me out there on the water and now I want to buy you a drink. I won't take no for an answer and that's that."

We argued for a moment in the dark entranceway near the open doors of the club. A ZZ Top song and a strong booze reek floated up the stairs from the depths of the bar. I told John about the first time I'd ever gone to a strip joint—a disconsolate occasion at a low ebb in my life—and how I was embarrassed by one of the dancers, who recognized me. I also told him about going to the Zanzibar Tavern on Toronto's Yonge street for a friend's stag, only to come across a father whose child attended my son's preschool, primping his hair in the bathroom mirror before returning to his spot on Pervert's Row. John laughed his barking dog laugh and tried turning me around into the club. Finally, I stopped resisting.

"Okay, let's go for a drink," I said.

We were about to enter when two women came up the stairs, eye-linered with tangled blond hair, heels, and short leather skirts; one of them petite, the other not. As they reached the top of the landing, their eyes suddenly grew wide.

"You're John McFadden!" said the smaller woman, a phrase that, because I'd only heard it expressed with venom, confused the excitement of their voices.

"I am," said John, stepping back.

"You're our hero," said the tall one, pressing her hands to her chest like Mary Pickford.

"Way to stand up to the cops, man," said the other woman, waving a fist through the air, unlike Mary Pickford.

John was speechless.

"C'mere," said the tall woman, gesturing with the crook of her finger.

She moved to John, gathered him in her arms, and hugged him. He hugged back, not quite knowing what to do with his hands.

The women asked where I fit in.

"He's my biographer," said John, lighting a smoke.

"You have a biographer?" asked one of the ladies.

Everyone laughed.

I went home.

John went inside.

30

THE WOMAN WHO SWALLOWED A CONTINENT

J ohn's trial date neared, then was moved slightly later after the mag- istrate, Judge Garth Malakoe, found a minor oversight in the defence's submission of papers, prompting the newspaper to change lawyers. The waiting sucked because so many people were being kept at bay, but at least John, the newspaper staff, and their visiting fake journalist (me) could enjoy the annual Folk on the Rocks music festival—Yellowknife's July rave-up—without worrying about one of their writers languishing in jail.

Musicians arrived from every corner of the country, including throat- singer Tanya Tagaq and spoken-word artist Shane Koyczan, both of whom had spent their formative years here. Dan Mangan, Shred Kelly, Corb Lund, Leela Gilday, and Terra Lightfoot were also scheduled to play, and after a turbulent summer punctuated with the volatility of John's arrest, scrapes between the houseboaters and the authorities, the declining econ- omy, and the thinning population—in the June 22 issue of *News/North*, Mike Bradshaw from N.W.T.'s Chamber of Commerce told Shawn, "I think it's safe to assume we're in a downward spiral here"—everyone was ready to forget their shit and have fun, if only for a weekend.

At the beginning of this book, I describe Yellowknife as lacking regional songs and having produced few performers of substantial reputation, but it was exactly this kind of southern-bias bullshit I hoped to shed during my time in the North. While it's true that Yellowknife didn't have a city band the way Kingston had The Tragically Hip or St. John's had Ron Hynes, the Northwest Territories still yielded a series of fascinating figures whose musical lives wouldn't have happened had they come from anywhere else in Canada.

For instance, there was the violin player Angus Beaulieu (pronounced "Bol-io" in the North), who grew up in Fort Resolution. When Angus was a young man, he travelled by twenty-foot skiff every spring to Hay River— "The trip took a day and a half if there was no ice," he said—where he played seasonal dances at a fellow named Johnny Lamalice's place (Angus also occasionally made the journey in December by dogsled, taking two and a half days to traverse the southern end of the Territory). One time during his spring trip, he realized halfway there that he'd forgotten his fiddle, but his companion—his grandpa—refused to turn around. When he arrived, he told the crowd that he'd left his rig at home, so people asked around the community trying to find one. They did—it was the property of a man named Frank Lepine, who was away at the spring hunt—but the bow had only a few hairs on it. Johnny told Angus they'd shot a horse with a bad foot just that morning, and so a group of men and women went into the bush to cut off the tail. When they brought it back, Beaulieu chose the longest hair and an old woman washed out the poop before hanging it above the wood stove in the kitchen. Since very few visiting musicians made it to Hay River, everybody stayed in the house waiting for the hair to dry—which it did—until Angus realized he needed rosin. He decided that spruce gum would work, and so the crew was dispatched again, where they combed the bush looking for spruce gum. After they found some, Angus prepared his bow, and, at five in the morning, the dance started; the sawing of Angus's violin and a great thunder of feet. The musician played for hours into the next day and the bow held fine.

There was another local man named Alex Czarnecki, who, before moving to Yellowknife, played in Pierre Trudeau's private campaign band, performing from an open-air limousine bus while the prime minister whistle-stopped and danced for his adoring crowds. Alex worked in many capacities in music in Yellowknife—musical theatre, Legion rock bands, brass bands—and, one evening in the nearby community of Dettah, he found himself in the middle of what can only be described as the most Canadian musical instance ever: jamming with two loons on the Slave Lake shoreline while playing Guy Lombardo's saxophone. According to a story found in the archives of the Prince of Wales Northern Heritage Centre, Czarnecki, who was given Lombardo's instrument at the behest of his son, said (I'm paraphrasing here): "I took [my saxophone] out and started playing, just running nonsense scales—*duo doo dat doo*—that echoed in the bay. Suddenly I heard a loon going *da doo da doo*. It came back. It was joined by a second loon and this dialogue between the little saxophone and these two loons went on for about twenty minutes. I would play and they'd do something back. They would dive down then come back up. It was like a dream. It was magical. Also, it was a time when I was healing from various things and so it was very spiritual to me. I played some last notes. I remember sitting on a rock. My wife, Carol, was watching all of this and the lake was dead calm. I went *doo da doo bum boo*. They went *do da la doo* and made some funny noises. They dove under and I never saw them again. We finished. That was it. It was the last time I ever played that sax."

One morning during breakfast at the Grange, I told a few of these stories to Indio Saravanja, who was the closest Yellowknife had to a non-Indigenous lyrical soul (Digawolf, along with William Greenland and Stephen Kakfwi, were the town's Dene voices). He'd written a handful of great songs about the city, including the residential school elegy, "First Communion," which he played across the North at the behest of the Truth and Reconciliation Commission, which had flown him to Inuvik to perform it.

In the 1970s, Indio's father, Elias, brought his family to the Northwest Territories from Argentina (think about *that* change of culture) on the promise of a job at Giant Mine. "He got the job by phone on a Wednesday, and we arrived on Friday, only to discover that they'd given his position away," said Indio, who found himself going to school with miners' and bureaucrats' kids as well as Dene children from nearby N'dilo, known as Rainbow Valley in the 70s and 80s for its multicoloured shacks. "When I grew up, I had a strong accent. I was an immigrant and there were three black kids in town. The Filipino kid was my best friend and we were picked on and bullied. My life was like a cross between *The Outsiders* and *River's Edge*. The Dene kids from Rainbow Valley spat tobacco juice at us in kindergarten, and I was terrified of them because of everything I'd seen on TV and in movies: cowboys and Indians, and all of that. They eventually became my friends. A lot of them are gone now and almost half of the boys are dead. I always say that 25 per cent of the kids in my class became jailbirds; 25 per cent became jail guards; 20 per cent died from drugs or violence before they turned eighteen; 20 per cent joined the local workforce, and maybe 10 per cent matriculated and became university-educated professionals and got the fuck out, sometimes returning as well-paid political elite. Still, it was PTSD for all," he told me.

For almost a full winter, Indio's family lived upstairs at the Gold Range. The Ukrainian owners helped them out while his dad looked for work, eventually landing a job at the mayor's car dealership where the *Yellowknifer* now stands. "After six years, Elias opened his own garage," said Indio. "He was one of the only mechanics who worked on vehicles from N'dilo. He fixed their cars and people came by with food—fish, caribou, moose—when they couldn't pay. We grew up with an underdog mentality and my dad loved the Indigenous communities. He was a Christian. He was the only guy who hired ex-convicts and gave jobs to Dene men who disappeared after their first payday. In my mid-20s, during a visit back to Yellowknife, I remember Elias telling me, 'I finally get it. I've been helping these people for twenty years, and they've been helping me, but I never understood them. Why they didn't stay with the job? Why did they leave so soon? Now I see that it's because they don't have a ghost inside them. They don't have the hungry ghost, the European disease, which we all have.

Instead, they have something else: the ability to laugh, to be generous, and to live in the moment.' My dad had more in common with the Dene than he had with the white community. They influenced our family forever." Indio's story echoed something that Samuel Hearne had observed during early contact with the Dene—"Nothing but personal or family calamities can disturb their tranquillity, while misfortunes of the lesser kind sit lightly on them"—although it's hard to know whether to trust the explorer, who, after meeting the Chipewyans, also wrote: "They pronounced me to be the perfect human being."

Indio played drums in a heavy metal band that performed six nights a week at various bars around Yellowknife. "In the mid-90s, there were fifteen live music bars downtown. Back then, the strip was different. There was a place across the street called the Rec Hall, and there'd be brawls every night when the bars got out. There were knife fights, blood and vomit, just brutal violence," he said, his voice quavering at the memory. One night, Indio found himself drinking at a bar called the Float Base. He went to the washroom and was confronted by an enormous Dene man who tried to pick a fight with him. "I thought he was going to kill me," he said, "and I didn't know what to do. I tried defusing the situation but one thing led to another and I thought, 'All right, I have no choice here, let's go.' The dude started swinging and missing and then all of a sudden he grabbed me close and hugged me. He was convulsing in tears, just shaking, and I spent an hour with him in the bathroom, listening to his story about what happened to him in residential school. The fucked-up thing was that I'd lived almost my entire life in Yellowknife, and it was the first time I'd heard about what happened to those kids in those places."

Indio left the Territories for almost thirty years—Spain, Montreal, Toronto, Mexico, Argentina—occasionally coming back to work, and then leaving again, continuing his love-hate relationship with Yellowknife. At one point, he settled in New York and became best friends with the gifted American singer, Jeff Buckley, who gave him five hundred dollars from his first record contract to help him get back up north. One evening in his houseboat on Yellowknife Bay, he pulled out a quarter-inch master tape and showed it to me: a reel-to-reel recording of him and Jeff singing together in an East Village apartment circa 1993.

On one of his returns to the city, Indio drove a cab in Yellowknife. "I lasted two months," he said. "The decay around me was devastating, like a bomb had blown away the downtown core. I wrote a few epic songs about it, then swore I'd never come back." Still, it's what he did, recently returning to work as a sound technician and living on the bay in a small wooden vessel built from two gold mine cabooses. "Yellowknife Bay transcends Yellowknife," he told me. "For years, I carried the memory of this place through the world like a map to a secret treasure in my back pocket, the legend of it. The same bohemian freedom and way of life I'd sought out internationally was here: affordable, wild, maverick, singular, and special. But I don't belong to Yellowknife anymore, and vice versa. It still summons me back, but now we're just old friends. Today, it's about my music and my daughter. The real world is calling. Partly it's the fact that so much of what I need from my career is south and east of here, and partly it's the feeling that, as an artist, I've written all I can about this place."

On Friday afternoon, the festival opened. There were camper vans with decals, hippies-not-hippies with guitars, families slugging blankets and coolers to main stages, golf carts ferrying performers down sandy paths blanketing the bare rock, tented local food vendors, and drum heads hit during sound checks—*goammm*—that footballed around Fred Henne Park, carried on the clean air and light so that even the people in New Town looked up, wondering who was outside booting their recycling bin. The first marquee show featured Tanya Tagaq, appearing just past midday on the wooden NWT Pride stage. Because Folk on the Rocks wasn't over-programmed with too many events competing against each other— there were no tiresome workshops—festival-goers could focus on one performer. Beer stalls were staked and bins filled with ice. People crowded the area in front of the stage and on picnic tables in the middle of the grounds, and, within a few moments, the show started.

In many ways, the slow awakening of Canada to its northern regions had been triggered by Tanya Tagaq's rise from independent and alternative music streams to the front page of Arts sections across Canada, as well as major touring productions in disciplines that included film and ballet and concerts. For people living in the Northwest Territories, the throat-singer's impact was profound. "Her sound is the sound of the North," writer Andrew Livingstone told me, "and knowing that she's reaching the rest of Canada through her popularity gives people hope that we're being heard, read, whatever." Because there was no performer like her in the world—at least no one as instinctively connected to the essence and power of the land—her gig at Folk on the Rocks possessed a certain intrigue and magic. It would be the first time she'd played there since performing as "a baby folk singer," which is what she told the expectant crowd as the band, led by master violinist Jesse Zubot, readied to begin its set.

Throat-singing makes you listen differently. There's no transparent narrative, or at least none that Southerners recognize, having been weaned on pop music structures and Johnny Winter lead breaks. Instead, you let the performer take you blindly to wherever they decide to go, lost in aural settings that are new and unpredictable and affecting. Throat-singing is musically transformative—the singer's circular breathing creates sound, melody, and noise from the body cavity that calls to mind the roaring of the natural world as much as it does, say, Thom Yorke and Radiohead—but it also clears a sonic cavity gummed up with car commercial jingles and sitcom themes. The ear opens, but the mind and heart open, too. Every time I've seen Tanya Tagaq perform, someone has been carried out of the room, having discovered something in their soul or corporeal being they were not prepared to experience or share.

The Folk on the Rocks audience—weighted with cousins, aunts, and longstanding friends, a gathering owing to the singer's childhood in

Cambridge Bay and to her teenage years spent in Yellowknife—laughed when the singer told us, "It's nice being in a place where I'm not the only Eskimo at the festival." Zubot—as severe-looking before the performance as Tanya was bright-faced and mischievous—stroked his bow across the gut of his strings and you could feel the crowd settle somewhere between calm and about to lose itself. The singer, who wore a blood-red silk dress, settled at her mark in the middle of the stage and crouched, holding the microphone to her face. She sucked in a breath, then another, before producing a low growl that reminded one of a waking dog pack. Over the next few moments, her voice swelled into a long howling chamber of sound, a person swallowing a continent. Sweat poured down her face and she drove her entire physical nature into the performance, squatting low to the stage until it seemed as if sound was exploding from the vessel of her body. After about thirty-five wholly improvised minutes—part Gilgamesh, part roaring sea, part wolf den, part Led Zeppelin, part playful sylph—she settled on a word—"Ma"—which she repeated over and over until it swirled about like a gyre. Someone in the audience screamed while others openly wept as the word tore through the music. It was one of the most profound live moments I've ever experienced, more so considering that it was created by an Indigenous woman in the Far North, in Yellowknife. When the piece ended, I asked a woman next to me what "Ma" meant in Inuvialuit. She turned to me, her face matted with sweat, hair, and tears.

"It means 'no.'"

Tanya Tagaq performed one last piece: a traditional composition that she sang with my landlord's daughter, Tiffany, and another friend. They held their mics close to each other and at the end, they burst into tears and hugged: old friends on stage in Yellowknife. I felt proud seeing someone I knew up there. The crowd cheered them on, desperate for more, but that was all. The stage emptied and we turned to the trees and the lake. We moved toward them.

Over the festival's two days, I counted seven performers doing songs about either Truth and Reconciliation or missing and murdered Indigenous women. Folk on the Rocks was profound with these issues. At one point on Sunday, I stood with Dëneze and Shane Koyczan and listened to them speak about what had happened, what had to happen, and what they thought might happen when it came to Canada's recognition of Indigenous people and the North.

"Everything changes with education," said Shane, speaking at a frenetic clip. "People have to believe they are powerful, that their vote is powerful and that they can change the nation and be empowered by democracy. You can be somebody working at Starbucks or somebody working at the highest level of a corporation, but we all have the exact same power. People need to be reminded of this daily, but instead people are reminded that they have zero power, that it's out of their control and out of their hands. Really, though, the opposite is true. People are sick of their taste of choice. Orange Crush, motherfucker."

"Canadians have never figured out how to create a government that makes sense in this part of the world," said Dëneze, keeping pace with Shane. "The mayor in Fort Simpson has to pledge allegiance to the Queen because even our conditioning has been conditioned. People don't even realize that what they're doing might be racist or discriminatory. It's important to learn your history. Like, where does Canada even have the title power to affect land claim negotiations when they were originally based on a sale from the Hudson's Bay Company and before that the North West Company? It comes down to the 'document of discovery,' a papal writ that decreed that any place landed on by Europeans that wasn't already Christian meant they could take the land as their own. They were empowered to do whatever they wanted to do to the heathens who lived there. That's what we're dealing with. The mentality exists a hundred years later."

Shane added: "People graduate from high school and get their university degrees and assume they have an understanding of what it means to be Canadian. But that's bullshit. There's a huge ignorance there, even for educated people, even for those who actually care."

"We're ignored and forgotten," said Dëneze. "The North is the last place where change happens, but there's the potential for us to be the first. Why not? We should be experimenting with all sorts of things. If stuff works in the North, it can work anywhere else."

Other festival-goers saw us talking and they ambled over, throwing out ideas and opinions. Travis Mercredi said: "The ultimate riddle is: how do we make this place work? There's no local economy, so how do we incentivize people's desire to lift things up, but also keep the bottom line? We're nomadic people, and circumpolar cultures behave in a specific way. You trap and hunt in the winter and in the summer you come back to known fishing spots and you have a pop-up community and you share work, and it's how it's always worked. It was convenient for the powers that be to establish their Western living model: pay for this, pay for that, and everyone gets a cheque. But, at its essence, that disempowers people no matter where you live. You have to nurture an unengaged populous. The social programs are bad and they're getting worse. You're starting to see younger generations getting more and more fucked up. It's a huge problem. We're just not going upwards."

As I stood with the group, the scene reflected the idealism that folk festivals promise but rarely deliver: people exchanging ideas and debating issues while a performer on a nearby stage—in this case, Deline's Leela Gilday—played a heavy song about the abduction and disappearance of a friend's sister. After a while, I turned away from the group, wanting to hear the music more closely. When I did, a person spoke to me.

"Hey buddy."

It was John, wearing a Run-DMC shirt. Together, we made our way through the grounds—one song from this stage, another song from that one—and eventually, we ended up at the beer garden. Dan Mangan played and the festival closed under dimming skies with the Dene drummers hitting caribou-skin drums and chanting while the crowd, as per the musicians' instructions, walked in a slow circle around the grounds. After the finale, we arrived at an end-of-festival party behind the stage, tight to the bank of Frame Lake. Beer was sold from an old fishing cabin lit by fairy lights while two deejays—the Funk Brothers from Vancouver—spun records from a makeshift tiki hut on a sandy 30-degree-sloped dance floor. All the performers were there, including the Dene drummers; Loren; Pat Kane, the brilliant local photographer; assorted volunteers; and dozens of people from town. Midnight grew to 1 a.m. which grew to 2 a.m. The Funk Brothers came on the mic and said, "Sorry, folks, the bar is closed." People groaned, but it was okay. I looked down to the end of a long dock on the lake and saw three women silhouetted against the moonlit water, their bodies swaying to the deejay's beats, arms wrapped around each other. It felt good leaving my imagination there, so I got up to leave the grounds and return to Old Town and the Allooloos' cabin, where I'd savour the end of my time in the North as if it were a Life Saver melting on my tongue. But just as I was packing away my notebook, the deejays returned to the mic:

"We have another announcement," they told the crowd. "The bar has reopened and all of the beer is free!"

People stormed the fishing cabin, emerging with armfuls of beer cans. The deejays grinded on and I thought I could hear another kind of music snaking from the speakers. I listened beneath the swirling electronica: a cement-mixer voice singing over a swampy drum beat with scrappy guitars cycling across major chords. Something about Vietnam. Something about the cops. I called to Loren through the crowd:

Creedence.

31

THE HEADLINER

I f nothing good ever happened again to John McFadden—if he was locked up in prison or barred from every tavern in town or assigned Rotary Club stories for life—he would at least know that his face had made it on to a T-shirt: FREE JOHN MCFADDEN, sitting above a cartoon illustration of the reporter in full jabber, selling for ten dollars a pop. A lawyer in town had made them in advance of the trial and you couldn't walk into a bar without seeing one. Some people bought them as a joke, some didn't, and orders had come in from Toronto, where former co-workers wanted to promote the cause. If John's place in Yellowknife and newspaper folklore wasn't already established, he was now immortalized the way every band has been: their shirts outlasting whatever reasons they were made in the first place.

It was a crazy few weeks leading up to the trial. Something new happened with each passing day. One moment, things looked great for John; the next day, not so much. Word reached him that police were tapping his phone calls—this raised the possibility of an illegal breach of privacy—when, in fact, the RCMP had been surveilling a known weed dealer and John's hoarse voice had shown up on clandestine recordings of him trying to score. Another twist came when the Privacy Commission consented to allow John and his lawyer to view the courthouse tape of him being man-handled by the sheriff, confirming what he'd remembered about the incident: the push, the arm lock, the way the security officer had tossed him to the carpet. John's lawyer thought it might be a trump card to play during his trial, but, in the end, no further viewing was granted. In a case where police had allegedly rousted the reporter and put him in jail, the film showing almost this exact thing was unavailable to the accused (John would later appeal the department's decision not to allow him a copy of the video). Making it worse was knowing that the incriminating tape existed, and that its submission could have potentially taken out the Crown's case at the knees.

If John couldn't get ahead, there was at least news that both he and Shawn had won national community newspaper awards, with John placing third in two categories. He'd been cited for two stories, including his Decheco King sword murder piece, of which the judges wrote: "Who stakes out the home of a man who is the sole survivor of a deadly attack that killed his best friend? Reporter John McFadden, that's who." John was proud of the recognition—he kept the paper with the award announcement on the dashboard of the company car—and it steadied him, I thought, if allowing a certain vindication for the ways in which he'd been criticized as a reporter. The award was also sweeter knowing how displeased the RCMP and Ms. Sturko had been during the reporting. At the time, she told John, "I don't like where the story is going," but he said, "There was a vacuum in the story and I had to get to the bottom of it. It was my job, for fuck's sake." Even better—and even steadier—Sturko announced she'd put in for a transfer to Ottawa, and at her going-away party, she and John exchanged a few words and, all of a sudden, they "hugged and got it all into the open. It was all very civil and she left on good terms with me, and me with her. I'm glad it happened; really glad," he said, expressing relief. I asked John if he still wondered whether Sturko had stonewalled him because someone from above had ordered her to maintain a hard line, but he said, "That's in the past now, buddy," relieved to be on the other side of at least one conflict before inevitably marching toward another.

With the beginning of the trial, everything about Yellowknife—the wild poetry of the land; the merry eccentricities of Old Town; the eternal madness of the Range; and the August sky with its grape-juice evenings and torn-mattress clouds—was sucked into an airless unblinking Territorial courtroom where reporters, lawyers, justice department officials, and friends gathered, among them Yellowknife's leading pot activist, Karen MacKearney, who surprised no one by giving John a long hug before the reporter moved through the gallery, nodded to the crowd, and took his seat beside his lawyer, with whom he shook hands. Every item in John's formal ensemble had been borrowed from someone else: dress shoes from Elijah; a white shirt passed down from a late uncle; dark unpressed pants left in the cabin by a previous tenant; and a black suit jacket with bits of dog hair along the shoulder that he'd found rolled up in a ball under his desk at the *Yellowknifer*. "But the tie," he told me, "the tie is mine."

John's lawyer was a man named Peter Harte, a seasoned barrister and flâneur with a shaved head, goatee, and wire-frame glasses, who wore a floral bow tie and a suit vest. He was opposed by the Crown attorney—a Québécois woman named Annie Piché—who was younger than Harte and who spoke English with a pronounced Montreal accent—she'd grown up and gone to school there before attending the London School of Economics—making Harte's work appear more Osgoode Hall professorial, and hers a little more like the trial was taking place in The Hague. Piché's wardrobe was muted—black and dark blues—and she possessed a generous, uncombative tone to complement the relative efficacy by which she examined the witnesses. If John feared attack from someone out of the lion's den, the profile didn't fit Piché. She flipped through her yellow legal pad and kept her line of questioning moving in straight lines, maintaining an almost mundane rhythm to the proceedings.

All Yellowknife media was in attendance along with a few members of the Justice Department, as well as Bruce Valpy and Mike Scott. Together we stood as the judge—Garth Malakoe—was buzzed into the chambers. John had hoped for a magistrate with a record sympathetic to cases concerning the people vs. the RCMP, or vice versa, but if Malakoe wasn't that, he wasn't *not* that, either. Everyone agreed he was a fair judge, and something about his face and eyes and manner confirmed this: reserved and focused, but gently so. To me, he looked like the actor Sam Neill, if less physically robust. He wasn't gavel happy, and not so self-absorbed that he excessively imposed himself on the proceedings, crowing "I'll remind people that this is my courtroom!" or other clichés I tried remembering from . . . *And Justice for All* or *To Kill A Mockingbird* or *Physical Evidence*, the Burt Reynolds/Ned Beatty/Theresa Russell comedy filmed in Toronto in the 80s in which I'd been paid fifty dollars a day to be an extra.

The judge straightened some papers on his desk, opened his laptop, and called the courtroom to order. The first officer called by the Crown was ten-year RCMP officer—and acting Watch Commander—Constable Bill Maxwell (as before, I've given the police officers aliases here), whom John had hardly mentioned to me, partly because he was the least threatening of the officers and partly because he was as flat as a tin of evaporated milk. If Officer DeMarco, the other constable testifying, was menacing in his physical space, Maxwell took the stand like a man looking for a pole to hide behind. He was as awkward in his suit as Harte seemed born to it; a barely middle-aged man with a thinning hairline and few of the qualities found in the jack-bodied and gym-hewn figures of modern policing, who look like what happens when you cross MMA with UFC. In the witness box, his body cheated to one side and his hands remained forever crossed at his belt buckle as if he'd been instructed by a parent. He never quite knew where to look, answering questions by turning to the judge, then to the Crown, then back to the judge. His uncertainties provided a reminder why the trial was unique: instead of being the questioners, the police were now the questionees. If workdays saw them uniformed and patrolling the streets, here they were exposed in court wearing the suit they wore to their cousin's wedding. With John seated beside his lawyer, and the police officer standing in front of him, the cop was at the behest of John's lawyer, and thus John, even though it was the reporter whose ass was on the line. To say that the process was humiliating might have stretched the notion, but Harte's cross-examination did nothing to pump the officer's tires. He was now down there in court with everyone else—the drunks, the drug dealers, the journalists—trying to piece together just what the frig happened on a certain Canada Day weekend in Yellowknife.

Questions were floated, and then stabbed at by John's lawyer. There was some disagreement about the nature of his client's sobriety and truculence, and whether an angry crowd had formed outside the Elks Club, proving a threat to police. The lawyer's pace and nature of questioning might not have seemed immediately purposeful, but you could see Harte wearying Maxwell, his words tapping at him like a felt hammer on a taut piano string. The lawyer's angle of attack found its target once Maxwell testified that there'd been a "bubble" around the van that John was told to not penetrate. Harte proved quickly that the idea of the bubble was unclear—that it was a "bubble" gave him plenty to work with: something invisible with an amorphous size. Harte wrote a few things down before raising the issue of the police officers' search of the van, in which they'd tried to secure the vehicle's papers as well as the VIN (serial) number. Harte questioned the legality of the search under the Motor Vehicles Act—suggesting they needed a warrant—and lingered over the legalese, clearly tiring the witness, the courtroom, and McFadden, who slumped a little in his seat. It was a mundane tactic, and it soaked up at least thirty minutes of the morning's session, effectively dampening the narrative of the charges, which Piché had tried to emphasize during her questioning of the constable. Harte also raised a salient point: if the police were merely looking for the van's documentation after locating the intoxicated owner—and after calling in the confirmed stolen plates—what exactly had the reporter been obstructing?

Harte circled back to the issue of John's behaviour. Maxwell insisted that John was causing a disturbance, at which point Harte asked:

"Was he charged with causing a disturbance?"

"No, he was not," said Maxwell.

"Was he charged with public intoxication?"

"No, he was not."

"Did you see McFadden enter the van?"

"No, I did not."

"Was his body inside the van?"

"No, it was not."

Throughout all of this, John sat beside his lawyer trying not to slouch, his suit jacket nonetheless bundling at his shoulders. If the reporter's personality generally made him seem greater than his height, he came across in court like any other nebbish at the mercy of the law, the mischief of his eyes and quirks of his expressions hidden from us. Even more discomfiting was watching him fall silent for such great stretches of time, although in a few instances, I noticed him look back to us while conferring with his lawyer—the hint of a raised eyebrow, the trace of a sardonic glance—before turning his focus back to the bench. This was most prominent after the officer described McFadden as an "angry man with a camera," which saw Shawn look over to me with a smirk that suggested an easy headline—ANGRY MAN WITH CAMERA!—one that John himself would have relished. The testimony confirmed something that John had said all along: only an immature police force would be threatened by a Nikon digital point-and-shoot. A lot of time was spent exhibiting the camera. They explored the length of its lens—Harte argued that the information was germane to whether a shot inside the van could be taken without thrusting it across the "plane" of the van's doors—and discussed the ability of John to get a decent shot while having very little comprehension or knowledge of how the digital device and its zoom worked. Walter had earlier submitted testimony in which he'd confirmed John's incompetence as a photographer. It had portrayed him as a kind of boob, but this was a slight he was willing to suffer.

Harte ended his questioning and the officer stepped down. Everyone agreed that if the other cops were as awkward-seeming as Maxwell, the defence would skate freely. The notion of reasonable doubt would be a two-foot putt.

Officer DeMarco was called next. He seemed sturdier, and he was, proving a tougher nut to crack than Maxwell, who'd been called first by the Crown because he was the least confident witness. DeMarco arrived at court in his uniform, but if this, along with shaved head, made him more imposing, his voice was surprisingly gentle, and he was, at times, forgiving when it came to his description of John, insisting that he hadn't used profanity nor was he very drunk after coming out of the Black Knight. He also said that he knew exactly who John was because, the previous year, he'd been called to McFadden's house to investigate a break-and-enter, and John had answered the door, seeming, according to DeMarco, "calm and friendly." If Maxwell had characterized McFadden as a drunk lunatic "yelling and screaming" and "smelling of liquor with slurred speech," it wasn't DeMarco's impression at all. Even though John described him to me as being the most confrontational of the officers and had sworn at him, it belied the constable's behaviour on the stand. Even when he was challenged on this matter by the defence, he told Malakoe that he might have said something along the lines of "Get lost, we're doing stuff here," which reads as preposterously juvenile but sounded plausible by the large man trying to appear soft, an act that shouldn't have worked, but did. Harte laboured to tear holes in his story, but because there was a calm about the witness and a confident ballast to his words, even a neutral observer would have found a certain credibility in his testimony. In the end, the impression left by police was level. The session concluded with neither side emerging over the other.

John headed across the street to the Black Knight, just a few metres away from where his arrest happened. If you didn't know him, you might have confused this for being a strident gesture remaining so close to the courthouse, but the truth is he wanted a drink, and so did the rest of us after the intensity of the session. John was cool to it all, reading the progress of the trial the way one might study a baseball game: wondering who the Crown had remaining in its lineup and how his lawyer might pitch to them. A few people came over—mostly lawyers and members of the GNWT—and said hello. One of them asked, "So, how you doing?"

"Not in jail," said John, his arms crossed on the table.

We played out the events of the day. At one point, Maxwell had suggested that John carried "the odour of liquor." I told John: "I think you've got the name of your autobiography right there."

"'Angry Man with a Camera' is better, though," he said.

"'John McFadden: Yelling and Screaming,'" I suggested.

"That would be good, too," he said, draining his pint.

When we returned to the courthouse, the next officer to testify was Constable Smith. He was cross-examined by video from Toronto, having taken a job there in the interim (whether he'd been shipped out of town because of the trial was a question to which nobody had a clear answer, and there were suspicions in John's camp that, because of the patchy digital hookup between the notoriously unreliable Northwestel and Ontario, video jumps and frozen images would challenge Harte's flow of questions, making it harder to engage the witness).

Smith comported himself somewhere between the two other officers. He was smaller than the others, but with a small, stocky build, close-cropped hair, and a stubborn chin, speaking from his stomach in low, masculine tones. He was the least eloquent of the officers, but the hardest to get inside. He painted a picture similar to DeMarco's: McFadden was combative; and the photojournalist came too close to the van after stepping off the sidewalk. Addressing the matter of the crowd in front of the Elks, Harte produced a set of photographs taken from John's camera in which two, maybe three, people were shown smoking outside the club. The lawyer asked the police officer to square this with his impressions, but he replied that there'd been a lot more people outside, you just couldn't see them. The lawyer dwelled on the relative emptiness of the image, but Smith insisted that the photo was incomplete. I looked to see if any of this was registering with the magistrate, but Malakoe's game face was such that you couldn't be sure of anything. Harte hammered awhile longer but the cat wouldn't chase the mouse. Piché objected to her opposite's line of questioning—her appeals were mostly sustained—and Smith kept parroting his answer. Harte reluctantly moved on. John rubbed his face, realizing that there was no blood in that stone.

At one point, the lawyer mentioned the *Yellowknifer*, the first time the paper was namechecked during the trial. That it had taken this long supported the notion that, even though northern media would be affected by the outcome of the trial, it was the reporter who would suffer the most from the fallout, at least until the next time something like this occurred. During proceedings, Harte never once raised the issue of freedom of the press—"Not a reliable precedent in this case," he told me later—and resisted turning the trial into an indictment of journalism. While Bruce Valpy attended every minute of the proceedings, and Mike Scott continued to pay the bills (Mike Bryant was at the shop chained to pumping out a newspaper twice a week), they were neither summoned nor asked to account for John's effectiveness as a reporter or standing as a citizen. As the lawyers headed toward calling the accused as the final witness, it became obvious: it was John's life that was on trial. Outside the courtroom, a screen displayed docket names like flight listings at an airport, but there was never any argument about who the headliner was. He even had the T-shirt to prove it.

Before John took the stand in his own defence, Harte drummed home to him the importance of remaining calm and professional and not rising to whatever bait the Crown offered as a way of getting him to support its portrait of an unprofessional drunk who'd gone out of his way to make a bad situation worse. Even though this was excellent advice, part of me hoped that John would express all the shit he'd had to deal with and rail against the problematic ways in which the city's forces operated. As he settled on the witness stand—moving from a desk facing the judge to one to his right, and sitting, not standing, revealing his weary profile to the gallery—I saw that, no matter whose shoes he was wearing or what kind of shirt he borrowed, he'd always be an outsider wherever he lived or worked—unpolished and brusque, as noisy as a crash cymbal flung down a flight of stairs—more so at a time when media personalities occupied greater space in the telegenic newscape, and where finish counted for more than process. In this sense, the trial wasn't only about whether cops had a right to arrest reporters for taking photographs. It was also about allowing room for fuck-ups who could sniff out and write a good story, and who didn't care what they looked like before, during, or especially after.

32

THE *YELLOWKNIFER*

Suddenly, it was autumn. The Chinese and Japanese tourists arrived—the airport produced them daily, mostly couples who, according to locals, sought to procreate under the northern lights, a superstition based on an old episode of *Northern Exposure* in which an Indigenous character promoted the idea that a male would be born if intercourse occurred under aurora skies—and the days chilled into fall jacket weather and gloomy skies. Occasionally, the canopy cleared to promise an evening light show, but you could never be certain when the phenomenon would take hold. On the evening before John's testimony, I stood on Elijah's rooftop talking about the Crown's strategy when, over John's shoulder, a wand of light swished across the sky. "Look!" I shouted. We bent our necks, mouths agape, as the aurora splashed in mint green waves from above.

"This is more than I've ever seen," said John, following the undulating light through eyes that, despite all that had happened, maintained a measure of surprise.

"I wonder how the Japanese feel about the aurora bringing luck to writers on trial for obstructing police?" I asked.

"Quick, guys, have sex!" said Elijah, gesturing to me and John.

It was a funny line, but nobody laughed. Still, maybe the lights were a gift. Maybe the North was giving John its best before he was lost to the sallow grey insides of the North Slave, or maybe it was promising something else. Or maybe it was nothing more than brilliant lights against a shock of dark sky, ethereal creatures dripping from the paintbrush of the gods.

The next day, the courtroom filled to hear John tell his story. Annie Piché, the Crown attorney, followed the defence's questioning of his client, and John met her officious cross-examination head-on, composed but for a single moment. This came during questions regarding the engagement between the officers and the reporter, which followed a submission that quoted the police on John being drunk with bloodshot eyes, a suggestion he batted away. Piché announced what DeMarco had said when he'd found the writer crossing the street: "Get lost, we're doing stuff here."

"That's not what he said," John told her.

"Are you saying that he said something else?"

"I am."

"What then, in your recollection, did he say?"

John cleared his throat and moved a little in his chair.

Pausing a moment between each line, he spoke:

"You're fucking John McFadden. What the fuck do you want? Get the fuck out of here."

The words hung there for a moment. Piché stood at her rostrum and John's eyes bore into her, as if repeating the phrase unspoken. Something about the mood of the courtroom was released, a bit of air escaping from a balloon. Despite the sharp curve of their blade, the word "fucking" followed by two "fucks" possessed a humanity that felt lost after days listening to uniformed men speak the way they are expected to speak in a legal setting. Here was John finally being John. He sounded real.

The reporter settled in to answer the rest of the Crown's questions. *"You're fucking John McFadden"* afforded him a sense of confidence the way a boxer finds his form after uttering an inspirational epithet—and maybe some *fuckings* too—into the knuckles of his gloves. Piché restated a few salient points and John corrected her each time: he'd not left the sidewalk; he'd simply followed his nose as a reporter investigating a story; and he'd behaved in the cells with the professionalism of a working reporter trying not to make things worse for everyone, no matter how distressed. Piché never found an edge in establishing John's behaviour as tempestuous or confrontational, and, no matter how she pressed on with efforts to paint John as an angry drunk, in the end "two pints and a Caesar" humanized, rather than demonized, the writer. After asking tough questions all his life, John proved expert in answering them, too.

Piché skidded to the end of her cross-examination—although, truthfully, she was as much out of gas as anything—and Judge Malakoe asked if there were any more witnesses. There were not. The lawyers took a moment to gather their mountainous stacks of papers for final arguments and the court adjourned before taking its final lap.

During the break—thirty minutes—I spared a moment to walk the town, knowing that I'd be leaving Yellowknife soon. The climax of the trial gave my time here a Hollywood ending, and my turn around the city was informed with a kind of melancholy. I passed by the main post office and said hello, then goodbye, to Bear and the others. He asked what had gone down in Tuk, and I told him about the the baseball game under the midnight sun. "You're a real Tukker now," said a small denim-jacketed woman from the far end of the busy flowerbed bench, with about a half-dozen people between them.

"That's what they call people from 'Tuk'?" I asked her.

"No, no, no," said Bear, hitting my knee with his catcher's mitt hand. "They call us 'Eskimos.'"

"That sucks," I said, not knowing what else to say, to which Bear laughed the kind of laugh that could only be produced from an enormous sedentary three-hundred-pound man. The laugh volleyed from one person to another in a hacking chorus of lung-burned sniggering, right there in the gritty heart of the city.

I went to the *Yellowknifer* and thanked Mike and everyone else for their time and openness, still waiting for the jeujing that would never come.

I went back to the printing press and watched and listened as the great machine roared, pushing out newsprint. I stood with a group of writers behind the building, including Glenn, who butted out his smoke and admitted: "John might be a loose cannon, but he doesn't deserve to go to jail." In a few months, Glenn would apply for a job in Edmonton and he'd get it, finally ticketed out of the *Yellowknifer*. Ewan would move back to Burlington, Ontario, with a woman—another reporter—he'd met at the paper, and Julius would start taking cross-fit classes, which had me worrying what might happen if he and John got into another fight (they would, finally forcing John to find another place farther into the city). Shawn stayed in Yellowknife, listening to his police scanner and breaking stories. He suffered John and the others as best he could, but I wondered whether the episode of the *Yellowknifer* vs. the RCMP had shown him what it took to be a lifer reporter, how the bramble of controversy had to be tolerated in order to live the full breadth of a writing life. If John ended up going to jail, it would be left to the young writer to carry the burden of a free press, at least until another talented and driven young person determined to freeze their ass off and write from a northern fishbowl arrived on the next plane north. Still, kids weren't exactly tearing down the shop trying to get in. If Shawn slid and John was sent away, there was no telling what the *Yellowknifer* might become.

I walked Peace River Flats and Old Town, soaking up great secret places that, if time, progress, and development—and writers from Toronto writing about it—meant anything, would become less secret every day. I went to the government wharf and stared out at the houseboats. I fought through the weeds—they'd drooped and fallen a little with the change of seasons—to see if anyone was around in The Woodyard, which they weren't, although something was always happening somewhere in the stacked cordwood yards and cabin hives even if you couldn't see it. I went to the edge of the Dene shore. I bent down to pass my hand through the water and looked over the lake, which, in six weeks, would be pure blue ice.

I called Assan, the cab driver who'd first brought me into the city. He collected me at the Narwal and brought me downtown to hear John's verdict. I climbed into the back seat and asked how things were going. "Good, good, good," he repeated. Then he rolled up the driver's window and *brrrr'ed* at me in the rear-view mirror:

"Winter's coming."

When I arrived back at the courthouse, I received a text message from John—"I'm nervous"—and found Bruce Valpy sitting outside the courtroom, pushing his glasses back as he read and checked his phone. I asked him if anyone had a contingency in place should John be required to dry out in his cell: Valium and B3s to help curb the effects of the DTs. But the managing editor *pfffted* and said, "It's not going to happen," confident that John would walk away a free man. Whether he was simply affecting the calm of a good leader—or whether he was, in fact, being a good leader—I didn't feel any less worried. This was Planet Yellowknife. Crazy shit happened. Things were different here.

The courtroom was packed for the reading of the verdict. I pushed out of my mind the image of John being handcuffed and led away, instead imagining all of us headed to the Black Knight and a party to end all parties, although, honestly, I needed to get my liver out of Yellowknife and put my head down and tell the story of all that had happened. I'd go home and play the story over and over and I'd try to flatten it, mould it, and order it before flattening it out in disgust and shaping it all over again trying to get it right, even though some Northerners would naturally resent that a Southerner had done this while others would grouse about how much I'd gotten wrong, which is inevitable because our impressions are our own and they're flawed and they're personal and we see things the way we see them. All I needed was an ending, and, in a moment, I'd get one. I stared at the last blank page in my notebook wondering whether I would write "Guilty" across it, or, perhaps, a better word. The judge entered the chambers. He nodded to the lawyers and the gallery. He spoke.

The judgement lasted over forty minutes. It was a detailed forensic account explained across sheafs of written material—twenty, thirty pages—which, in the magistrate's slow, careful, and measured tone headed toward its resolve like an evening drive through the countryside pointing to a destination you can see glimmering across a patchwork of fields but aren't sure when or how you'll get there, or what awaits you when you do. The justice spelled out the details of the arrest as if explaining it to a child: who was there, what they were doing, and what they said. He ordered the characters and assembled the backdrop: a cargo van, an investigation, and a reporter with his camera, who, he said, "stepped out of the Black Knight pub in the evening and lit a cigarette," which made me smell the tobacco and feel the midnight light on my face. Malakoe then waded into some legalese, beginning with "It's necessary to provide an overview of the laws of obstruction" before establishing three pivotal questions: What were the levels of his intoxication? Was John yelling and screaming? And did any part of his body enter the van? It was upon these the hills that the RCMP and the Crown had fought its case. Malakoe asked: "Did any of these actions constitute obstruction?"

He made sure that the court knew, in his words, that "anyone who obstructs police is guilty of an offence" before explaining that the *Criminal Code* did not specifically define obstruction, a moat over which John and his lawyer had hoped to vault. There was an early statement that made John's heart leap—"Just taking a photo does not make [a person] culpable"—after which Malakoe said that the police—or rather, the Crown's—argument that John had produced the camera in an effort to make the RCMP's life more difficult seemed implausible against Officer Smith's testimony, which, he implied, had holes and tears, the cop's exaggerations and evasions being "a concern to [him]" because of his tendency to "enhance testimony." The judge told us that "the court's confidence is diminished because of inconsistencies," and, using restraint, he upbraided the officer for refusing to directly answer questions about how a crowd could have existed without evidence of there being one, among the handful of times Smith had filibustered through Harte's line of questioning. After this happened, the lawyer took out his pen and wrote something on a piece of paper. He passed it to John. It read:

"You know that we've won, right?"

Malakoe moved on to discuss the conflicting testimony of the other officers, how John was portrayed by one person as a "glossy-eyed" drunk and another as "showing no co-ordination problem." He tried on John's chorus—"two pints and a Caesar"—and concluded that, to his mind, he did not "accept that he was slurring his speech," arguing that, if John were intoxicated, he wouldn't have remembered how many drinks he'd had, or what had happened to him in such exact detail. Malakoe repeated what Officer DeMarco had, allegedly, said—*"You're fucking John McFadden. What the fuck do you want? Get the fuck out of here"*—and if I didn't know any better, I felt like he was saving a measure of fun for himself, his "fucks" cast about the room.

John and his lawyer did nothing with their body language to express that they knew, but they knew. Since at least two of the officers had told the court that McFadden could take pictures as long as he stayed on the sidewalk—good policing, all told—Malakoe determined that he could, and that he had. Finally, he quoted Smith's testimony in which he said he'd seen John craning into the van, the judge deciding that, if the van's doors were open and John was visible, there's no way he could have lurched inside, passing the critical plane that the officers had suggested during testimony. He also raised issues of the absence of police tape, the neglect to arrest for public mischief, and the failure to administer a breathalyzer test. In the broad light of the Territorial courtroom, the RCMP were being eviscerated.

If Peter Harte saw John as having already crossed home plate, none of us in the gallery were entirely certain, partly because you never knew where the judge would settle when he got to the end of his decision, whether the destination on the other side of the field would be a house filled with people pouring beers and lighting bongs and dancing to Creedence, or whether it would be sad and empty, with only a trace that someone lived there. There was a little more legalese, more plumbing of the concept of obstruction—citing other cases that had been tried in Canada—until, finally, the judge reset the pins:

1. Was John yelling and screaming and agitating the alleged crowd?
2. Had he angrily produced his camera in a confrontational way meant to obstruct?
3. Were the officers forced to stop their search?
4. Had John contaminated the crime scene?

Beginning again at the top, he answered every question resoundingly: "No." And then he told the court:

"I cannot find that John McFadden obstructed the police."

We looked to John. Because his back was to the gallery, we couldn't see his expression. What I noticed, instead, were his white socks drooping below his pant leg, showing his bare ankles. Malakoe repeated himself to be clear: "John McFadden did not intend to obstruct police." John came off the balls of his feet, and his pant legs hiked up a little higher. He could move again.

Malakoe announced an acquittal of the charge. John lost himself, crying into the sleeve of his borrowed jacket. He stood up and turned, hugging Sarah before making his way outside the courthouse into the cool of the North, where he stood and talked to cameras.

"I'm just looking forward to going back to being a reporter," he said in his Skilsaw voice, if with a tired motor pushing the blade. "My job is to write stories and to tell the truth. That's what I'm going to do."

John would forever bitch and complain about Planet Yellowknife, but there was nowhere else that would have him for who he was. He was part of the story now—the city's story—and, as time passed, people would point back to how, in the case of John McFadden vs. the RCMP, the court found the writer innocent of being himself: loud, belligerent, colourful, difficult, and a glorious pain in the ass. He wasn't close to perfect, but maybe that was the point.

After following John to the *Yellowknifer*, I doubled back to the Gold Range Bistro, where I sat down for one last cup of diner coffee and to ruminate on everything that I'd experienced. I'd come to the North wanting to discover this largely unwritten region of Canada through a newsroom, and to have my fears allayed that print and reporting was in its death throes. All of that had happened, but I'd also stepped inside the story of a writer and a place, and the relationship between them. One of things I'd learned was that both the Dene and the city—its paper and the writers—didn't take shit from anyone, and in swirling modern times, they possessed tenfold what everyone else was searching to find: identity. All of this from a place that, before coming here, appeared to have no identity at all, at least as viewed through my southern lens. But Yellowknifers were distinct and true in all of their imperfections, and they taught a lesson one can never be too smart to learn: it's okay to be yourself, whether anyone's noticing or not.

After getting home and working on the book you are now finishing, I thought about what I wanted to do with whatever remained in my life as a writer and an artist. So I started a newspaper, the West End Phoenix, which we home deliver throughout our community, trying to give voice to the legions of writers, photographers and illustrators who, like myself, used to do this kind of thing all the time for other magazines and newspapers whose names we are starting to forget. We're published once a month on newsprint that rolls through a press like the one in the back of the old newsroom, and it allows me to go to work every day pretending I'm in Yellowknife, with John over there in the corner, Deneze riding up from N'Dilo, the Woodyarders paddling across the gut to someone's butterscotch coloured houseboat and Lorne coming down 50th street, producing his recorder to capture the story of the person who just blew into town from a distant frozen place many people have never heard of and maybe never will, but it doesn't matter.

After finishing my coffee, I looked up to find a kid standing beside the table, a yellow strap crossing his shoulder, a heavy yellow bag at his side. I closed my notebook and waited for him to speak.

"Excuse me, sir. You wanna buy a paper?"

ACKNOWLEDGEMENTS

The author wishes to acknowledge the support of Charles Alexander and the Chawkers Foundation, the Ontario Arts Council and the Toronto Arts Council, as well as Northwest Territories Tourism, without whom this book would not have been possible. Thank you, as well, to everyone at the *Yellowknifer*, especially Bruce Valpy, Mike Bryant, and Mike Scott; Scott Sellers, who deftly edited this book and provided endless support to me working through it; and Doug Pepper, who helped the idea come to life. Also, thank you to my family, and especially my wife, who kept life running while I was thousands of miles away.

There are a few time sequences, particularly in the case of the trial, that have been compressed so that the comings and goings of the author to the North—I made seven visits to the Northwest Territories over eighteen months—weren't dragged out. I have changed a few names and done my best to maintain the spirit of dialogue, even though many conversations happened in Yellowknife bars with bands playing CCR in the background. Thank you to CBC North and Loren McGinnis, who helped employ me in a few instances while I was there, and to Jessica Johnson of the *National Post*, who ran a few dispatches from the North. Most of all, thanks to John McFadden, although he didn't have to get himself arrested for my benefit. "It'll be a great ending for your book if I go to jail," he told me before the trial. But this ending was fine. I hope the rest of the book is okay.

A NOTE ABOUT THE AUTHOR

≡

Author and musician Dave Bidini is the only person to have been nominated for a Gemini, Genie, and Juno as well as CBC's *Canada Reads*. A founding member of Rheostatics, he has written thirteen books, including *On a Cold Road*, *Tropic of Hockey*, *Around the World in 57 1/2 Gigs*, and *Home and Away*. He is a three time National magazine award-winner, and his play, *The Five Hole Stories*, was staged by One Yellow Rabbit Performance Company, touring the country in 2008. He last book was *Keon and Me* and he is the publisher of the *West End Phoenix* community newspaper in Toronto.

A NOTE ABOUT THE TYPE

The body of *Midnight Light* has been set in Perpetua, a typeface designed by the English artist Eric Gill, and cut by the Monotype Corporation between 1928 and 1930. Perpetua (together with its italic partner Felicity) constitutes a contemporary face of original design, without historical antecedents. The shapes of the roman characters are derived from the techniques of stonecutting. Originally intended as a book face, Perpetua is unique amongst its peers in that its larger display characters retain the elegance and form so characteristic of its book sizes.